Educational administration

Third Edition

Written by members of
the Society of Education Officers
and the Association of Directors
of Education in Scotland
and edited by Kenneth Brooksbank
and Keith Anderson

Longman

1A468

Published by Longman Group UK Limited
6th Floor, Westgate House,
The High, Harlow,
Essex CM20 1YR

First published 1980
Second Edition 1984
Third Edition 1989

British Library Cataloguing in Publication Data
Educational administration. - 3rd ed.
  1. Great Britain. Education. Management
  I. Brooksbank, Kenneth II. Anderson, Keith, *1939*-
  III. Society of Education Officers
  379.1'54'0941

ISBN 0-582-03339-X

Typeset by Kerrypress Ltd, Luton
Printed and bound in Great Britain by
Biddles Ltd, Guildford and King's Lynn

Contents

          PRACTICE   171

9   Practical management of a Local Education
          Authority's system   173

10   Office organisation   192

11   Rules, regulations and procedures   217

12   Management at institutional level   235

13   Communication and consultation   256

14   Equal opportunities and race relations   275

15   The administration of education in Wales   282

16   Administrative considerations arising from the
          separate nature of the Scottish educational
          system   291

17   Manpower Services (Training) Commission:
          education and training   314

          APPENDICES

1   Budgeting for expenditure on education   337

2   Source of statistics   343

3   The role of Local Authority Associations in the
          education system   347

          Further reading   352

          Index of Statutes   355

          General index   356

Foreword

Educational Administration was first published in 1979 and the Second Edition followed in 1984. There were many changes between the First and Second Edition, but even more will now be apparent in this one because not only will it take into account changes which followed from the 1986 Education Act, but it will cover the massive changes which will follow the implementation of the 1988 Act. The whole basis of the partnerships upon which educational administration has rested, traditionally, for the last 100 years will be very significantly altered as a result of this Act. The Secretary of State, on behalf of the Government of the day, will have a very much higher profile in terms of powers to determine policy matters than ever before. Local education authorities on the other hand will find their role restricted in many ways, but still vital in terms of determining strategy, carrying out monitoring and inspectorial duties; and for influencing those parts of the service which are not affected by the 1988 Act. Governing Bodies and Heads of Schools and Principals of Colleges will have far greater powers in determining the day to day running of schools and colleges. There will be a National Curriculum to be put in place and the Local Management of Schools and Colleges has to be effected in the early 1990s. These weighty matters alone will involve great changes, not only in powers and duties to be carried out by Education Officers on behalf of local councils, but also in terms of the culture, as it were, of the service as a whole.

As Richard Knight said in 1984 in his Foreword, the public education service involves a great many people in varying capacities. It involves teachers, lecturers, pupils, students, research workers, voluntary organisations, governors, administrators, parents, the Churches, and so on. The knowledge which these various partners bring to the service is an extremely valuable resource.

The future seems to hold a devolving of responsibility to school and college governing bodies on the one hand, and an undertaking of more direct responsibility and power by the Secretary of State on the other. However, the role of the local education authority remains paramount in terms of securing the provision for primary and secondary education and further education. It remains the responsibility of the local education authority to plan a strategy for its institutions; to establish a formula costing to allow the devolution of individual responsibility to particular schools and colleges; to establish a National Curriculum and to monitor it, and to remain as the employer for staff, both teaching and non teaching, as well as to implement the demands of a capital programme over the years. It will therefore continue to be of vital importance that the service can attract into it young professionals of outstanding ability able to advise, to guide, to organise and to manage whether as teachers and lecturers, administrators, inspectors, careers officers, indeed in the many professional capacities in which they will still be needed. There is an outstanding challenge to be faced and an absorbing task to be undertaken.

It is hoped that this book will be a valuable resource for all the partners in the education service, and it is also certainly hoped that perhaps it will play its part in the campaign to bring the partners closer together to work as a team. If it does that, it will have made a major contribution to the service.

I should like to thank all those in the Society of Education Officers who have helped in the production of this book. The exercise has been a mammoth task, it has been particularly demanding, bearing in mind that they have had to cast their eyes towards the future even more than ever in this edition to take account of the matters which are likely to follow upon the implementation of the 1988 Education Act.

Peter Boulter

President
Society of Education Officers 1988-89

Chief Education Officer
Cumbria

Contributors

General Editor

Kenneth Brooksbank	Former Chief Education Officer, Birmingham
Keith Anderson	Chief Education Officer, Gloucestershire
Richard Clark	County Education Officer, Hampshire
Andrew Collier	Chief Education Officer, Lancashire
Gordon Cunningham	Former Education Officer, Association of County Councils and former Chief Education Officer, Cambridgeshire
Martin Davies	Director of Education, Newcastle
Donald Fisher	County Education Officer, Hertfordshire
Gordon Hainsworth	Former Chief Education Officer, Manchester
Jackson Hall	Former Director of Education, Sunderland
Gareth Lloyd-Jones	Secretary, Welsh Joint Education Committee
John Mann	Former Chief Education Officer, Harrow
Mike Nichol	Director of Education, Wirral
David Semple	Director of Education, Lothian
Ivor Slocombe	Chief Education Officer, Wiltshire
Chris Tipple	Director of Education, Northumberland
Keith Wood-Allum	Director of Education, Leicestershire
Bill Wright	Chief Education Officer, Wakefield

Introduction

The third edition of 'Educational Administration' appears as the Education (Reform) Act 1988 is beginning to be implemented. No individual Act has had such potentially far-reaching effects on the educational system of the country since 1944. There are those who claim that one of the major objectives of the Act was to destroy local education authorities. Certainly, one of the greatest of LEAs will disappear as the Inner London Education Authority ceases to exist and its functions are transferred to the councils of the Inner London Boroughs, reversing the 1974 position and creating more smaller LEAs. Significant areas of education are removed from the control of local authorities as polytechnics and some other institutions of higher education become corporate bodies entirely independent of the LEAs. Within each authority individual schools may, with the approval of the Secretary of State, acquire grant-maintained status which means for most purposes separation from the local authority's system. An Act therefore which provides for the total elimination of the country's largest LEA, for the removal of control of higher education from LEAs, and grant-maintained status for some schools clearly is intended to diminish the powers of LEAs, and the question may legitimately be asked as to whether educational administration in the local authority context has still any meaning or importance. The answer is that, not only is educational administration important, but that it becomes even more significant as the 1988 Act is implemented. The cornerstone of our educational system remains what it has been since 1944 when Section 1 of the 1944 Act laid upon the Secretary of State the duty to promote the education of the people of England and Wales.

> . . . 'and to secure the effective execution by local authorities under his control and direction, of the national policy for providing a varied and comprehensive educational service in every area'.

While the fundamental statutory position of the local authority is acknowledged, the reality is seen by some as quite different. The 1944 framework remains: the Secretary of State formulates national policy, the LEA determines the system within its area, and the governing bodies of schools and further education institutions regulate the affairs of the individual schools and colleges. But emphases have shifted. The Secretary of State has more and greater powers; for example, by instituting the national curriculum he may exercise much greater direct control over what is taught and what standards should be attained by children and students. His powers relating to admissions to schools increase his potential to control school provision within the authority's area; the creation of institutions virtually independent of the LEA such as city technical colleges and grant maintained schools allows scope for more direct and detailed interest by central government; and the Secretary of State's involvement in examinations and testing could prove to be a serious regulator on the work of the schools. These few instances demonstrate, if demonstration were really necessary, that the era following the full implementation of the 1988 Act could see greatly increased and more immediate power of central government.

Powers only become reality when they are exercised and since the ultimate point at which power is effective in education is the individual school or indeed the individual pupil, the 1988 Act provides for the management of schools by governing bodies. The conduct of the school is under the direction of the governing body whose constitution is so determined as to preclude control by the LEA. By 1993 LEAs will have had to implement their schemes delegating financial and managerial responsibilities to governing bodies of many schools. Then, the Act provides for major decisions (including staffing) affecting schools to rest with governors where parents and representatives of the community will play a major role.

It is argued, therefore, that squeezed between the upper and nether millstones of central government and governing bodies, the LEA is drained of power and that educational administration is discounted. Alternatively some see a fundamental change to a new role for the local authority which loses its executive function for that of a strategic control. Both views are erroneous. Historically the LEA has had both a strategic and executive role and both will continue, as long as the local authority is responsible for providing efficient education for all within its area.

It is conceivable that local authorities could be superseded by area boards or some similar organisation, but this is not at present envisaged and until a change of that order comes about, the LEA and its administrative arrangements remain the vital core of the education system. All finance – both capital and revenue – to enable the local education system to operate is the concern of the LEA, whether such finance is raised locally, from central government, from other national agencies, or by grant. In making allocations to schools LEAs must exercise their intimate knowledge of their area and of their schools; they must monitor the application of delegated finance. The responsibility for ensuring that no part of the system fails through misapplication or mismanagement of resources rests with the LEA which is finally publicly accountable for the efficient discharge of its duty to provide. The fact that some of the authority's financial and managerial powers are devolved on other agencies complicates the task of efficient control of resources but in no way relieves the LEA of its central responsibility.

In certain areas the responsibility of the LEA remains unchanged. The Careers Service, often underrated but extremely important, particularly as awareness of the relevance of education to employment increases, rests with the LEA. Capital expenditure, i.e. new buildings, extensions, major modifications, major items of equipment, is the LEA's concern. So too may be responsibility for structural repairs, field centres, the psychological services, education welfare, educational advisers, home to school transport, and peripatetic teachers – a wide range of services necessary to support an efficient service. Moreover, when attention is focussed on the innovatory provisions of the Act such as the creation of grant-maintained schools which can 'opt out' of the LEA system and financial devolution to governing bodies, it has to be remembered that many smaller schools will continue to be maintained, without financial devolution to governors, as at present. So too will special schools.

What of the schools and institutions where financial delegation is required? Here the situation is less clear, and certainly care will be required before the extensive changes envisaged can operate smoothly and universally. When the change is satisfactorily completed, the task of the administrator may well be different. No world is perfect and it must be assumed that schemes will provide for the educational administrator to retain some contingency funding, for example to guard against failure of governors to operate effectively within the financial limits prescribed, whether through unforeseeable accident, through incompetence or through deliberate protest. Whatever the cause and whatever the remedial action necessary, the duty of the LEA to maintain the service to the whole of its population remains and the administration must provide to ensure that this is possible.

The government auditors have already warned that much planning and early training of governors will be necessary if governing bodies are to be capable of fulfilling their obligations. It is ironical that the government should be seeking to raise standards in schools by involving parents more closely in the control and financing of schools, and at the same time pointing to lack of parental control and interest as a major element in the indiscipline of youth. Nevertheless, the LEA and the administrators have the arduous function of training governors to govern schools efficiently, effectively and economically within tight financial constraints. If they succeed, it will be an executive responsibility well discharged.

If they do wholly succeed, then the LEA administrator will need constantly to monitor the financial operations of institutions to sustain governors with advice, guidance and professional support and to intervene as necessary to prevent collapse. They will need also to be in a position to mount salvage operations as policies of governors, movements of popular tastes, edicts from the Secretary of State on school admissions, lead to redundancies and school closures.

If they do not wholly succeed, then it is possible to envisage a variety of undesirable situations. It may prove impossible to recruit governing bodies for some schools if governors are coerced or persuaded to serve reluctantly. They may prove incapable of discharging their functions and some governing bodies may first prove to be hopelessly incompetent. In such circumstances, the LEA may find itself exercising control of schools or institutions temporarily or even permanently despite their best endeavours to return functions to governors. Executive as well as strategic functions will clearly then need to be exercised by the educational administrator.

The precise future is impossible to forecast. What is certain is that the delivery of education in the school or college will become more complex. The devolution of responsibilities may prove to be more costly. Not only will the Education (Reform) Act create many new situations requiring guidance, regulation and policy statements to help institutions, but other regulations such as the local government acts dealing with finance and competitive tendering will add new degrees of complexity. Education is best delivered against a background of stability and tranquility. The task of educational administration will be to maintain such a background for governors, teachers and lecturers so that amid the turmoil of innovation and change, children and young people can learn to fulfil their potential. The need for accurate, relevant information and data for clear-sighted policy making and for efficient communication will be greater as changes are implemented. Evaluation of what is taught and learned, assessment and improvement of performance in this constant quest for higher quality will above all emphasise the paramount importance of personnel management.

Indeed, in whatever perspective the era following the Education (Reform) Act is viewed, it is clear that the realisation of the high objectives of the legislation depends in no small measure on the maintenance of sound educational administration in the LEAs.

Every effort has been made in this edition to ensure that references to educational procedures, policies and practices, are in line with the provisions of the 1988 Education Act. However, some of the detailed implementation of the legislation will be the subject of subsequent circulars from the Department of Education and Science.

The Local Government Finance Act 1988 introduced the Community Charge to replace domestic rates. The Community Charge comes in from 1 April 1990, but to avoid confusion, the book has been written as if the Community Charge system had been in operation from the time the book was published.

Finally, during the course of preparation of this edition, the Manpower Services Commission was redesignated the Training Commission. Both designations are used in the book.

Part 1 The framework of educational administration

1 The nature of educational administration

With the possible exception of rate demands, few, if any, activities of local government have such a profound effect on the lives of most citizens as the education service and its administration. Few elements of local government are so little understood. All parents will be affected by the educational system and most will at some stage come into direct contact with their local education administration. Parents of young children may be dissatisfied with the provision for nursery and pre-school education and not infrequently such dissatisfaction may lead to parental organisations bringing pressure to bear on the administration. Once a child is of statutory school age parents become involved with the administration in securing a place in an acceptable school for their child, in obtaining grants of various kinds to assist them in providing adequately to enable the child to profit from his or her education, in obtaining school meals, in guidance towards a career and work, in the obtaining of professional qualifications for their children and themselves, and not least in securing recreative activities and continuing education for themselves.

The impact of educational administration on most members of the community is not only wide but deep. As the status of the United Kingdom has changed very rapidly from a wealthy world power to that of a highly developed industrial country competing to maintain the standard and quality of life of its citizens from its own resources, so a deeper awareness of the vital need to develop the skills and talents of young people to the full has spread throughout our society. The education service is seen as a most significant factor in national economic survival. Currently the perception is finding expression in the activities of bodies such as Universities, Polytechnics and the Training

Commission and informs the vast legislative programme designed
to achieve education for all children and adults which is of higher
quality and more relevant to the demands of our increasingly
complex technological society.

Parents are involved in increasing numbers in the management
of institutions charged with the delivery of the improved quality
of education.

If so many people are so acutely conscious of the importance
of educational administration and the educational system which
it provides, it is reasonable to ask why the nature of educational
administration should be so little understood. There is probably
no satisfactory single answer to the question, but it is the hope
that the consideration of the nature of educational administration
in the succeeding chapters will help to elucidate the problem.
First it is necessary to look at the framework within which
educational administration operates.

Educational administration

It is significant that the first sections of the Education Act 1944
are concerned with the administration of education. No
subsequent legislation has amended them. Part I of the Act is
concerned with **central administration** and Section 1 provides
as follows:

> It shall be the duty of the Secretary of State for Education and
> Science to promote the education of the people of England and
> Wales and the progressive development of institutions devoted to
> that purpose, and to secure the effective execution by local
> authorities under his control and direction of the national policy
> for providing a varied and comprehensive educational service in
> every area.

Part II of the Act, is concerned with the statutory system of
education, and deals first with **local administration** as follows:

> [Section 6.2]
> 'The local administration of the statutory system of public
> education shall be conducted in accordance with the provision of
> Part II (of the First Schedule to the Act)' which provides that:
> 1. Every Local Education Authority shall, in accordance with
>   arrangements approved by the Secretary of State, establish such
>   education committees as they think it expedient to establish for

the efficient discharge of their functions with respect to education and . . .
5. Every Local Education Committee of an LEA shall include persons of experience in education and persons acquainted with the educational conditions prevailing in the area for which the committee acts.'

The authority for educational administration clearly establishes the central and local areas of the system and the interdependence of the two, although the position of central government as the senior partner is implied by the duty imposed on the Secretary of State to secure action by local authorities, and by the unequivocal responsibility to promote the education of the people. Subsequent variations of the detail of national policy have not affected the fundamental administrative provisions set out clearly in 1944. Before turning to consider the administrative functions of central government, it is appropriate here to mention the third statutory element of educational administration – the Chief Education Officer. Section 88 of the 1944 Education Act laid upon an LEA the duty of appointing a fit person to be the Chief Education Officer and after considerable debate during the period in which local government reorganisation was under review, this duty was retained by specific provision under the Local Government Act 1972. This statutory appointment (the only other office established by statute is that of Director of Social Services) at once gives the education service an appearance of uniformity and of difference from all other local government services, which has not always contributed to a full understanding of the public education system.

Central administration

The duties of the Secretary of State are deceptively simple, but in practice are fraught with difficulties. Nowhere in the Education Act 1944 or in subsequent legislation is the term 'education' defined. The Education Reform Act 1988 goes some way towards definition by prescribing the requirements which must be satisfied by the curriculum of maintained schools. Since the curriculum is that which the school intends to teach, the requirements for the curriculum must broadly equate with what the school and the community regard as education. Those requirements are expressed in the 1988 Act as follows:

> The curriculum for a maintained school . . . is a balanced and broadly-based curriculum which
>
> (a) promotes the spiritual, moral, cultural, mental and physical development of the children at the school and of society; and
>
> (b) prepares such pupils for the opportunities, responsibilities and experiences of adult life.

Central government, through the Secretary of State for Education and Science, has extensive powers to prescribe elements of the curriculum, programmes of study, arrangements for assessing achievement, and to revise the National Curriculum as it is deemed necessary. Local authorities and governors are accountable to the Secretary of State who is advised and informed by various agencies such as HM Inspectors of Schools, the Curriculum and Assessment Councils, and such other bodies of enquiry as he may commission. To assist local authorities and governors in the task of delivering the curriculum he may issue instructions which have the force of law, circulars which are for guidance, research findings and special papers on specific aspects of the curriculum. He has considerable power to develop particular areas of study, e.g. science, through financial arrangements and by controlling the supply and training of teachers.

The 1988 Act has sharpened the Secretary of State's powers and duty to promote the progressive development of educational institutions, e.g. by giving corporate status to Polytechnics and other Colleges of Higher Education, and by supporting the providers of City Technical Colleges. New administrative mechanisms are also brought into existence, e.g. the Polytechnics and Colleges Funding Council, all of whose members are appointed by the Secretary of State to support education and research in the Polytechnics and Colleges. City Technical Colleges are controlled by the agreement made between the Secretary of State and the promoters and by financial payments from the government. On the financial control of LEAs comment is made in a later chapter.

No less significant is the current accent on the importance of all pupils having some qualifications when they leave school. Here the Secretary of State is able to exercise considerable influence on the nature and content of education in schools by virtue of the fact that no course of study leading to an external qualification may be provided unless the qualification has been approved by the Secretary of State or by a body designated by him.

The Secretary of State appears therefore to have vast powers to enable him to fulfil the duties specified in the 1944 Act and amplified by subsequent legislation, notably the 1988 Act. Some dilemmas are already apparent. While for children in maintained schools a balanced curriculum is required, their contemporaries in City Technical Colleges are not offered a balanced curriculum but a broad curriculum with emphasis on science and technology. A consensus of opinion as to the responsibilities of adult life rarely exists and is of short duration. Within the space of less than fifty years the emphasis has shifted from physical fitness, to high technology, to skills required for industry, commerce and finance. Similarly the cultural patterns of society have changed during that period as have the predominant values of the adult population. At the same time individuals and voluntary bodies have through persistent and devoted work brought about changes in the attitude to children with special education needs which have found acceptance and embodiment in government policy.

Agreement on the purpose and nature of education is achievable in the broadest of terms. Acceptance of that agreement in a stable society rests on a basis of commonly held values, attitudes, cultural awareness and aspirations which are deeply felt but not readily definable. The paradox for the Secretary of State is that he must use precisely defined powers with sensitive, delicate and at times almost intuitive perception of the subtleties of essential shifts on that basis, if central administration is indeed to promote the education of the people and to secure effective execution of national education policy by local authorities.

Local education and administration

Local education administration may not be a flawless jewel but it is a thing many-faceted and of rare distinction. To avoid confusion it will be helpful to look separately at some of the main facets.

First it may be well to dispose of an issue on which much energy and time has been and will be spent – the almost metaphysical questions arising from the roles of the elected member and the Chief Education Officer. Where shall policy be made and where is the place of understanding is the sharp edge of the chisel with which critics seek to split the hard secure stone of local government. Occasionally members and officers tend to facilitate the cleavage by claims that policy is made exclusively by one or the other. Fortunately behavioural science has taught us that our assessment of our own role may be very different from the assessment of our role by another. Both have elements of validity and the reality of policy-making as distinct from the mechanics thereof seldom rests solely in one area. Moreover the Education Acts of 1986 and 1988 provide for the delegation of powers by the LEAs to governing bodies. Policy making in some areas is required by law to be a function of governors, e.g. whether sex education shall be given in the school, and if so, how. A further gloss on where policy is made is thus added, namely that policy as it affects the operation of a single institution may be made by its governing body. Local educational administration is therefore considered as the totality of all involved although inevitably much of this book will appear to reflect most strongly the viewpoint of the officer.

The most restrictive view of local educational administration is that which looks solely at the light reflected by the facet facing central government. Basically this view is that local government's function is simply to apply locally central government instructions. It is of course true that local government must operate within the limits prescribed by law and exercise only those powers which it is entitled by law to exercise. Powers exclusive to an individual LEA may be conferred by a Local Act or by bye-laws made by an authority by virtue of powers conferred by Parliament. Thus, for example, the bye-laws governing the employment of children may differ somewhat between one authority and its neighbours. But that in no way derogates from the principle that authorities must act within and fulfil their duties under the law. Indeed, in addition to the safeguards applying to all local government undertakings, the laws of education prescribe machinery for individuals to secure redress against unreasonable exercise of powers by LEAs and for the Secretary of State to enquire into any part of an authority's activities and to direct an authority to carry out a duty in case of default. Furthermore the 1988 Act provides for other bodies to assume powers to manage schools formerly maintained by the LEA while, at the same time laying on the authority a duty to carry out certain functions in respect of those schools.

The law not only imposes duties, but also confers powers. In many matters the authority is empowered to act if in its judgement it is beneficial so to do. For example, an authority may provide board and lodging otherwise than at boarding schools or colleges if it is satisfied that only by so doing can an individual receive suitable education.

The nature of educational law

At first sight the law of education may appear quite precise. It is certainly voluminous. The Education Act 1944 (which still remains the principal Act concerning the education system) has been amended or amplified by more than 20 subsequent Education Acts, including that of 1988, which is exceptionally detailed. Within that body of law are sections laying down the principles governing the provision and government of schools and the curriculum of primary and secondary schools, sections prescribing the provision for those with special educational needs, for school attendance, further education, medical inspection and treatment and finance. The rights of individuals, groups of individuals, parents, trustees and local government electors in respect of the educational service are set down and supplemented by other legislation, e.g. the Local Government Act 1972, which defines the rights of the community to use school premises. The laws prescribe penalties for non-compliance with certain requirements, e.g. that parents shall cause their child to receive education either by attendance at school or elsewhere, and empowers the Secretary of State to make detailed regulations which have the sanction and force of law. It could well be supposed therefore that any ambiguities or imprecisions in the legislation have been cleared up or disposed of.

This is not so and the latitude of interpretation of the law remains wide. At the very core of the legislation lies the fact that 'education' is nowhere defined. Such definitions as do exist are tautologous, e.g.:

Primary education, that is to say, full-time education suitable to the requirements of junior pupils;
Secondary education, that is to say, full-time education suitable to the requirements of senior pupils.

The 1988 Education Act goes some way towards definition by describing the curriculum of schools and laying down the core and foundation elements of the National Curriculum which are to form the major part of the curriculum to all schools. But even the core and foundation elements are qualified by the requirement that the knowledge, skills and understanding in each subject shall be attuned to the abilities and maturities of pupils. The duty imposed on LEAs therefore carries the responsibility of determining how and what educational provision shall be made in their areas, where decisions as to what shall be taught are made and how the needs of their areas are best understood and met. This is the great reality of educational administration demanding intelligence, vision, a lively appreciation of history, powers of analysis, synthesis and organisation, but above all depth and catholicity of understanding of human condition and human aspirations. These are the qualities which the law implicitly requires of educational administrators although the one attribute specifically required is that of reasonableness.

A glance at the existing situation soon confirms that within the framework of the law, powers are exercised individually by individual education authorities in the manner just described. When, in the reorganisation of local government in 1974, existing authorities were amalgamated into larger units considerable variety of practice between the constituent authorities was revealed. In some, children were transferred from primary to secondary schools at the age of 11, in others, children attending middle schools from age 8 or 9 years were transferred to secondary at 12 or 13, while the pattern of adult education varied from college-based to a diffused institutional pattern. As the former West Riding approached its end it published a paper which drew attention to the adequacy (or perhaps inadequacy) of the diverse provision made by some of the existing smaller authorities. Dramatically 1974 raised the curtain on educational administration and raised expectations that assimilation of authorities would lead to the adoption of the practices of the most enlightened. It also underlined the latitude which individual authorities have within the general framework of the law.

Changes in the law and in the application of the law affect the relationships between local education authorities and central government. The Secretary of State uses his powers to earmark expenditure to ensure that the development of certain aspects of education is accentuated. The 1988 Act gives the Secretary of State wide powers in many areas, notably in relation to the National Curriculum where he can establish and vary specific requirements. At the same time curriculum development work may be carried out at the instance of a local education authority with the Secretary of State's consent. Fears that financial constraints and inducements from bodies such as the training commission might unduly modify the curriculum at some stages of education have proved baseless. But the advent under the new legislation of institutions directly funded by central government yet part of the provision for the area will undoubtedly generate new situations for the administrators charged with the duty of providing a varied and comprehensive educational service for their area. Given the dedication of the Secretary of State to the promotion of the education of the people of England and Wales, and the provision of adequate resources, local administration has to use the whole framework of law to provide an economic, efficient, and effective educational system in its area.

Regulations

It may be thought that the regulations made by the Secretary of State by virtue of powers conferred by law would in fact prove to be a more prescriptive framework carefully defining the limits and nature of powers to be exercised by local authorities. To an extent this is so. The Schools Regulations for example lay down that 'in every school or department there shall be a head teacher'. It is not open to an authority, however reasonable it may appear, to organise schools without a head teacher. But two other prescriptions of the same regulations may be quoted as indicating the need for vigilance, adaptability and accommodation to change in educational administration.

Classrooms shall not be overcrowded
A pupil shall not be refused admission to or excluded from a school on other than reasonable grounds.

Given the needs of certain pupils and the methods desirable to meet those needs, a classroom which only 20 years ago was designed to house up to 40 children may reasonably be deemed capable of accommodating no more than 20. Educational administration must therefore constantly re-examine needs and practice to match resources to perceived requirements.

The second prescription illustrates the need to be aware of adjustments to the framework within which administration operates. What constitutes reasonable grounds for refusing admission rests primarily with the local authority but on appeal the Secretary of State may and does on occasion reject the authority's view. Gradually therefore, through case determination, practice establishes new known limits within which an authority may work. As no two cases are exactly similar the educational administrator must, being aware of practice and precedent judgement, determine how far such judgements limit the exercise of discretion in dealing with a particular case.

Departmental circulars, letters and guidance

Strictly speaking circulars, letters and other forms of guidance issued by the Department of Education and Science have not the force of law. Nor in the strictest sense are they statements of national policy. Despite the sometimes strenuous efforts exerted to persuade local authorities to comply with the guidance offered, it is nevertheless convenient to be able to withdraw such guidance quietly and unobtrusively. Thus while recognising the genuine desire of central government to be helpful to local authorities called upon to deal with the unfamiliar as people from widely differing cultures become resident in this country, the convenience of being able to withdraw such advice by administrative process when events had demonstrated its unsuitability must not be overlooked. While, therefore, guidance in the several forms adopted by central government constitutes a less definable part of the framework of educational administration, it would be unwise for local administration to ignore such advice even though after due consideration of the circumstances it is decided not to follow the guidance offered.

Case law

Practice reveals aspects of the law which are subject to a variety of interpretations, the final determination of the meaning of the law rests with the courts. After all the processes of appeal have been followed, the decision of the court is binding and compliance therewith obligatory. It is sufficient here to observe, that as the courts deal with specific cases, the law becomes clarified through judicial decisions and the educational administrator must be aware of the increasing definition of the framework in which he exercises the vast powers of interpretation alluded to above.

Other legislation

The many facets of local educational administration arise from the responsibilities which it must assume. The legal framework within which it operates is not merely that set by Education Acts. Certain powers, such as the power to employ staff, arise from the Local Government Acts and the position of the LEA as an employer means that it is subject to the law governing employment, protection of employment and insurance as is every other employer. In many authorities the direct responsibility arising from such legislation may fall on the Establishment or Personnel Committee, but no educational administrator relating to such diverse occupations as teaching, caretaking, building, engineering, secretarial work, technicians or school meals work, can afford to be ignorant of the provision of such legislation. The whole structure as well as the welfare of the staff or work force can be seriously affected by considerations arising out of employment legislation.

The Health and Safety at Work Act 1974 bears even more directly on the person as well as on the work of the educational administrator. Failure to comply with the provisions of the Act can be attributed to the individual ˙responsible with the corresponding personal liability. But even more seriously the requirements of the Act can, it appears, operate so that the curriculum of an institution may be affected or even that certain activities in the institution have to cease. They must cause anxiety and concern for every educational administrator.

Legislation for the protection of the individual or of groups of citizens will continue to be enacted and in view of the wide range of educational activities will impact on educational administration. Two pieces of legislation deserve specific reference: the Sex Discrimination Act 1975, which has already had some effect on the curriculum of schools, and the Race Relations Act 1976. The latter is particularly significant for the way in which it permeates and requires positive action in every aspect of educational administration by requiring that local (education) authorities 'make appropriate arrangements with a view to securing that their various functions are carried out with due regard to the need . . .

> to promote equality of opportunity, and good relations between persons of different racial groups.

Limitations on educational administration

Within the vast framework outlined the educational administrator is called upon to exercise powers with imaginative informed interpretation, but educational administration is subject to check. Of financial checks and audit more will be said later. Here it is necessary to refer to the safeguards against irrational use of power. The first and most far-reaching lies with the Secretary of State who can, if satisfied that an LEA has failed to discharge a duty under the Act, issue directions and secure their enforcement to ensure that the duty is carried out. This power has not yet needed to be exercised.

Any person may complain to the Secretary of State that an LEA has acted or is proposing to act unreasonably and if the Secretary of State is satisfied he may give directions to the LEA. This procedure has been invoked especially in connection with the placing of children in particular schools.

The Local Government Act 1974 set up the Commission for Local Administration with Commissioners (Ombudsmen) with powers to investigate complaints of injustice in consequence of maladministration by or on behalf of a local authority. Increasingly the exercise of functions by LEAs has been restricted by successful challenges to specific actions in the Courts, and by edicts from the EEC.

Needs of the population of the area

In considering the framework within which local educational administration occurs, it is necessary finally to refer to the duty laid upon LEAs to secure 'that efficient education throughout those stages (primary, secondary and further education) shall be available to meet the needs of the population of that area'.

The powers and duties of an LEA cover practically the whole span of human life. To meet the needs of the population implies an involvement in every level of human activity and endeavour. Even the apparently simple function of making adequate physical provision to enable the various stages of education to take place has been and is complex as later chapters will indicate but the task of ascertaining the spiritual, moral, mental and physical needs of the population is of enormous compass. Yet however vast and apparently beyond achievement the task may seem the educational administrator is from time to time called to account for his stewardship in this respect.

Investigations carried out by Committees of Enquiry and similar bodies have thrown light on good and indifferent practice in LEAs. Such investigations engender national and local debate which, at some point, almost invariably leads to a call for an appraisal of the contribution made by local educational administration. National perspectives also exert their influence on the provision looked for. Thus when there was grave concern arising from the rapid growth of sophisticated technology in certain nations, attention was focused on the ability of this country's educational system to produce men and women scientifically and technically equipped to generate an even more advanced technology here. More recently, when there was a widespread mood of depression and disillusion, the tendency to point to the failure of the educational system at all levels and to demand a reckoning of educational administration has been strong. Accountability for the operation of the education service is required – schools must declare their programmes and their success in achieving objectives (as measured by examinations); any person may be required to give or produce evidence to the Select Committee of the House of Commons and Her Majesty's Inspectors' reports are to be made public.

Alongside this 'market-place' attitude to the relationship of education to the community is to be set the impact of the media.

On the one hand there is serious educational provision and information, e.g. Open University, Open Tech, numeracy and parental guidance programmes, and on the other entertainment and documentary feature programmes which often reinforce the image of education as a failure, at best irrelevant and wasteful and at worst harmful. The problems of anticipating, meeting and interpreting the needs of the population of the area are therefore an extremely important part of the framework of educational administration and will be a constant theme implicit or explicit throughout the chapters which follow.

How educational administration is, in fact, carried out and within the framework outlined is the theme of this book, and it is fitting that, in considering a service which is fundamentally concerned with people, we should first turn to look at the administrators themselves.

2 The Local Education Authority

Historical background

Arrangements for local machinery to provide a public education service in England and Wales date from the Education Act of 1870. This created new public bodies elected for the sole purpose of providing elementary education and known as School Boards. By the end of the nineteenth century there existed 2,568 of these Boards and they had done much to fill in the gaps in the school system, previously regarded as the preserve of the churches.

The 30 years of life enjoyed by the School Boards also saw the evolution of a structured system of local government, itself a term almost unknown until the second half of the nineteenth century. By a major Act in 1888 the Government established 62 new County Councils and thus was born a division between Shire County administration and that of the Cities and Boroughs. At that time a County Borough usually needed a minimum population of 50,000. In 1889 both the County Councils and the County Borough Councils were given certain powers in education by the Technical Instruction Act.

During the 1890s it soon became clear there was uncertainty about powers and responsibilities for education and the urgent need for a major reorganisation was recognised by the Education Act of 1902. This abolished the system of School Boards and brought the education service into the mainstream of local government. The County Councils and the County Borough Councils were given full powers over technical and secondary education and for the first time the term Local Education Authority (LEA) was in common use. In addition these councils inherited from the School Boards the responsibility for the elementary schools, which they were required to share with other boroughs that had over 10,000 inhabitants and with those urban district councils that had 20,000. These latter councils, with powers only over elementary education, were known as Part III authorities. As a result there were in all 315 LEAs, all with powers over the voluntary schools that were granted only after fierce parliamentary struggles. The 1902 Act required each LEA to appoint a statutory Education Committee which must include co-opted members from outside the ranks of elected councillors.

This structure lasted until the Education Act of 1944 which reduced the number of LEAs in England and Wales to 147. It abolished the Part III authorities, though in many county areas their separate identity was partially preserved by the introduction of a network of Excepted Districts and Divisional Executives. It was a principal feature of the 1944 Act that each of the new LEAs had full responsibility for each stage of the education system, then defined as primary, secondary and further. This is the arrangement that is often spoken of as 'the seamless robe' of responsibility.

Twenty-five years later when the local government system of England and Wales was examined by the Redcliffe-Maud Royal Commission the education service was in the hands of 79 County Boroughs and 45 County Councils. The London area was excluded from this study as it had been separately reorganised in 1964. This figure of 124 LEAs has to be set against the fact that there were some 1,200 local authorities in all so that already responsibility for education was vested only in a small minority of the larger units of local government. Even so 32 of the 124 LEAs had less than 100,000 inhabitants and as many as 65 of the County Boroughs and nine of the counties had less than 250,000, a figure then widely regarded as the minimum appropriate for ensuring proper educational provision. The report of the Royal Commission was published in 1969; a Local Government Act followed in 1972; and a new system was born on 1 April 1974.

For the education service one of the main changes made was the abolition of the system of Divisional Executives and Excepted Districts despite strong resistance, itself reminiscent of the unsuccessful struggles to avoid extinction by Part III authorities in 1944 and School Boards in 1902.

In 1990, education in Inner London is to be reorganised. The 1988 Education Act provides for the abolition of the Inner London

Education Authority on 31 March 1990, and for each Inner London Council to become the LEA for its area.

Present structure

There are at present 104 LEAs in England and Wales. The main groupings are:

I *London* (21)   The present structure dates from a reorganisation in 1964. Each of the 20 Outer London Boroughs is a full LEA. In the centre of London education is the responsibility of the unique Inner London Education Authority which is the largest single LEA in the country. Its geographical area covers that of 12 London Boroughs which therefore do not have responsibility for education. The position of the ILEA was included in the review of the government of London published by Sir Frank Marshall in 1978. No structural change was recommended in this report. However, a late addition to the 1987 Education Reform Bill proposed the abolition of the ILEA and the transfer of its educational responsibilities to the Inner London Boroughs. The new LEAs are required to prepare and publish educational development plans showing how the education system within its area is to be maintained, and in doing so, to consult the local authorities for adjacent areas where it appears that one authority on its own is unable to make suitable provision for particular areas of the service.

II *Metropolitan Districts* (36)   The 1974 reorganisation of local government established six Metropolitan County Councils in England centred on Birmingham, Leeds, Liverpool, Manchester, Newcastle and Sheffield. Responsibility for education is not, however, vested in these six Metropolitan County Councils. Instead the 36 Metropolitan Districts of these six counties are the LEAs with full powers. At one stage during consideration of the Royal Commission Report it seemed likely that the six Metropolitan Counties would themselves be given responsibility for education but this view did not prevail and the designation of Metropolitan Districts as LEAs was in line with the view expressed by the Royal Commission in its recommendations.

III *Shire Counties* (47)   In England 39 and Wales eight counties are the LEAs, with no responsibility for education being vested in the district councils established within those counties. In 1978 proposals to return responsibility for the education service to nine former County Boroughs currently within shire counties were formulated by the then Labour Government

under the name of 'Organic Growth'. They were not
implemented.

ILEA is a single purpose authority established solely to provide
an education service for the central area of London. All the other
LEAs have a number of functions of which education is one.
In these authorities it is the full elected Council which is the
LEA. It is thus on the floor of the Council Chamber itself that
decisions of major educational policy are taken and they will
inevitably reflect the balance of political parties at that level.
In general it has been noticeable in the period since the mid-
1960s that local government in England and Wales has become
more and more political in its activities. With major areas of
social policy such as housing, social services and education vested
in local authorities it has also been remarked that the headquarters
of the Conservative, Labour and Liberal parties have all
significantly increased their activities in influencing the policies
of local authorities, both individually and collectively through
the associations of local authorities.

It is the normal practice of each political party in a local
authority to elect one of the members as leader and to meet
regularly in private as a party 'caucus'. It is on these private
occasions that a majority party will determine its policies and
attitudes to matters of importance so that in practice educational
decisions on major issues will be made in the caucus and not
in the Education Committee or its sub-committees. The extent
to which this happens will vary according to the nature of the
authority and the effectiveness of the party whip system within
it. Often the whips in County or Town Hall are now as active
as they have long been at Westminster. It is essential to understand
this aspect of the work of an LEA in the later sections that deal
with the relationship of senior members including chairmen of
committees and chief officers.

The emergence in recent years of 'hung' councils has made
more complex the policy making process. The ruling group may
have to seek an alliance with one of the other parties in order
to secure the implementation of its policies, and the partners
in that alliance may differ according to the issue under debate.
Chief Officers have to be alert to these changing patterns of
partnership, and may more frequently find themselves
participating in public debates alongside politicians, particularly

where there is a chance that the issue itself rather than politics will determine the outcome of that debate. The complexity of the situation can only be heightened when lack of agreement between the parties can lead to there being no permanent committee chairman but instead a rotational chairmanship arrangement or even the appointment of chairmen meeting by meeting. In such circumstances, and in order to demonstrate publicly that there is strong leadership for the education service, the Chief Education Officer may need, at times, to play a more obvious role in respect of policy making as well as in its implementation.

In addition to coming more under the influence of party politics local authorities have also been affected since reorganisation in 1974 by various theories of corporate conduct. The readily understood need for the activities of service committees, including the Education Committee, to run in harmony has at times given rise to needless interference with the effective operation of the services themselves. The strengthening of central activities, such as financial control and policy co-ordination, can be a source of strength to an authority when handled sensibly and this has often been the experience from which the education service clearly benefits. There are indeed signs that excessive enthusiasm for practices that were unwisely corporate has largely moderated to achieve a sensible balance though still in a few areas it is the services that alone justify the very existence of local government that have appeared most at hazard from pointless and unthinking bureaucracy.

The obligatory delegation of financial management to governing bodies of schools and colleges following the 1988 Education Act will necessarily affect the relationship of central departments to the education service and its establishments. For example, where central personnel committees were responsible for approving the establishment or appointment of non-teaching staff in a school or college, that function will now become the responsibility of the individual governing body within the limits of the overall resources available. Similarly, governing bodies will have power to deal with day-to-day maintenance of buildings, a function that had previously been discharged by the Property Services Manager. Just as the relationship between the Education Department and its establishments is changing, so also will that of central departments to education.

A local Council is empowered to provide a number of services and has a duty to consider fairly the needs of all the inhabitants of its area. Councillors therefore have to balance many competing claims for resources. Sometimes this involves weighing the demands of one service against those of another, while at other times the balance of priorities will be between different areas of the authority. Thus the specific rate-raising duty of the Finance or Policy and Resources Committee will oblige the Education Committee to do its work within broad financial guidelines that are prescribed for it. This and other constraints on the local working of the education service are not always at first appreciated by teachers, students and parents whose particular concern is only with educational provision. Thus at a particular period a Council may decide quite rightly that its level of provision in housing or the needs of its services for the elderly shall have priority over all other requirements. As a result legitimate needs for money or staff on behalf of schools or colleges may be deferred or rejected. It is on such occasions that the reality of the position of the education service as part of a wider local authority whole has to be understood and acknowledged. It is a vital part, and by many indices, the largest single element. It is nevertheless but a part.

The Education Committee

The appointment by an LEA of an Education Committee was a requirement of the 1902 Act and has remained on the statute book in subsequent legislation. The need for such a constraint on the freedom of a local authority to determine its own internal structures has often been questioned, most recently in the debates on the 1972 Local Government Act, but the opponents of the statutory provision have not prevailed.

Members of an Education Committee are of two main kinds. A majority must be drawn from the elected members of the Council itself and they are normally chosen to reflect in the committee the balance of party political interests in the Council itself. As councillors these members will have many other interests and commitments and some undoubtedly find the demands on their time and energy by the Education Committee difficult to sustain. Moreover those who make the determined effort to accord priority to that committee so that they become prominent members are rarely able also to play a leading role in the work of the other related service committees, such as Housing and Social Services. At times this can mean that the focus of the elected member is service dominated and a positive barrier to the attempts to run the Council's affairs in a corporate manner. It is now usual for there to be a party-based education caucus that meets in advance of meetings of the Education Committee to determine party policy and the majority party will normally choose two of their number to be Chairman and Deputy Chairman of the Education Committee.

The other main body of members are those who are co-opted from outside the ranks of councillors. These are to be 'persons of experience in education and persons acquainted with the educational conditions prevailing in the area for which the committee acts'. Legislation does not specify in more detail, though when this broad statement was included in a schedule to the 1944 Act the Ministry suggested that authorities might appropriately include representatives of the teaching profession, of religious interests, and of industry, commerce and agriculture. It was of course the fears of the church in 1902 that had much to do at that time with the origins of the arrangements for Education Committees to have co-opted members as such.

At times the position of teachers as members of the Education Committee causes argument. They clearly serve as members of the profession employed by the authority and not to speak or act for sectional interests or particular unions even though they may have been elected in contests between nominees of the different unions. Moreover in serving at all teachers are exempt from the general provision of the 1933 Local Government Act which bars employees of a local authority from membership of it. This special provision is not uniformly popular with politicians and effective service on an Education Committee as a teacher member requires a very special blend of resolve and restraint.

In general the position of co-opted members as a whole has become more difficult as the party divides and LEAs have grown. The Acts ensure that the elected members on the Education Committee have a majority over their co-opted colleagues, but that provision on its own will not normally protect the majority party members from in theory being outvoted by a combination of the minority councillors plus the co-opted members. So in many LEAs now it is usual to co-opt enough persons willing to take the whip of the majority party and to attend its caucus to protect the voting strength of the party in power. Others seek further protection for the party in control of the Council by the adoption of procedures and standing orders that in practice severely restrain the powers of the Education Committee to act unilaterally. Both the co-option of party faithful and the restriction of delegated powers may be adjudged contrary to the spirit of the Education Acts, but they nevertheless reflect the reality of power in local government today.

An Education Committee will appoint sub-committees to conduct much of the business and typically these will be for stages of the service (e.g. Primary Sub-Committee; Further Education Sub-Committee) or for broader aspects (e.g. Sites and Buildings Sub-Committee; Careers Service Sub-Committee). A total of five or six sub-committees is common and the frequency of meetings will vary considerably from one area to another. Monthly cycles of meetings are widespread particularly in urban areas, so that 11 or 12 meetings a year of the Education Committee and its sub-committees is usual. Elsewhere, particularly in counties, committees may not meet more than four or five times a year, though since 1974 reorganisation the general trend has been for more frequent meetings and thus to increase the burden on those who serve on Education Committees.

The agenda for the typical meeting of a sub-committee of an Education Committee will contain 15 to 20 items, all of which involve papers and reports prepared by officers of the education department or of other departments of the Council. Some items will arise from initiatives that the officers wish to propose, or from communications from central government or one of the many national bodies that have dealings with LEAs. Some may relate to a review of a major area of activity at the authority level while others may arise from meetings of governors or from cases put forward by individuals that raise issues of principle. The sub-committee's meetings can last up to three hours or even more, and there may well be taken one or two decisions that will later be debated again at the meeting of the full Education Committee. The occasional issue may go further and later still cause argument at the full Council. It cannot automatically be assumed that at these later stages the decision of the sub-committee will remain unchanged.

Voluntary bodies

Local government has the duty of providing a wide variety of services and in many of these, such as Highways and Fire Brigades, the local authority has a monopoly. In other services, of which Education is a prime example, local government is not the sole provider but shares the task with voluntary agencies. This gives rise to complex legal arrangements to define the relationship of LEA and voluntary bodies. In part this is a matter of history where churches and charitable organisations were the first to establish schools or clubs for young people and the statutory authority came later on the scene. As standards have risen and inflation of costs has bitten deep the voluntary bodies have increasingly needed to seek financial help from the public authorities. Thus the Acts of 1902 and 1944 were significant steps in redefining the relationship as a measure of independence was exchanged for the comparative security of financial support from the public service.

An LEA's main partners are the Roman Catholic Church and the Church of England. Both have significant numbers of schools, whether Aided, Controlled or Special Agreement and also a big stake in the training of teachers in denominational colleges. They have denominational Diocesan Directors of Education with whom the authority's officers work closely in planning ahead to meet the shifts in population. At the parish level whenever there is an R.C. or C. of E. School the local Clergy will also have a part to play and in some areas there will be the occasional school of the local Free Church or of the Jewish community. On the whole these complex relationships work well and are not as difficult in practice as a study of the formal structure might suggest. There is an atmosphere of tolerance and mutual understanding that resolves most difficulties without the kind of strain that might have been foreseen from the debates that preceded the compromises of the 1944 Act. This is the more notable in those areas where the moves towards comprehensive education in the past decade have required much co-operation and have obliged LEAs to move ahead with sensitivity in matters of conflicting and strongly-held opinions. Interestingly, debates within the House of Lords during the passage of the 1987 Education Reform Bill provided opportunities for leading Church figures to speak strongly, not just about education, but on behalf of LEAs.

In matters of community, youth and recreational provision the activities of voluntary interests are more diffuse and difficult to summarise. Here an LEA may discharge its obligations by direct provision (e.g. a Civic Youth Club or a Sports Centre) or by co-operating with a voluntary agency to which financial help is given (e.g. West Indian Centre or the local branch of the National Playing Fields' Association). Many voluntary bodies are part of well-established national or local organisations of many years' standing and the nature of the partnership is well understood.

In addition there is a multitude of other voluntary agencies that are more ephemeral and may exist only for the period of interest and enthusiasm of a small local group or even of one energetic individual. Some of these arise spontaneously as part of a sense in a community of deprivation or injustice in the distribution of resources, but it ill-becomes the local authority to ignore or seek to suppress such initiatives. Indeed, in the drive to revive community life in inner city areas of the mid-1970s it has been part of the policy to seek out spontaneous groups, to offer them advice and financial support and to encourage them in a small way to be active in filling gaps in existing facilities. There are inevitable risks that time and resources will be ill-used but these are not adequate reason to suppress local initiatives. Here in a small way on the fringes of their mainstream provision LEAs have the opportunity to stimulate people to do things for themselves as opposed to passively waiting for the authority to do everything for them. In a very real sense the frontiers of development for an LEA shift from one generation to another as progress is made. The frontiers in the 1970s were most fluid in the whole area of community education and participation by a miscellany of voluntary groups.

The Chief Education Officer

Section 88 of the 1944 Education Act required each LEA to appoint 'a fit person' to be its Chief Education Officer. Though an earlier Act in 1921 had given LEAs general powers to appoint appropriate officers this was the first specific reference in law to the office. Moreover it remained on the statute book when the Local Government Act of 1972 was passed despite opposition from those who believed the clause to be an undesirable constraint on local authority discretion. The debate was similar to that about the appointment of a statutory Education Committee. The 1972 Act did, however, remove another provision of the 1944 Act which had given powers to the Secretary of State to prohibit the inclusion in the short list of candidates for interview of any person regarded by him as unsuitable to be Chief Education Officer. In the debate within the House of Lords over the abolition of the ILEA and the transfer of its educational powers to the Inner London Boroughs, the government introduced a clause giving the Secretary of State the right to approve senior education appointments in the Boroughs for a limited period.

School Boards have been served by clerks who were not normally educationists. The transfer of responsibility to the new LEAs under the 1902 Act, however, was soon followed by the appointment as their chief officers of men who had been Head masters or Principals. This new breed fought tenaciously to free their authorities from the tight central control that the Board of Education hoped to establish. Men such as W. A. Brockington in Leicestershire and Percival Sharp in Newcastle and Sheffield had, however, by the 1920s firmly established the importance and influence of the office variously designated Director of Education, Chief Education Officer or simply Education Officer. It was recognition of the significance of the work of such men when the 1944 Act included provision to make the office statutory.

There are at present 104 Chief Education Officers in England and Wales, of whom five are women. Local autonomy inevitably means that the nature of the work done varies considerably and there is also some scope for differences of style and personality to affect the manner in which the duties are discharged. Despite this it is possible to make some broad generalisations about the work of a Chief Education Officer.

First and foremost he is the principal educational adviser to the Council as local education authority. He is expected to be in touch with major educational developments both locally and nationally and to ensure that the authority responds appropriately. His main access for giving advice is through the sub-committees of the Education Committee to which written reports are submitted to obtain decisions or to promote initiatives. Often a written report is preceded by some informal discussion with the chairman and other senior members who at times may decide first to obtain a preliminary reaction from the caucus of the majority party. There will be other reports that have been called for by the Education Committee or the Council on the initiative of a group of members or as a result of earlier debates. In many matters the written report will end with a clear recommendation so that the professional judgement of the Chief Education Officer is stated, but at other times the report will try to give a balance of advantages and disadvantages for alternative courses of action and leave it to the debate in committee to decide what best to do. In most authorities elected members prefer that officers, whenever possible, should be prepared to frame a clear recommendation so long as the officers in turn acknowledge that it cannot be assumed that their views will necessarily prevail.

The second broad area of work lies in implementing with care and accuracy the decisions and policies of the authority as expressed in meetings of Council and Education Committee. These decisions over the years become the framework within which the Chief Education Officer and his colleagues administer the service and many people will look to him to interpret individual circumstances and issues within the framework so that they can speedily assess their position. Here clearly the need is for skills of management and administration that are sufficiently flexible to cater for unusual factors yet not so relaxed that there is an impression of total absence of policy and principle. Since too the Chief Education Officer must never in public be critical of, or unenthusiastic about the decisions of the Council for which he works, the general public do not always draw much distinction between the elected member and the officer. This confusion is often noticeable at meetings for public and parents to explain schemes for secondary reorganisation, where it is normal for the platform to be shared by the Chairman of the Education Committee and the Chief Education Officer.

It can be seen from these broad statements that the post is both educational and managerial, but the latter function operates within an educational setting where there is considerable independence of action at institutional level. The typical profile of a Chief Education Officer that has emerged from surveys is that of a man with an arts degree who trained as a teacher and taught full-time for five or six years, nearly always in a secondary school. One survey in 1973 found that only 14 per cent had any full-time teaching experience in further or higher education. It has been usual to enter local government service from teaching at about the age of 30, to serve in two or three different LEAs, and to become a Chief Education Officer at about the age of 46. There are a number of significant departures from this norm, including some who have been appointed between the ages of 35 and 40, and others whose previous experience in teaching has been much longer and included service as Headmaster or a member of H.M. Inspectorate.

The requirement of Section 88 to choose as Chief Education Officer a 'fit person' has never been put to the courts for interpretation, though the profile already described indicates that much custom and practice has developed in the past 35 years. In the past a small number of Authorities have sought to advertise for a Chief Education Officer in terms that emphasise the managerial functions and attach insufficient weight to educational experience. Sometimes these incidents have had some relationship to a structure of management in the authority that is associated with a system of directorates where one Director assumes overall responsibility for such matters as Education, Libraries, Art Galleries and recreational services, and there is an understandable wish to open the post to all relevant professions. More recently, such proposals have reflected a growing view amongst some politicians that the industrial or business model of a Chief Executive whose credibility is primarily based on managerial skills, is badly needed within the education sector. On such occasions the combined efforts of the DES, the Society of Education Officers and the teacher unions have succeeded in establishing the position that to be a Chief Education Officer a 'fit person' must have first-hand experience in education. The post is thus for an educationist with managerial skills and not for a professional manager who, however competent, is not acceptable if he lacks an educational background.

A Chief Education Officer's first duty is of course to his employing authority but the key external relationships of the authority which are later covered represent a significant part of his work. He has both regional and national duties which few of the 104 post holders can ignore. In addition to serving on various committees as a representative of his authority he is likely to have opportunities to serve in an individual capacity on DES initiated working parties and as a member of bodies such as MSC Area Manpower Boards. Indeed the demand is such that many Chief Education Officers can accept only a small proportion of the invitations to serve that are received, though in some cases their senior colleagues are acceptable alternatives. To some extent the educational world in its expectation of personal involvement has not wholly adjusted to the fact that the 1974 reorganisation reduced the number of Chief Education Officers by one third. They are also in demand as speakers at courses and conferences, as advisers to the local authority associations and for international work with such bodies as the British Council and the Organisation of Economic Co-operation and Development. One result is that the allocation of his time between competing claims is a constant concern of the Chief Education Officer and there are today few who claim to find it easy to control and balance their diaries of engagements.

The Education Department

The work of local government is carried out through departments of full-time officials and there is usually one department for each of the main services. In addition there are a number of Council departments for functions such as finance and legal matters. Each LEA has a central Education Department under the direction of the Chief Education Officer and the larger or more scattered authorities may also have satellite area or district officers for a particular part of their territory. Others may not have general area officers but will establish them for specific functions such as Education Welfare or Careers.

Most of those who work in Education Departments are administrative and clerical officers who have chosen a career in local government either on leaving school at 16 or 18 or as part of a developing graduate entry. Initially their assignment to the

Education rather than to another department of the Council may be fortuitous but many of these officers spend all their working life in the Education Department and become very experienced and knowledgeable members of staff. Since however they do not have teaching experience they are debarred from reaching the top as a Chief Education Officer, though many of the school-leavers acquire qualifications up to and including degree level through a variety of day release and other training schemes. These officers will hold posts with such titles as chief clerk or administrative assistant in which they will have considerable responsibility for payment of grants, or maintenance of buildings or servicing of committees. In many Education Departments some of the more senior positions as Assistant Education Officer will also be open to those without teaching experience and these will typically cover matters like sites and buildings, finance or personnel.

Most of the senior administrative posts in the department are held by former teachers who have joined local government after a period of work in schools or colleges. These provide the professional top of the department, starting on entry as professional or administrative assistants and moving on to become Assistant Education Officers, deputies and chiefs. An Assistant Education Officer will normally have charge of one of the half dozen or so branches into which the work of the Education Department is divided. A typical branch designation will be Secondary Education or Further Education. Those senior officers share with the Chief Education Officer the task of ensuring that the policies and practices of the Authority are in accord with national regulations and, as far as possible, local perceived needs, and in addition to their own section responsibilities, they will form part of the senior management team of the department. While Assistant Education Officers cannot avoid heavy office duties their work is in no sense desk-bound. Much of their time is appropriately spent in professional discussion and consultation, both with heads and teachers, and with officers of other departments of the Council. Regular contacts with union representatives, with elected members of the Council and with aggrieved individuals dissatisfied with the service will feature prominently in their work.

At the level of Deputy Chief Education Officer the role is more that of trouble-shooter, handler of major initiatives such as secondary reorganisation and co-ordinator of the half dozen or so branches. Increasingly departments also have a separate Assistant Education Officer less encumbered by daily administration who is in charge of development or forward planning. Where this provision exists the holder will work closely with the Deputy.

In addition an Education Department will have groups of field officers whose main task is to deal with individual cases and who need to act closely with schools and colleges. Two such are the Education Welfare Officers whose duties involve close co-operation with the Council's separate Social Services Department and the Careers Advisory Officers who liaise both with employers in the area and with members of secondary school staffs in charge of careers advice. Because a single central office is not adequate for these services to contact parents and pupils it is usual for these officers to work in area teams, often with bases in schools or in small area offices.

An LEA will also have its team of inspectors or advisers. They will have been former teachers, and recruited from posts of departmental or greater responsibility. They will typically carry both a general responsibility for a group of schools and a specialist phase or curriculum responsibility for the whole Authority. Most of the main areas of the curriculum will be covered in this way, although the size of the advisory service can range from a mere handful to a force of 50 or more in the largest authorities. Increasingly, advisers are being supported by teams of advisory teachers, a number of whom will have been appointed as a result of education support grant initiatives. The 1988 Education Act charges LEAs not only to provide or secure the provision of services, but also to monitor and evaluate that provision. LEAs could well in the future, therefore, be looking to separate the advisory and inspectorial functions, but it will be the function principally of this team, in whatever guise, to provide advice, guidance and support to advance the standards of the service, and further to secure those standards through a process of monitoring and evaluation. Much of the time of advisers will be spent on working with heads and teachers within schools, planning and managing programmes of in-service training, giving advice and recommendations to the Chief Education Officer and administrative colleagues as well as keeping elected members informed. They are likely to act on behalf of the Chief

Education Officer in being involved with the appointment and promotion of teachers, and will have particular responsibilities in connection with the appraisal of teachers and the preparation and implementation of the Authority's own curriculum policy.

All the work of an Education Department is the responsibility of the Chief Education Officer although he will delegate many of his responsibilities in practice and in name to senior colleagues. He is accountable for the work of the department to the Education Committee where any departmental action is open to questioning or challenge at the public meetings. In such a large organisation working to the public both directly from a central office and through the running of several hundred varied educational institutions there is a premium on clarity of communications and accuracy of information. While mistakes and misjudgements are inevitable the overall record of competence and sensitivity is commendable and certainly bears favourable comparison with similar contemporary bodies, both in the United Kingdom and in education internationally.

Internal relationships

In every large and complex organisation certain internal relationships will be crucial to its effectiveness. For the Chief Education Officer of an LEA four groups in particular will require his constant personal attention even though colleagues will share the load with him. It is his personal success or failure with these relationships that will significantly determine whether or not the authority functions constructively and harmoniously.

First there are the working conditions established between the members of the Education Committee and the officers of the Education Department. These are unlike those of civil servants and ministers for the local government officer works closely with all members and not only with those of the political party in power. He is available to advise and give information direct to all councillors and other members of committees and this requires great mutual trust and understanding. In a public Council debate it is likely that members of both sides will be using facts and figures obtained by calling at the Education Department to see appropriate officers. The key relationship is that established between the Chairman of the Education Committee and the Chief Education Officer.

A chairman is the politician who needs to be in touch with his colleagues, to interpret their wishes to the officers and to ensure that the education service is properly treated in the majority party caucus. He need not necessarily have a profound knowledge of the education service but he needs to know and be known by the people of the area and to have a sense of their priorities. Unlike the Secretary of State, however, a chairman has no position in the statute books and all his actions must be such that they can command the support of the Education Committee. Since the burdens of the office are heavy he must be careful not to allow himself to be endlessly side-tracked by trivia while remaining accessible to any individual with a genuine grievance. The chairmanship of an Education Committee is today a formidable responsibility and very time-consuming. A councillor with a full-time job, particularly one in a small concern that relies heavily on personal involvement, can sometimes find it impossible to serve for long as Chairman of the Education Committee.

The Chief Education Officer must always beware of himself becoming a politician, though at all times sensitive to the political climate. He must warn the chairman in good time of rocks discerned ahead and keep himself in touch with how the thinking on future policy is going in the party caucus. He will not, however, normally attend the caucus meeting himself. As the permanent official the Chief Education Officer may in time serve as many as half a dozen chairmen and will need to adjust his role with each to ensure an effective partnership. Some may seek contact several times a week or almost daily while others adopt a style with much less frequent communication. While one may ask for as much as possible to be put on paper, another chairman may prefer the periodic informal conversation or phone call and shun paper work. The relationship is one of the most fascinating and crucial in the work of an LEA.

The second area of relationships for a Chief Education Officer is that with the other chief officers of the authority. He is likely to work with them as a group through some kind of management team that meets on a regular basis under the chairmanship of the Chief Executive or the Town Clerk. Here, too, there is an infinite variety of practices from weekly meetings with long agenda to a much more informal and occasional structure, but even in this latter case there is a corporate role that cannot be neglected. On an individual basis the other chief officers (Social Services, Recreation, Culture and Housing) will all be involved to some extent in joint working. The Planning Officer's staff will work closely with the section of the Education Department that deals with sites and development but the Chief Education Officer personally will not so often be involved with him or with the Highways Engineer.

In addition the Chief Education Officer will need to establish sound personal relationships with the Treasurer and with the Chief Executive himself, though it is unusual for the latter to seek heavy involvement in the education service save when particular issues seem to be causing difficulties beyond the Education Committee. Most chief education officers find in practice that fellow chief officers are only too ready to leave them to cope with what they rightly judge to be the formidable management problems of the education service.

A third group is made up of the several hundred Principals and Heads of the colleges and schools that are maintained by the authority. To them the Chief Education Officer is their professional leader and they look to him to exercise this role while respecting their institutional autonomy. Their number will include Principals of large colleges at one extreme and Heads of small infant or nursery schools at the other. While it is clearly impossible for the Chief Education Officer to know them all in any real sense, he is wise to be available and accessible to any one of them who seeks a personal contact. He will also usually have systematic arrangements to meet all heads of establishments in groups that are not too large or formally convened to inhibit a frank exchange of views. At any one time it is likely that a small number of Heads will be deeply anxious either about a personal or a professional matter and at such a time in an authority however large it is important that the chief officer should be available and willing to be personally involved in the attempts to resolve the anxiety. Personal interest by the Chief Education Officer in the concerns of Principals and Heads can do much for the morale of this group who sometimes feel isolated in their institutions and in need of understanding support from the top of the authority.

Fourthly a significant feature has been the growth in activities in each LEA of the various unions, both of teaching and other staff. At national level there is some rivalry and manoeuvring between the teacher unions and this is inevitably reflected locally. It is important that the Chief Education Officer should be personally accessible to the officers of the main unions, who often will act in consultation with the teacher members of the Education Committee. While much of the routine work can be handled by other officers the Chief Education Officer should be ready to act personally if appealed to on a specific issue. In addition he is likely to play some part himself in the periodic formal meetings for consultations that are held with all the unions as a preliminary to submissions of reports to sub-committees. His contact with the unions is likely to be underpinned with informal and social contacts through attendance at receptions and dinners arranged locally by associations and at times by attending their national conferences and there contacting the local delegation. Practices vary here, too, but in those LEAs where the Chief Education Officer personally gives some priority to these contacts with the unions the benefit to mutual understanding and trust in the work of the authority is often considerable.

External relationships

An LEA does not exist in a vacuum and its network of external relationships has an important influence on how it does its work. Successive Acts have sought to establish a system of government with a careful arrangement of checks and balances. Powers are shared at different levels as a deliberate protection against autocracy and in particular to avoid the dangers of an over-centralised system. The classic definition is that of 'a national system, locally administered' in which the LEA is the middle tier between central government and the individual institution.

External relationships are therefore of critical importance, particularly in defining the frontiers with central government, as represented by the Secretary of State and the Department of Education and Science. The theory of the 1972 Act, espoused in the parliamentary debates, was that local discretion should be enhanced and the new-style local government was to be freed from the minutiae of detailed control by Westminster and

Whitehall. In reality the period of economic difficulties that marked the mid- and late 1970s made it essential that local government expenditure was tightly controlled. Education, as both the largest revenue spender and the biggest employer of all local government services, has not been free from exhortation and monitoring by successive Secretaries of State, some of whom have lamented their lack of powers to influence events more directly through a greater measure of specific funding. At times too the LEAs have been under simultaneous attack from teachers in schools and Secretaries of State who have made common cause against them. Thus the area of genuine local discretion has seemed so slight that some have lamented that LEAs have declined to become mere agents of the DES. Following the 1988 Education Act, the balance of power between these three partners will change significantly with the LEA while still the middle tier, seeking to discharge its responsibilities rather through influence and exhortation than control and instruction.

The Education Act 1980 relaxed ministerial control of the local education authorities in comparatively minor matters such as provision of recreational facilities, the determination of boarding fees, provision for conducting educational research or the mounting of educational conferences, while at the same time taking powers by regulation in a more significant way, to prescribe, for example, precisely what information shall be given to the public about individual schools, for example detailed examination results. The replacement of the Schools Council by the Secondary Examinations Council and the Schools Curriculum Development Committee provided the Secretary of State with an opportunity to assume a much closer influence over what is taught in schools. The increased potential power of the Secretary of State is evident in the Education Act 1988 wherein there is provided for the Secretary of State a very wide range of enabling powers, far in excess of anything previously experienced, together with authority, for a limited period at least, over teachers' pay and conditions, but also over the appointments to the new Secondary Examinations and Assessment Council and the National Curriculum Council which have been established to implement the national curriculum proposals in the new legislation. Responsibility for the curriculum is now shared between the government in its control of the national curriculum, including programmes of study and attainment targets, the LEA with its overall curriculum policy, and individual governing bodies in their determination of the curriculum for each school and pupil. But the Manpower Services Commission, too, has a role, for example in promoting vocationally orientated schemes for the curriculum of 14–19 year olds, designed to give a much greater technical and practical bias to the latter stages of the secondary school curriculum. These initiatives are now linked into the work of further education colleges, and thereby overlap the contribution of MSC to authorities' work related non-advanced further education provision. Moreover, membership of the European Community has meant that the DES and in turn the LEA are required to conform with directives of the European Parliament or the European Courts. The EEC directive on language teaching for the children of migrant workers and the issue of corporal punishment illustrate the ways in which the powers, both of the LEA and of individual schools may be circumscribed by a DES requirement, stemming from a European Community decision. The establishment in 1992 of Europe as a single market area is bound to have further implications for the education system, both in the content and delivery of the curriculum, its relevance for future employment, and the recruitment of staff. Overall, the intended devolution of responsibility into individual establishments is being accompanied by a strengthening of centralist policy and decision-making which is bound to create tensions.

LEAs have two main avenues of communication with the DES. The structure of the department assigns a Territorial Officer, normally at Principal level, to keep in close contact with a group of authorities. Routine correspondence, telephone contact and occasional meetings between an authority and the department will be handled through this Territorial Officer. Some meetings will be in London but at times the officer will visit the area of his authorities to see for himself conditions and to meet the authority's officers. Usually elected members are not directly involved, though a major difference of opinion or difficulty over school reorganisation proposals may result in a formal deputation to see senior officers of the department or even Ministers.

The second point of contact is through members of H.M. Inspectorate. Each Local Education Authority is assigned one HMI to act as its District Inspector for Schools and another who deals with Further Education. Although these HMIs are locally based so that over a period they become well versed in the particular features of the LEA and are in a position to advise their colleagues in the department of its needs, increasingly they are being committed to central office and national projects with the result that some of the personal and local contact is being lost.

The DES also has a role to investigate and arbitrate on the actions of an LEA in those cases where there is an appeal to the Secretary of State. Section 68 of the 1944 Act was framed to ensure that an LEA exercises its powers in a reasonable manner and under it any individuals or group may approach the Secretary of State direct if they believe that this has not happened. It is not necessarily required of the LEA to prove that these actions have been those that the Secretary of State would have chosen.

In addition to the general duty placed on the Secretary of State by Section 1 of the 1944 Act and to the appellate function under Section 68, the DES can rely on two other provisions in its dealings with LEAs. Under Section 92 of the 1944 Act the Secretary of State has the power to call for such reports, returns and other information as he may need from an LEA to enable him to exercise his functions. This power is reinforced under Section 17 of the 1988 Act. This is a sweeping power that is sufficiently wide to give the department access to all the information that it may need as those authorities initially disposed to dispute the right to information on the curriculum that was called for in Circular 14/77 were reminded. More significant is the power under Section 99 to allow the Secretary of State to make an order that declares an LEA (or Governors) to be in default in respect of the execution of their duties.

This relationship with the department is the most important single external contact but it is by no means the only one. A number of other national organisations, such as the Equal Opportunities Commission, will also be an important element. Some of these bodies will have locally based staff with whom the officers of the authority will need to keep in touch. Certain national voluntary bodies will also have local branches that seek to influence the authority in its actions and in particular in its resources allocation. In addition, the Local Government Ombudsman may undertake investigations into the processes by which local authority policies are determined and implemented with a view to determining whether or not there has been

maladministration that has prejudiced in some way the rights
or opportunities for the pupil, parent, or member of the public.
A third main area of external relations is that which involves
co-operation and negotiation with other LEAs. At national level
nearly all the shire counties belong to the Association of County
Councils while the London Authorities and the Metropolitan
Districts are members of the Association of Metropolitan
Authorities. Both have Education Committees and their own
Education Officers, though while every member of the ACC is
an LEA the membership of the AMA includes authorities such
as the Metropolitan Counties and the inner London boroughs
which do not currently have educational functions. The elected
members of the two Education Committees are usually chairmen
of their own Education Committees and both also invite a number
of Chief Education Officers to act as their advisers. In addition
in 1974 a joint Council of Local Education Authorities was
established, with its own administrative officer and membership
drawn from the Education Committees and the advisers of the
two associations. This meets quarterly, provides members and
officers for a number of national negotiating and other bodies
and each July holds an annual three-day conference open to
representatives of all LEAs.

LEAs also have arrangements to act in concert on a regional
basis. In big conurbations such as London and Merseyside there
tends to be very close inter-authority co-operation, while in other
parts of the country the arrangements may be less intensive. In
addition to their own separate contacts authorities act through
membership of bodies such as the Regional Advisory Councils
for Further Education and the Examining Groups for the GCSE
examinations. Much of this level of inter-authority working is
at officer level but at times meetings of chairmen will be held
regionally to receive and determine proposals of officer working
groups. Any such decision is not binding on an individual LEA,
though with students in particular often crossing authority
boundaries it is in the general interest to endeavour to ensure
some comparability on such matters as fee levels.

From 1944 to 1974 there was legal provision for two or more
authorities to set up a Joint Education Committee with the
approval of the Secretary of State. As the 1972 Act gave local
authorities a general power to establish joint committees for
specific purposes, this separate education power was no longer

needed and it was repealed. In general, these powers have not been widely used, for one of the objects of local government change in 1974 was the creation of fewer but stronger individual authorities. That may change now following the transfer of ILEA responsibilities to the Inner London Boroughs, and there have been some other interesting joint ventures. Two particular examples in recent years have been the creation in the early 1970s of the Royal Northern College of Music in Manchester by the joint action of four LEAs and the establishment in 1978 in Barnsley of the Northern College of Adult Education by a consortium of the five LEAs in South Yorkshire.

The 1944 Act was perhaps the high-water mark of agreement on the purpose and nature of educational provision. Since then our community has become more complex and less homogeneous and as our economic status in the world has declined, so the concept of the purpose of education has diversified. Reports such as the Scarman Report and the Toxteth Report have underlined the social variety, the multiplicity of expectations, and the depth of unease (even at the Primary School age) within our society. Young people, facing prolonged unemployment, have voiced their disillusion at the inadequacy of the educational system which has failed to secure them a job. HMI have reported on the weakness of educational provision for the less able child while officially, increasing stress is being placed on examination success. Crime, particularly crimes of violence, has increased, and gnaws away at the fringes of social morality, gradually inducing an indifference to or disregard of the integrity of the individual.

Ethnically, culturally and politically, our society is vastly different from that of 1944. It is small wonder therefore that there is a lack of clarity on the course which the LEA should adopt to fulfil its new statutory duties, or indeed on defining exactly what those are. The task of .the LEA and of its administrators, particularly in the areas of communication and public relations, is more difficult than ever.

Part 2 Principles of educational administration

3 Educational planning

Planning is the fundamental activity of educational administration in all its various aspects and at all levels of operation. To fulfil their legal obligation of effectively executing the national policy for providing a varied and comprehensive educational service in their area, Local Education Authorities must create an efficient organisation. Careful planning is the instrument by which such an organisation can be created. Nothing in life is static and no organisation is sufficient for all time. The continuing need to plan in an education service arises because things change continually. In order, therefore, to understand the planning processes in educational administration, it is first of all necessary to look at the dynamics of the system – the major sources and causes of change.

The dynamics of the system

Four major categories of pressure for change or adaptation in the education system can be identified: political; professional; demographic; and changes in related services.

Political initiatives

Education law places with the Secretary of State the responsibility to promote the education of the people of England and Wales and the progressive development of institutions devoted to that purpose, and to secure the effective execution by local authorities, under his control and direction, of the national policy for providing a varied and comprehensive educational service in every area. These words prescribe very succinctly vast and complex responsibilities. The exposition of those responsibilities in the 1944 Act probably represented the closest approach to political consensus on the aims and scope of the educational service which the country has experienced in the last 50 years. It was generally accepted therefore, that although education is administered locally and, as will be seen, large policy initiatives have been taken by LEAs, the many aspects of the service are now settled by Westminster and Whitehall.

Major political initiatives have been taken since 1944 by central government; for example, reorganisation programmes to eliminate all-age schools, legislation to enable the establishment of middle schools, the introduction of comprehensive secondary education, bringing the most mentally handicapped children within the scope of the education service, the development of higher education in the public sector and its later removal in large parts, the virtual disestablishment of mono-technic teacher training institutions, and the raising of the minimum school-leaving age on two occasions. All such initiatives require considerable planning for their implementation by local authorities.

In more recent times, governments have become much more interventionist, most notably in the shape of the 1988 Education Act. The national curriculum and testing, arrangements for substantial delegation of powers to governing bodies in schools and colleges and proposals for open enrolment have re-emphasised the sometimes latent power of the centre to take major initiatives. Indeed the nature of the 1988 Act lays much emphasis on the LEA's planning role. Whilst detailed administration is devolved to individual schools the LEA is expected to concentrate on strategic planning issues, such as monitoring and delivery of the national curriculum, and overall plans for the delivery of work-related non-advanced further education. In addition, an armoury of specific grants such as those for In-service Teacher Training and Education Support have appeared. Often funded by siphoning off part of the education element of the block rate support grant, these have provided central government with a much more direct leverage on educational developments at local level. But the local authority will continue to have an important role in planning the delivery of such schemes. Specific grants are no longer confined to DES; the Department of Employment, the Training Commission, the Department of the Environment and the Department of Trade and Industry have also become active in this field. As examples 2 and 3 at the end of this chapter demonstrate, the development of bids to central government based on detailed and far-reaching plans has become a very important task for education departments.

Within an LEA itself political initiatives may arise from the education committee or the council, from governing bodies of schools and colleges or from voluntary bodies such as the churches, parent-teacher associations or specific pressure groups. Whatever their source, they become policy when they have been considered and approved by the authority. Examples of local initiatives in which the principle involved is so urgent as to require its adoption regardless of all other consequences are extremely rare. Generally speaking therefore any such initiatives should be examined carefully and thoroughly planned before the policy decision is taken. The planning process will include consideration of all the factors – including resources – necessary to the implementation of the policy arising from the original initiative.

It is perhaps, in this respect that the two kinds of 'political' initiative most importantly differ from the point of view of the Education Officer of the LEA. Any new policy or adaptation of existing policy approved by the authority itself ought, by definition, to have understanding and support for its implementation among the relevant professional and political groupings in the authority's area. The planning for the change takes place within a framework of known resources, well understood objectives and an agreed timescale. Consultation prior to the decision merges into planning groups and working parties subsequent to the decision. Representatives of those responsible for the implementation of policy are likely to have been aware of the initiative from its inception (and frequently party to its promotion). The planning required is therefore likely to be advanced through existing structures and to be well within the capacity of those involved. Feedback from those introducing the change is likely to be relatively easy to achieve. School reorganisations and local curriculum initiatives belong in this category.

By contrast, initiatives taken by central government, even if they have been the subject of consultation with local authority associations, are unavoidably more remote from the officers, members and teachers of the LEA. Sometimes they are politically unwelcome to the majority group on the council. Nonetheless, if they are a legitimate fiat of central government their introduction has to be planned for by the LEA. The details of the planning processes are considered in a later chapter. The necessity to use senior staff time and skill, to ensure adequate memoranda and explanation to the committee, to lay bare resource implications and to set forth the limits of LEA discretion within the proposed national policy all do however require emphasis here. The planning processes set up in consequence of national initiatives frequently need to be specifically created for their purpose; to include members as well as officers from an early stage; to ensure considerable consultation with teachers and the public; and involve the necessity to reach agreement with treasurer, architect, planners and others within the authority about resource implications. The development of formulae for financial delegation to schools and colleges as required by the 1988 Education Act provides a prime example. So too do the preparations for the introduction of competitive tendering in the areas of school meals, cleaning and grounds maintenance now required by legislation. The process of planning in response to central government initiatives is not essentially different from that involved in responding to local initiatives, but it is often longer, more demanding of senior officers' time, and more complex. This is because central initiatives cannot reflect the variety of local circumstances. Moreover, in responding to a central political imperative such as parental choice as expressed in open enrolment policies or the opportunity for schools to opt out of local education authorities altogether, such initiatives can, by their very nature, make efficient planning at local level very difficult indeed.

Of course, political initiatives, whether of central or local government, do not arise out of thin air. They emerge from the existing state of the service and the climate of opinion in 'the political nation'. This climate is partly created by the other three parts of the dynamics of the system, which we must now consider.

Professional initiatives

The 'profession of education' is properly wider than many professions. Central to the service are professionals such as teachers, advisers, administrators and academics. Less directly or exclusively involved are workers in allied fields of human science and behaviour, such as philosophers, economists, political scientists, sociologists, paediatricians and psychologists whose work nevertheless can have a direct bearing on the objectives and methods of the education service. Those concerned with educational provision have therefore to be sensitive to contemporary research and practice both in pedagogy and in other related professional fields which influence the contemporary view of human nature and what the state should attempt to offer its citizens.

Professional initiatives affecting the education officer may arise from, for example, national or local curriculum developments or research, the teachers' associations, HMIs, advisers and administrators. DES requirements to issue a major statement on the whole curriculum, policy statements on the place of science or modern languages, curriculum development initiatives, such as the projects on economic awareness and oracy and education support grant activities such as rural schools or information technology, all require LEA planning. But these are only a few of the outstanding manifestations of the constant search for more appropriate, and surer ways of educating all the children within our schools. The search by well-informed, highly dedicated and energetic people is almost limitless in range and variety. It is part of the professional expertise of the educational administrator to be aware, as extensively as possible, of this incessant quest for improvement. More important, he must be equipped to distinguish the most promising among many possible innovations, know how current practices may be modified to benefit from such innovations, understand what, from the past, needs to be jettisoned and through channels such as training courses, reports to committees and briefs to architects, ensure that new approaches are thoroughly understood and beneficially applied. Increasingly he needs to know how to shape and prepare plans which will be acceptable to those at the centre of responsibility for allocating specific funds.

Demographic change

The dynamic caused by population changes is always with us. Any account of the education service since 1944 very soon involves describing how 5 million school pupils in 1947 became nearly 10 million in 1972 (including the raising of the school leaving age first to 15 and then to 16); how 207,000 teachers were employed in schools in 1950 compared with 404,000 in 1974; and how the population of England and Wales shifted internally from old urban areas to new suburbs and new towns so that to the problems of providing for growth were added those of providing for redistribution.

Population growth was the general theme until the mid-seventies. Since then, however, a major trough in numbers has developed, passing through the system to reach the upper end of secondary schools in the early 90s. It is not a symmetrical trough. Current births and future forecasts do not promise a return to the peak numbers of the past. Superimposed on these national patterns are local variations, sometimes very marked, together with a wide range of future forecasts. Such a complex and changing situation means that educational planning at LEA level needs to be constantly reviewed and monitored.

Other services and co-operative action

One of the most striking features in the field of social provision since the last war has been attempts to bring about co-operation between discrete services. The intellectual origins of these attempts lie in focusing upon the client or client group rather than upon the service organised predominantly around a single professional discipline. Consideration of the needs of the young child and his family, for example, transcends the confines of any one discipline. Doctors, health visitors, teachers, and social workers may all be involved in the welfare of the child and family. And once inter-disciplinary thinking has been accepted inter-disciplinary working becomes an imperative.

Of course much had already been done within the limits of individual authorities. An excellent example is the close co-operation between the pre- and post-natal health services, the hospitals and the education services to provide a diagnostic and supportive service to handicapped children and their parents.

The tremendous advances in the education of deaf children owed much to this co-operation. Intermediate treatment depends for much of its success upon co-operation between social services and education; whilst co-operation between education and the police service and the initiatives taken by the Training Commission over the Youth Training Scheme and, most recently the Employment Training Scheme for older unemployed require a considerable response from the further education service. Such developments represent the acceptable face of corporate (that is, co-operative) planning in local government and allied services. They demand in the educational planner a wider vision and secure professional roots.

The constraints upon planning

The greatest constraint upon educational planning is the inevitability of starting from where you are. Virtue in educational planning consists partly in acquiring and making use of a profound understanding of the existing system and partly in accepting realistically that most change, however carefully planned, will be gradual and unspectacular. This should not obscure the fact that from time to time the various dynamics already mentioned lead to a situation where planning and planned change must be so urgent and immediate that their effects are sudden and disturbing. The restructuring of teacher training to match the falling school populations or measures to deal with youth unemployment are examples which come readily to mind. Nevertheless it is true that plans should never be based on any starting point other than present realities. They should provide for the evolution of the existing system so that it has some new, desired capacity. For this reason it seems likely that 'the planning function' in an education service should never be too far divorced from the experience and understanding which comes from taking responsibility for day-to-day administration. The 'thinkers' and the 'doers' should not be allowed to drift far apart from each other. Five different kinds of constraint, or rigidity, in the existing system may be analysed.

Existing policies

The authority will probably already have a policy upon the matter which the planner is about to tackle. It may be a policy to have no policy; or it may be a policy which needs changing; but in either case it will have collected around itself a set of public expectations, political implications and assumptions in the clerical and administrative staff which together constitute a formidable inertia. These factors need consideration early in the planning process, for they exercise a powerful influence on the preparation, presentation and implementation of plans. Minorities or an ill-informed administration can substantially frustrate change earnestly desired by the majority.

Existing procedures

The explicit or implied policies which have just been mentioned will be enshrined in clerical and administrative procedures ingrained in the staff of the authority. The power of procedures – whether written or conventional – should never be under-estimated. It is of vital importance to the administrator, therefore, that staff, at all levels, should be adequately trained and alert to the need constantly to ensure that procedures are the most efficient instruments for effecting policies and that they do not degenerate into rigid constrictions of desirable improvements.

Existing staff

Neither should the impact upon staff, whether clerical, manual, administrative or teaching, of asking them to change their ways be underestimated. Planning, which is an instrument for improving a service for people should always provide for the human elements, although there is an understandable tendency for the concrete issues of providing buildings, equipment and transport to assume an undue prominence.

The education authorities of this country have experienced over the last 45 years an unprecedented amount of change. Curricula, school and college organisation, teaching methods and forms of administration and political authority have all been radically realigned. As we seek evidence of the effectiveness of much that has been attempted, the importance of understanding how the 'critical unit of work' really works (the teacher in his classroom, the head with his staff, and adviser in his team, the education officer in his hierarchy, the committee in their divided world of care for the service and fear for the rates) is being driven home to us more and more. Where things seem to have gone wrong, there is often to be found at the root a failure really to understand what the innovation was for and to make a commitment to it and feel a new sense of motivation. This is especially a danger when the planning has been prompted by external, unwelcome forces for change. Where it has had to be 'reactive' rather than 'proactive'. Perhaps worst of all have been the half-understood innovations which have led to good ideas being introduced in a superficial way and with lack of rigour so that they become discredited. Educational planners must face these traumata of their psychological past and yet must avoid feeling too scared to take any bold decisions. Instead they should provide in the future more sensitively for preparation and training of those who have to make new systems work.

Existing buildings

The procrustean bed is never more starkly revealed than when the existing stock of buildings seem inappropriate for its future use. Fifteen per cent of the country's primary schools still date from before 1903; many secondary schools are on split sites; colleges of further education are working in annexes and makeshift accommodation. The qualitative problems are, however, greater than those of quantity. The 'open school' is hard to achieve in a railway carriage of classroom compartments; integration of departmental effort in a college of further education is difficult to achieve when departments are spread over several sites. The planner must judge what it is reasonable to expect the staff to achieve against the odds: get it right and you raise people above themselves; miscalculate, and you destroy morale.

Finance and budget forecasts

The planning process requires some realistic estimate of the future flow of resources into the sector of the services under consideration. This is often the most difficult of all the variables to assess. Buildings, numbers of staff, their state of training, the theoretical objectives, can all be researched and known fairly accurately. This is especially the case when local government finance is manipulated by central government for purposes of national economic management. For an individual LEA the more significant factor in finance planning is often the rate support grant, not local views about service levels or willingness to pay the rates. Locally expenditure is generally determined for one year only and this one year at a time. The politically-fraught revenue budget of the local authority system is inimical to good planning. The creation of a five-year forecast budget, rolled forward each year looks fine in theory but presents far too many hostages to fortune in practice for it to have been widely attempted. Whilst the financing of local government is now to be reformed, it is unlikely to present the educational planner with a much firmer basis for his work. With the community charge contributing a much smaller percentage of their income to most authorities than rates, their dependence on finance outside their direct control will become even greater.

The planning process

We can now see what good educational planning ought to involve. It should mean deriving from the dynamics of the system things which either should be attempted or which those in power are determined to attempt (the two are often the same thing) and proposing workable ways of doing them, in the light of the constraints.

Logically, four stages can be seen. In the real world, of course, they often turn up in a different order or occur simultaneously in different parts of the authority's deliberative processes – so that the planner has the additional task of bringing some order to the process and keeping the appropriate groups and individuals in touch.

Choice and first thoughts

At any one time a Senior Education Officer is probably aware of a dozen potential and pressing initiatives which would meet some or all of the criteria set: they would gain political support;

changes in demography or teaching methods make them desirable; they could be achieved within existing or likely future resources. Increasingly they are influenced by central legislation. But it would not be possible to sustain so many initiatives simultaneously. There appears therefore to be a need for a kind of standing policy review process. It does not always require the formality of a sub-committee of the education committee; yet it is essential that there is some member involvement. In practice, in most authorities, it is the Chief Education Officer and the chairman reflecting together and exchanging ideas and information from their two overlapping worlds who carry out this review process. It is reinforced by the general network of relationships between officers and members, especially between heads of branches and sub-committee chairmen. The chairman may be backed up by regular meetings of all members of the controlling group at which policy is discussed. Where there is a 'hung' council all or most political groups will be involved. Equally the Chief Education Officer has various policy planning and review groups which maintain the health of the professional network through their contacts with advisers, schools, academics, HMIs and the literature. Both are regularly stimulated, indeed often nettled, by a flow of advice and criticism from practitioners and the public.

From this continual (and often half-incidental) review of the existing state of affairs, there emerges a manageable flow of ideas or projects which merit working up into discussable form because they appear to meet needs that are real in ways that would gain professional and political support. At this stage they are written up by the appropriate education officer as discussion documents, or consultative papers or draft committee memoranda.

To make this over-rationalised picture real, it is necessary to add that much important policy-making is done against the clock, because, say, a new specific grant is announced or curtailed by some central government department at short notice, or because a legal case or ombudsman report requires urgent consequential action. Most likely of all, it will be because of last minute changes in budget provision. In such cases chairmen and education officers must rely on their experience in coming to a decision and the process of 'getting the feel' of the political and professional climate has to come at later stages when first drafts may need radical revision.

Political decisions about policy and resources

When preliminary consultation and redrafting have finished, the policy proposal gets its first exposure to the formal consideration of an education sub-committee. That may lead either to a crisp decision, if the subject matter makes it possible, or to a more formal series of consultations with interested groups – especially teachers, governors and parents. Each of these will require from the education officer careful timetabling, preparation and recording, eventually leading to a further comprehensive report to the committee.

Increasingly the education officer will need to think about policy at two levels, that of the LEA and that of the governors and individual schools. As much greater delegation to schools becomes a feature, the ways in which a central LEA policy will be shaped and interpreted at school level will also be of considerable significance and there will certainly be interaction between the two levels.

Professional decisions about methods

Once the policy makers have decided the outlines and objectives of the new policy, the professional is faced by the need to choose the optimum method for bringing it into the authority's practice. Again, a sharp, clinical distinction between 'professional' and 'political' cannot be made. At the extremes there is no difficulty: the Chief Education Officer can assume that he is free to decide how to administer policy for the employment of part-time assistants in school kitchens. At the other end of the spectrum, the method by which existing schools are converted into a tertiary system, for instance are as much part of the public–political decision pattern as is the principle of comprehensive education itself. Between extremes, issues which would appear to rest entirely within the jurisdiction of the Chief Education Officer may because of topical interest become socially or politically charged and implementation of policy then requires a more open exposition.

Agreement about a plan

The final stage is the agreement among those whose assent is required. With the greatly increased central powers conferred by the 1988 Act on the Secretary of State, this may mean the holder of that office. In this case preliminary soundings will have been made with DES. It may require a committee report, whose preparation will involve consultation with teachers, other Council departments and any other interested parties. At a lower level, it may simply require a clear memorandum to all concerned in which the plan and any consequential administrative measures are explained.

At this point the necessity to write clear administrative and clerical instructions and train staff in their application becomes paramount.

Feed-back

All planning, to be realistic, needs feed-back from current experience of attempts to implement plans. And any particular policy needs to have, built-in, a servo-mechanism by which its application is refined in the light of experience.

To achieve this it is essential that the educational administrator should always be firmly in touch with daily practice whilst retaining, amid the mass of detail, clarity of vision, insight and imagination.

The structure of the LEA administration should be created with this need as one of the criteria. The complexity of the modern education office is itself considerable; add the necessary connections with teacher-groups, other staff-groups, voluntary bodies and with other local government departments or extra-local government services and the need for good management becomes obvious. Later chapters will analyze key planning tasks of an LEA in more detail. But perhaps a few examples chosen from the fields, co-operation with other local services, curriculum development and response to a national initiative will helpfully complete this 'overview'.

Examples

*1. A joint venture – education, health, social and voluntary
services*

The 'Children's House and Playpark' in a northern industrial
town was built by the LEA under an urban aid programme and
involves education, health and social services in its functioning.
The direction of planning was undertaken in the education
department and illustrates all the main dimensions.

In the late 1960s the Council had made a survey of day care
facilities for the under-fives and declared its belief that, wherever
possible, health, education and social services should be co-
ordinated and should emphasise also the contribution of
voluntary organisations and especially participation by parents
themselves.

When the opportunity of an urban aid project appeared there
was added to these objectives that of providing safe, open and
imaginative play space on the model which had impressed a
recent Council visitation to Scandinavia.

The project was, therefore, complex and novel. It involved
finding a suitable site in a declining urban area; pooling the
ideas of three statutory agencies; learning about adventure
playparks; surveying the voluntary groups of the chosen area
to see how far present needs were being met; working closely
with the building and landscape architects; and maintaining a
tight cost-control system. At a later stage, as the scheme emerged
from the discussions and sketch plans, considerations of
appropriate staffing, management and administration had to be
solved. Finally, the decision was taken to let the venture develop
slowly and free from publicity so that the first two or three years
of operation also became part of the planning process with much
important development of the use of the buildings being done
through the process of experience.

Following the initial approval of the concept, site and cost
limits by the committee, a project team under the leadership
of the Assistant Education Officer for Primary Education was
created consisting of education advisers, playing field officers,
project architect, head of the adjoining primary school, the
District Education Officer and the local parks officer, social
services and health service representatives and representatives of
the various local voluntary organisations associated with the pre-

school child and the family. From a series of fairly unstructured meetings there emerged the elements of a possible scheme which was then worked up into an architect's brief and interior finishing and design brief.

Local neighbourhood support was essential to the success of the scheme; not everyone would necessarily welcome a children's playpark adjacent to their home and the existing play groups or mother and toddler groups might feel threatened if they thought the statutory services were merely moving in with well-resourced alternatives to their existing efforts. Steps were taken, mainly through the existing primary school, to work with and through parents of young children in the area. The site was designed to add a visual asset to the area; the use of the building would not be a conventional nursery school but more of a 'drop in' centre where families could develop their own efforts with the help but not the dominance of professional teachers. It would also be a place where they could meet representatives of the local health and social services without a special journey and in relaxed circumstances which made it more possible to understand their purpose and value. Most of all, the Children's House would try to help young parents as they faced the problems and joys of bringing up their young children.

By the end of two years the building and playpark were ready and a small permanent staff, already known to parents in the area, and the local primary school staff, appointed. The furniture had been selected to add colour and texture. Floor coverings, cushions, curtains and easy chairs absorbed noise and gave an air of home. Parents and young children found it easy to enter and work in the various rooms and spaces. Their relationships with the staff were direct and on more equal terms than is common in school, office or clinic. The local health visitor found her contact with mothers and very young children especially easier.

But this was still in the planning stage. The first summer holiday's operation of the playpark taught a great deal; the community began to reveal new capacities which required new styles of organisation. The decision to avoid publicity and visitors paid off: all those working at the centre concentrated on the job in hand without the self-consciousness that questions posed by visitors might have aroused. The senior advisers of the authority kept in close touch and ensured that the adjustments of furniture, operation or relationships with 'the office' that became necessary were deftly achieved. The planning process probably lasted at least two years after commissioning the building, as well as the two years beforehand.

2. *Planning the delivery of WRNAFE (Work Related Non-Advanced Further Education)*

Throughout the 1980s the delivery of vocational further education has been subject to close scrutiny from a variety of bodies, including the DES, Audit Commission, TC and local authorities. Particular attention has been focused on the efficiency of the delivery by reference to such indicators as staff–student ratios but recently attention has also focused on the effectiveness of delivery, i.e., are objectives being met.

This movement to a more rigorous assessment of the performance of further education providers has, of necessity, led to consideration of the planning mechanisms of the delivery of further education. The MSC in particular have required LEAs to produce an annual development plan for NAFE. In this particular case study we see how the local authority moved from ad hoc arrangements to a more systematic and structured approach which directly relates the planning process to the allocation of resources.

When the MSC (now the Training Commission) announced in 1984 that LEAs would be required to produce an annual NAFE development plan, the local authority found that it did not have the staffing resources or systems in place to tackle the production of the plan in other than an ad hoc way. Statistical information was requested from the authority's colleges and was collated and drawn into a draft plan by a degree student on placement from a local polytechnic. The draft plan was then edited by a senior officer. Information was not collected in a structured way. Lines of thought on important development issues were not clarified before the information was requested. Colleges did not identify with the plan or accept any ownership of it. When finalised, the document was not so much a plan as a series of general and position statements which, in themselves, did not require action nor did they put forward a strategy or clear objectives.

It became clear to all concerned that a radical change was necessary if the plan was to achieve its objectives of ensuring that course provision reflected the needs of the local labour market, that courses were provided efficiently and effectively, and that development needs were identified and solutions proposed. Therefore, the format was changed so that

(a) The document was a plan of intended action (not a position statement) setting clear objectives against which performance could be assessed.
(b) The document established mechanisms to ensure that the objectives stated were automatically considered as part of the Council's budget process.
(c) The plan established systems to ensure that it was regularly reviewed and performance evaluated.

A secondment was arranged with the MSC whereby an experienced member of their regional NAFE planning team was based in the Education Department and under direction from the Assistant Director (Further Education) took responsibility for producing as a discussion document a first draft of a three-year plan. A NAFE Planning Group comprising Principals of Colleges, the MSC Further Education Officer, the Assistant Director FE and the seconded officer was established.

In view of the experience gained, the team recommended that a Planning Group be established on a permanent basis with the membership as above but with the addition of the College Industrial Liaison Officer, the Authority's Planning Officer and the LEA Adviser for staff development, all of whom had a significant input into the production of the plan.

The group established an annual planning cycle, as outlined overleaf, which was designed to produce the plan in a structured, coherent manner and also incorporate the Authority's response to the joint efficiency study on managing colleges efficiently. The Authority's response to the issues identified in the report was to strengthen planning procedures generally, to plan and monitor course provision and projected student numbers, and to allocate resources to colleges, not on the basis of historical budgets but by reference primarily to full-time equivalent student numbers. As the WRNAFE plan established projected FTE student numbers its conclusions fed automatically into the allocation of resources to colleges. At the same time the Authority introduced new management controls which allowed college managements the opportunity to benefit from the planning process. Virement and net budgeting in particular were introduced.

The impact of the changes is yet to be assessed in detail but will be considerable. The strategic role of the LEA will be enhanced as it will now be provided with comprehensive reports upon which it can establish priorities and assess performance.

College management are aware that planning documents now determine resource allocations and, as a consequence, specific plans have to be established for marketing, staff development and curriculum provision. These must relate to the overall WRNAFE plan.

It is intended to monitor closely the effect of these changes, particularly on the demands of senior management and to consider what, if any, changes are required to reflect the new approach.

The table opposite shows, in summary form, the overlapping processes involved as between WRNAFE planning with the Training Commission (column 1), the College's total course provision planning arrangements (column 2), and consequential budget adjustments (column 3).

3. Management of specific grant-aided provision: LEA Training Grants Scheme (LEATGS)

In promoting its policies for education during the 1980s, the Government instituted specific grant funding for a number of programmes managed by LEAs. In all such schemes, funding is subject to the acceptance by the funding agency of detailed LEA proposals, normally related to indicative expenditure allocations or other spending targets. The LEA Training Grants Scheme is one such scheme and provides grant aid at the 70 per cent rate in national priority areas of training and 50 per cent in support of locally determined needs.

Limited specific grant aid for in-service training of teachers was introduced in 1983–84 in support of training in national priority areas. That scheme was further extended in the years that followed. The 1986 Education Act established the LEA Training Grants Scheme by abolishing the teacher training pool and giving the Secretary of State new powers in respect of the funding of in-service training for teachers and other groups. The

Work related non-advanced further education planning

Date	WRNAFE Planning with TC	Budget Process	
		Planning	Budget
1987 September	Planning guidance issued by TC for 1988–89 plans. First formal meeting (TC/LEA Planning Team).	1988–89 Budget prepared on basis of historical cost plus adjustments for developments.	
October	Course starts determined. Programme revised/confirmed.		
December	Second formal meeting. Planning Team begin preparation of 88–89 Plan.		
1988 January	First draft of plan to TC. Third formal meeting		
February	Planning Team. Amendments to draft.		
March	Submit plan to TC.		
April	Fourth formal meeting Planning Team. Plan agreed and approved. Second monitoring review of current programme (87–88).		
September		1988–89 academic year commences.	
October		FESR return. Numbers determined.	Planned budget determined for 1989–90 FTE numbers.
Nov 88– March 89		Three year rolling total provision plan updated (89–90) (WRNAFE and other courses).	
April 1989		Projected FTE students agreed.	Colleges begin 1989–90 financial year.
September		1989–90 academic year commences.	Colleges advised of projected adjustments to 1990 financial year.
October		FESR returns actual FTE student numbers determined.	Colleges advised of planned budget for 1990–91.
November		WRNAFE plan revised in light of actual course starts/enrolments.	
Nov 89– Mar 90		Three year rolling total provision plan updated (1989–92).	
1990 April November		Repeat above process.	Colleges begin 1990–91 financial year. Colleges advised of projected adjustments to 1991–92. Repeat process above.

process by which one LEA implemented the scheme gives an example of the planning and management processes involved.

The Authority already had an extensive in-service programme before the onset of grant-related in-service training. Thus an INSET Advisory Committee constituted under the Teachers' Consultative Committee had been in place for several years.

In the summer of 1986, the Education Committee approved a paper from the Director of Education outlining the nature of the scheme and recommending that a proposal be prepared. They received a detailed 'policy for INSET' which had been drawn up by the Advisory Committee. A detailed plan was then produced by advisory staff based on advisory perceptions of need, a survey of schools and colleges, and the views of teachers' associations and regional INSET providers. These national aspects were managed by an Assistant Education Officer having responsibility for specific grant projects. The preparation of the LEAGTS proposal required a great deal of advisory time during the months of July and September 1986. The proposal was submitted at the beginning of October 1986 and notification of the outcome was received by Christmas 1986, just three months before the start of the 1987–88 financial year in which the scheme was to operate. The final scheme was approved by Education Committee in January 1987.

The secrets of successful planning demonstrated in this appendix are:

(a) to start early and build on existing curriculum policies;
(b) to build in the administrative and management costs;
(c) to meet the criteria in a way which anticipates local needs;
(d) to have effective mechanisms for consulting the clients;
(e) to be responsive to change with as much flexibility built in as possible;
(f) to ascribe sufficient staff time to the job;
(g) to have an effective senior management team to ensure that the advisory and administrative divisions work closely together;
(h) to be aware of the need for monitoring and evaluation of what is to be provided;
(i) to lay the ground work for a comprehensive INSET data processing system which can become part of the data base shared between the LEA and schools in local financial management.

4 The Management of educational plant and resources

Section 8 of the Education Act 1944 lays upon the Local Education Authority the duty to secure provision of primary and secondary schools:

> It shall be the duty of every local education authority to secure that there shall be available for their area sufficient schools (a) for providing primary education . . .; (b) for providing secondary education . . .; and the schools available for an area shall not be deemed to be sufficient unless they are sufficient in number, character and equipment to afford for all pupils opportunities for education offering such variety of instruction and training as may be desirable in view of their different ages, abilities and aptitudes . . .

Section 41 of the Act lays on LEAs the duty to provide adequate facilities for Further Education, that is to say:

(a) full-time and part-time education for persons over compulsory school age, and
(b) leisure time occupation in such organised cultural training and recreative activities as are suited to their requirements, for any persons over compulsory school age who are able and willing to profit by the facilities provided for that purpose.

It is to be noted that the Act does not impose on LEAs the duty of *providing* all the schools necessary to enable them to discharge the duty imposed by Section 8. Indeed, most careful and detailed consideration is given in the Act to the provision of voluntary schools (mainly by the churches) and to the use which may be made by an authority of independent (or private) schools. The fact remains that by far the greater number of schools are provided by the LEA; and it is of interest to speculate whether anyone involved in drafting the Bill which became the great Act of 1944, or involved in its passage through the House of Commons, had any idea of the scale of school building which would be required to carry out the duty imposed by Section 8.

In fact, it launched the education service on an operation bigger than any seen in any other part of the public sector; an operation which far outstripped the great wave of educational building which followed the Education Act of 1870. The growth in the number of children born in the post-war years, reinforced, in some parts of the country, by numbers of immigrant children and everywhere by the raising of the school leaving age to 15 and then in 1973 to 16, established school and college building as a major part of the work of all education offices. For nearly 40 years it has been one of the pressure points in educational administration as authorities have struggled against the calendar, and sometimes even against the clock, to keep up with rising school and college rolls.

It has to be remembered that education is the only one of the public services where the law requires a place to be provided for *every* member of its client group so far, at least, as the provision of schools is concerned. We may have as many prisons, as many hospitals, as many old people's homes, and as many houses as at any moment society believes it can afford and, if the supply falls short of meeting the demand, so be it. We shall do better gradually over the years. But where schools are concerned every child presented by his parents *must* be accommodated at least until he has reached the leaving age of 16. The effort needed to achieve this has been immense; the accumulated expertise, educational, financial and architectural, which is now a common feature of all education authorities, is unique in the public service. The country can justly be proud of what has been achieved and the great number of teachers, administrators and politicians who from all parts of the world, come to visit our schools are an indication of the international recognition of those achievements.

But now things have changed, not least as a result of the demographic trends which produced an initial dramatic fall in primary school numbers. While they are recovering (but not to their previous levels) the numbers in secondary schools continue to decline. In the post-16 sector, Government initiatives to control the number of students have affected establishments in the public and private sectors. Furthermore, contraction is in part, at least, responsible for a number of other developments which are affecting and will affect the design and equipping of educational buildings. These include for example, the wider development of nursery education, the most effective ways of developing/ remodelling secondary schools to serve merged schools and the needs of the modern curriculum, the development of comprehensive education, wider community use of schools, the need to cope with areas of educational and social disadvantage, the requirements of the 1981 Education Act concerning special educational need and, of course, the intervention of the MSC via the TVEI pilot schemes and the YTS for 16+ young people. It is obvious that all these new factors, together with the strains imposed on the system by the 'opting out' clauses of the 1988 Act make the management of educational plant and resources a very different matter from the expansionary requirements of a rapidly growing school population between 1945–71, when the pre-eminence of what is termed 'basic need' i.e., the provision of 'roofs over heads' was virtually the sole gauge of capital investment in educational buildings and resources.

To set the scenario for this chapter, it is important to devote some time to a more detailed consideration of falling rolls, and the surplus places which this phenomenon produces. 'Contraction' may seem negative and pessimistic in terms of educational development, but it offers opportunities for educational reform and development at least as great if not greater than the rapid 'expansion' of educational institutions and resources managed so wonderfully well between 1945 and 1971. In the second half of that 'expansion' period, significant advances were made in the design of new secondary schools to meet the needs of comprehensive secondary education as an alternative to compressing children of all abilities into the existing and often inadequate grammar and secondary modern school buildings designed for a bi-partite, selective system of secondary education. Equally, great strides were made between 1961 and 1971 in the design of more versatile new primary school buildings, eliminating unnecessarily lengthy corridors, assisting teachers and children to work together in more flexible, open groupings than was really possible in the single teacher, single class group, cellular classrooms designed with the objectives of the 1870 Education Act in mind rather than present day objectives. Even though the task of making the nation literate and numerate was thought to have been substantially completed before the Second World War, the method of training teachers allied to public and parental expectations based on the education they had experienced, ensured that generally new educational plant was reproduced up to 1945 with little design alteration. Much progress has been made throughout the country in redesigning new educational plant since 1945, due in no small measure to the work of the Architects and Buildings Branch of the then Ministry of Education. Nevertheless, much remains to be done in remodelling existing schools and in designing new schools to take account of all the new factors mentioned earlier in this chapter. With far more limited capital resources available we need to ensure the most versatile and efficient use of materials, furniture and equipment to enable new curriculum development to take place.

Falling rolls and surplus places call for careful management of educational plant and resources which could bring about improvements in the way in which the LEA fulfils its legal obligation to meet the needs of the population of its area. It has been estimated that nationally the total school population of England and Wales may fall from approximately 9 million in 1979 to about 7½ million by 1990. Within this national picture there will be much local variation. In some cases there will be a permanent fall as people migrate from the area; in others the fall will be followed by a rise in due course as a consequence of the birth-rate; in some areas there may, by a combination of factors, be a net gain in population. The effects of new housing developments have to be gauged carefully to try to judge whether the number and type of houses will result in overall increases in the school population or to internal migration, both within and between individual school populations. Each LEA must therefore carefully plan and forecast the needs not only of the total area, but also of individual localities within its area.

The effect of recent government legislation, which increased parental choice and limited the control over annual admission limits that the 1980 Education Act had allowed local authorities to exercise, is likely to make such forward planning far more difficult.

In planning, the administrator must have regard primarily to demographic factors, but these will be very radically influenced by social, educational and financial considerations. Financially, the case for closing schools or taking surplus places out of use is compelling. The Department of Education and Science estimated that for every 100,000 places taken out of use savings of approximately £10 million could be made – excluding savings on teacher salaries. If savings made on the heating, lighting and other maintenance costs of buildings could be applied to other elements of the service improvements in the provision of resources such as books and equipment could be looked for. While the full extent of such benefits does not always accrue to the LEA, it is nonetheless detrimental to crucial educational provision if money is unnecessarily expended on maintaining surplus places.

Increased resources are not the only educational benefits which might be looked for. Closure of small schools could lead to the transfer of children to larger schools where, for example, multi-age groups could be eliminated, a larger range of curriculum options could be offered, better technical and craft amenities could be enjoyed and obsolete buildings not well suited to modern needs could be dispensed with. At the sixth form level concentration of pupils into fewer, larger units has obvious advantages. These are some of the factors which the administrator will bear in mind when reviewing the provision of buildings and resources.

Social factors also are important. Accessibility of schools must, as always, require careful consideration. Long fatiguing journeys will not be good for children or acceptable to parents. Crossing of busy roads – particularly by young children – is dangerous and undesirable. It may therefore not be feasible for the LEA to close some small schools and, indeed, the Government has begun to recognise this fact. Schools are more than the sum of places that they provide. Parents hold schools in esteem and reinforce their views by seeking to secure the admission of their children to those schools. Reasons for parental preferences are diverse – not solely related to examination success. Some schools are by design community schools catering for the interests and involvement of the community they serve. Others are community schools by tradition and local acceptance. Some indeed are the focal point of the social and cultural life of the area. All these factors must be in the mind of those managing buildings and resources when they contemplate taking them out of use. This will frequently involve a nice balance of judgement before reaching a decision, particularly in view of the provision of the 1988 Act which strengthens the ability of the community to make choices.

The Act requires the admission limits of schools to be set at a level not lower than they are physically capable of accommodating using an admission level not lower than their standard number, as defined by the admissions to the school in 1979 or for schools established since 1979 (i.e., subject to the publication of Notices under Sections 12 or 13 of the 1980 Act) the number fixed when they came into being. The Act also gives governors increased powers, including the right to appeal to the Secretary of State to be allowed to change the standard number. The consequences of this legislation for less popular schools and the communities they serve will pose new problems for the administrator and further inhibit the application of any form of planning which attempts to make the best use of resources for the overall benefit of an Authority's clients.

To close a school or to reduce the number of places in a school, the LEA must publish its proposals in accordance with Section 12 or Section 15 of the 1980 Act. Objections to those proposals may be submitted to the LEA by ten or more local government electors for the area within two months of their publication. These must be transmitted to the Secretary of State who must take them into account in deciding whether to approve the authority's proposals. Despite indications from the DES that the Secretary of State would do his best to expedite the formal procedures, there is often a considerable lapse of time between the expression of the need for action because of falling rolls and the carrying out of necessary action.

The DES requires that consultations should take place before any notices are published. Good public relations are essential at every stage: all concerned, governors, staff of the affected schools, parents and the general public of the area should be given the opportunity of being acquainted with the facts and the bases of decisions. Objections to proposals to close schools have generated a substantial volume of case law, particularly with respect to the amount of detail that has to be given to interested parties in the consultation process. It is now accepted that consultations based on a number of options are not sufficient; detailed proposals of the exact intentions must be made clear. This inevitably leads to the need for a number of rounds of consultations before the actual proposals are published in the form of public notices.

Falling rolls and the consequent management of plant require the concentrated exercise of many skills which are referred to more extensively in another chapter – sound statistical information, thorough understanding of the geographical area and of educational issues, political and social awareness, ability to balance delicate matters and to formulate reasoned conclusions, power to communicate and the power of setting out salient facts clearly and concisely. The extent of the consultative processes and the timescale required for the publication and implementation of notices can be a cause of great strain and uncertainty for teachers and parents, so above all the administrator must have a patient and sympathetic understanding of the many personal problems that will· inevitably arise from any school closure or reduction of school places and which may well come directly to him for resolution.

At this point, it is important to glance back in time at what is still the legislative cornerstone of our educational system, the 1944 Education Act. Section 11 of that Act required each LEA to prepare and submit to the Secretary of State a Development Plan for Primary and Secondary Schools showing the action which the authority proposed to take to see that there should be sufficient primary and secondary schools available for its area and the successive measures by which it proposed to accomplish that purpose. The section also prescribed very carefully the nature of what was clearly intended to be a most detailed and thorough examination of the educational needs of the nation. Each LEA's Development Plan (and there was one also required for Further Education entitled 'A Scheme for Further Education and Plan for County Colleges') was of inestimable value and the major guideline for the development of educational institutions during the expansionary period up till the early 1960s. It has perhaps slipped into desuetude since that date, but nonetheless it is clear that every LEA must continually review the provision of buildings and other resources to meet the constantly changing needs of the population of its area.

Fundamentally it matters not whether the thoughts of 1947 are the same as those of today. What matters is that education authorities came to recognise the value of a Development Plan in one form or another. Such a plan needs constant up-dating and revision but it should exist to provide the essential framework within which the planning of individual schools can be undertaken.

In creating that framework, the authority must necessarily identify its needs in some detail – its need to build to meet basic need (i.e., the need to put roofs over the heads of children who would otherwise be without a school place); its need to build for the reorganisation of secondary education; its need to replace the worst of the worn-out primary schools, many of them more than 100 years old! Basic need has always been with us and continues to be so in some areas of new housing. After a decade of falling birthgroups, the recent upturn in some areas, though not to previous high levels, will mean that inevitably the meeting of basic need must remain the permanent first priority. The importance of other types of need has varied over the last 40 years, and has reflected the changing emphasis which successive governments have attached to the different aspects of education development. For, given the constraints upon the national purse, priorities there must always be, and, in broad outline at any rate, they must be determined nationally.

The chosen mechanism of central government control has been the approved building programme, generally an affair of annual allocation but occasionally an attempted three-year rolling programme designed to help authorities to plan ahead with a greater measure of certainty. Unfortunately, this has almost invariably had to be withdrawn during the three-year cycle as a result of financial crisis.

In inviting submissions by authorities (whether of single or three-year programmes) central government has indicated the types of project acceptable at that particular moment. At the end of the Second World War, priority went to projects for repair and re-building of bomb-damaged schools; in 1947 raising of the school leaving age was a major preoccupation. In 1960–65 the emphasis switched to the elimination of all-age schools and the provision of accommodation in secondary schools for science and technical studies. From 1968 onwards programmes were devoted to the improvement of conditions in inner city schools. For three years from 1971, there was a modest attempt to replace worn-out primary schools, and the raising of the school leaving age to 16 took place in 1972. From 1974 onwards nursery programmes were established following the White Paper 'A Framework for Expansion'; in 1977–79 there were programmes of special projects to aid the reorganisation of secondary education and, since 1979, there has been emphasis laid on the development of facilities in schools in areas of special educational and social need and, more recently, projects that will enable surplus places to be taken out of use or to replace buildings which, after a long period of poor levels of maintenance, are rapidly becoming dangerous.

In this way, the major building programme has acted not only as a financial regulator but as a steering mechanism ensuring, as governments have come and gone, that the truly massive resources ploughed into school building have promoted their policies – political as well as educational.

It is a common misconception that, in allocating to an authority a building programme of a certain value, central government is 'granting' the authority that amount of money. In fact, an allocation by way of a building programme is nothing more than a permission to spend that sum of money. It guarantees that approval to borrow money (in layman's terms to take out a mortgage) will be forthcoming.

The basis on which bids and resulting allocations are made was fundamentally altered in the light of the new capital expenditure control arrangements introduced by the Local Government Planning and Land Act, 1980. Previously, each government department was responsible for making a separate and self-contained allocation to each local government service and so far as the education service was concerned, this was based on very detailed bids for individual projects. The 1980 Act changed the whole concept of control of capital expenditure and, while involving new and more complex procedures, did in fact give a greater degree of freedom to local authorities to plan their overall capital programmes. It is important to understand the principal innovations introduced by this Act.

First and foremost, allocations of what is known as 'prescribed' expenditure – broadly speaking expenditure on the acquisition, construction and improvement of land, buildings and plant – are made in five main blocks to local authorities. These comprise education, housing, transport, personal social services and other services. Though these block allocations are still announced separately, once they have been made local authorities are free to spend them as they choose and to vire them between services. They are also free to augment them in two ways. They may overspend an allocation by 10 per cent in one year and this may then be carried forward to the following year provided it does not exceed 10 per cent of that year's allocation. Conversely, they may underspend the year's allocation by 10 per cent and carry forward the underspend on the same understanding that the sum carried forward is not more than 10 per cent of the following year's allocation. More importantly, however, and this is a very significant element in an authority's freedom to plan its capital programmes, it may enhance its government allocation by the use of a prescribed proportion (as low as 30 per cent in some years) of capital receipts that it has accrued by sale of existing building stock or land.

The method of controlling capital expenditure was also fundamentally altered by the Act and it is now based on the total of capital payments that may be made within each financial year rather than on the value of work started within that year. Traditionally, under the old system, provided a project had actually started, or the contract had been signed before the 1 April of the starts year, it did not matter how much or how little of the total cost was incurred within that year. Under the new system of control payments rather than starts are critical.

To try to increase the amount of capital that they are permitted to spend, authorities have made various attempts over the years to use creative accounting, particularly in respect of arrangements for leasing and deferred purchase. Not surprisingly successive items of legislation have been introduced to limit such opportunities. In addition, there has been an increase in the amount of central control of some educational expenditure, through Educational Support Grants. The capital consequences of these, whether in respect of the LEA's contribution or that funded by Central Government, have all to be set against the Authority's capital allocation, thus limiting the amount remaining for other purposes.

The annual allocations show approved spending limits for three years: the first year consists of a figure that includes within it the aggregate of all expenditure committed from projects started in earlier years as well as an allocation designed to enable new projects to start; the following two years give an indication of expenditure that will be committed as a result of projects that will not have been completed in the first year but they do not represent a guarantee of future years' allocations. In other words, if an authority wishes to start a £1 million project in Year 1 without a guarantee that its allocation for Years 2 and 3 will be adequate for the project to be completed, it can only do so if it is confident that funds from capital receipts or virement will enable the completion of the project should the government allocation be inadequate.

The new system requires the local education authority to show in its annual submission to the Department of Education and Science both its spending plans and its outstanding committed expenditure from previous years. Similarly the local authority as a whole must make overall calculations for the whole range of its services, unless it has continued to regard government allocations as self-contained for each separate service. If it has exercised any degree of virement between services or has used any of its own capital receipts to enhance its spending limits then it clearly must keep a careful account of its total spending patterns.

The new arrangements are considerably more complex than those they superseded, insofar as they require close and regular monitoring not only of the progress of individual projects but of the actual payment of accounts, since - and this has to be emphasised - payments rather than work completed are the critical factor in the new procedures. Delays and slippage of projects for whatever reason - be it difficulties in acquiring land, changes in political decisions, delay in approvals by the Secretary of State, staff illness, etc. - can seriously affect spending patterns, and if projects are not quickly substituted as the need arises and payments for completed work are not expedited, then capital allocations may be underspent by more than the 10 per cent tolerance referred to earlier. This could have the consequent effect of requiring greater use to be made of, say, capital receipts in the following years.

Conversely, however, the advantages of the new system are that it enables the individual authority to plan its capital spending as a whole; to decide its overall priorities within the totality of funds available from the two sources, i.e., government allocation and capital receipts; and to avoid the traditional scramble to get work started by the 1 April each year. It may well seem to those operating the system on a day-to-day basis that similar freedom could have been achieved with less complex procedures to be observed but nevertheless the overall flexibility the individual authority now has to plan its capital programmes is to be welcomed.

Unfortunately, so far as the education service is concerned, there is a further complexity that does not apply to other services and that lies in the procedures relating to capital expenditure at voluntary aided and special agreement schools. These are separate from those relating to all other educational expenditure but are nevertheless under the aegis of the education authority.

In brief, the governors of aided and special agreement schools must submit their requests for all improvement projects costing less than £2,500 directly to the DES for an allocation under its rationing scheme. All their requests for improvement projects costing more than £2,500 must be submitted to the local education authority for it to forward to the DES. The authority must indicate the extent of its support for such projects and make provision within its own capital allocation for those projects it is prepared to support and for such LEA contributions as are required. The allocation made by the DES for the voluntary schools is quite separate from that made to the authority for other educational capital work, but is announced on the same three-year basis described earlier, i.e., Year 1 comprising previously committed as well as new expenditure and Years 2 and 3 committed expenditure outstanding from Year 1. The allocation for the voluntary schools does not, however, include any expenditure on these schools for which the LEA is responsible and this must be met from within the authority's total 'prescribed' capital expenditure allocation.

The LEA is required to submit similar details about committed and planned new expenditure in respect of aided and special agreement schools as for its other educational projects but an added difficulty arises, insofar as the authority itself has little or no control over the progress of work at voluntary schools. In order to compile its submissions to the DES it has to obtain information from diocesan authorities and it must not overlook the existence of aided schools that are totally separate from any diocesan arrangements. (These are usually old-established grammar school foundations.)

So far as submissions to the DES are concerned, these too have been fundamentally revised to take account of the greater freedom now vested in the local authority. Formerly, the Department called for very detailed annual returns of information in order to calculate the precise deficit of school places in growth areas, according to very specific criteria. Information about basic need is still requested but in a less detailed form and confined to a brief statement of the total number of new places required over a planned three-year period, related to three age groups, 5-11, 11-16 and 16+. Authorities are asked to provide supporting information to help in the Department's analysis of the figures. So far as improvement projects are concerned, the Department takes account of the information it asks authorities to supply from time to time about the number of pupils accommodated in very old or unsatisfactory buildings – broadly pre-1903 primary and pre-1919 or substantially pre-1945 secondary buildings – and the number of pupils in areas of educational and social disadvantage. It also seeks information on the extent to which surplus places have been taken out of use and particular projects which will enable further places to be removed.

The forms on which this simplified information is requested would in themselves provide a very inadequate basis on which the Department could form a judgement about an individual authority's needs and it recognises this by suggesting that authorities may submit supporting information which they consider may be of assistance to the Department. It is clearly in the interests of individual authorities to do this, particularly if the DES allocation continues to play a significant part in the amount of capital building the authority is able to undertake.

In addition to its bids for primary and secondary schools, the LEA is asked to submit bids for other areas of the education service – nursery, special, further and higher education – though these are judged not on a formula basis but on their individual merits and needs.

When the DES announces the authority's allocation for the following year, on the three-year spending basis, it indicates how it has been built up by reference to the separate sectors of the service, namely schools, further and higher education. It makes it clear, however, that this is no more than a guide to the education authority: the disposition of the allocation is entirely a matter for the authority itself, which is also free to vire between the education block and any of the other capital expenditure blocks announced by other government departments. It may in a sense seem anomalous that the DES should still be showing the separate elements of the education authority's allocation when the system has changed so fundamentally and it may well be that this procedure will itself be varied as the procedures take firmer root.

For the time being, the separate break-down serves as an indication of the way in which the Department has judged the education authority's needs in the light of national policies.

As far as the capital programme is concerned, there are two factors which impose constraints on the time-tabling of the building process. The first relates to the statutory approvals which are required whenever a local authority intends to establish a new school, ceases to maintain a school, or make a significant change in the character and size of a school. These regulations (Sections 12 and 13 of the 1980 Act) involve the local authority in the publication of Notices so that the Secretary of State may receive comments and objections upon proposals: the resultant timescale will vary significantly according to the nature of each proposal.

The second major influence on the timescale lies in the timing of capital allocations. The Notices require implementation dates to be stated but, as these may prove to be incompatible with the extent of the capital allocation in any one year, the planning process can be further complicated and preliminary design work may have to be done in the knowledge that it may eventually prove to be abortive.

In 1985, a report of the Efficiency Scrutiny of the DES's Architects and Buildings Group recommended that most LEA building projects should no longer be subject, as a matter of course, to professional examination and assessment by the staff of the A & B group. As a result, the limit for minor works was increased to £200,000 and simpler procedures now apply for major works costing less than £2 million.

For these, if not the subject of Section 12 or 13 notices, no submission is required. For those subject to Section 12 or 13 notices, Form ABBX has to be submitted at tender stage. This requires a short description of the project, details of the relevant Section 12 or 13 notices and an undertaking that the works will conform to the requirements of the Education (School Premises) Regulations 1981 and to the Department's constructional standards as specified in AM 2/85. It is intended that these projects will be approved after the receipt of the specified particulars, provided these are in order, without examination or assessment by the department's professional staff.

Where, for some reason, the Authority foresees difficulty in being able to meet the regulations and constructional standards on any major works the Department needs to be informed of the particular circumstances at the earliest possible stage. This requirement also applies to minor works projects, which otherwise require no formal approval. Where, however, a series of minor works is to be carried out at an establishment, and the sum of those works exceeds £200,000, then the submission requirements relating to major works must be met.

For projects costing in excess of £2 million, the accelerated approval procedure applies. This relates to cases where the Authority anticipates that the cost will fall within plus or minus 10 per cent of the appropriate net cost, calculated by reference to the guidelines. The appropriate forms, together with sketch plans have to be submitted and a gross cost agreed as a result of consultation between the department and the authority prior to the submission of tender details. At tender stage it is necessary to submit further information. If at that stage the gross cost is met and a certificate of undertaking can be provided, formal approval will be given without further discussion. If not, the gross tender cost will need to be specifically agreed with the Department.

The relaxation of the approval procedures does not, however, mean that an LEA has a totally free hand. Annex A to Circular 1/86 makes it clear that the Secretary of State attaches importance to the need for continuing dialogue between DES building professionals and officers of the LEAs in support of the achievement of value for money. For example, authorities are asked to look at alternative solutions to such problems as school closures to remove surplus places, including the cost of keeping schools open. In such instances it is likely that building work would still be required to bring existing buildings up to modern day standards, resulting in the need for additional architectural services and associated fees.

The Secretary of State also reserves the right to require the submission of additional information and to introduce professional appraisal of projects from an authority whose performance appears to him to fall consistently far below a reasonable standard of value for money. Accordingly, therefore, LEAs are asked to submit details on the appropriate ABB forms of all major projects for which formal approval procedures do not apply.

Automatic approval is not given to projects at voluntary aided schools, but voluntary bodies and/or governors of voluntary aided schools can seek 'accelerated approval' by agreeing a gross target cost with the Department prior to the submission of tender details. Formal approval would then be given without further discussion if the gross target cost were met on tender and the local education authority confirmed that the project complied with the Standards for School Premises Regulations and the Department's current recommended constructional standards.

The Education (School Premises) Regulations 1981 represent the most recent version of regulations which first appeared in 1945. Minimum recreational areas, areas of playing fields, minimum interior areas of teaching accommodation, minimum numbers of sanitary fittings and washbasins, and more general regulations on the required provision for staff rooms, ancillary accommodation for staff and accommodation for meals are all laid down. Many of the requirements are expressed in terms of minima, but in a period of constantly escalating building costs minima more and more tend to be regarded as the most that can possibly be achieved. Thus it is that since the middle 1950s the architect has been more and more relentlessly ground down between the upper millstone of financial limitations and the nether millstone of minimum regulation requirements.

From what has gone before the reader might well have gained the impression that the Department of Education and Science is a restrictive, constraining body. This would be a travesty of the true position. As the agent of central government the department has a duty to monitor closely (which often means to limit) the cost of school building, always an unenviable job. It must ensure that minimum standards are achieved: a task which must be rigorously undertaken in the interests of educational, technical and hygiene standards. But these monitoring roles are but a part of its involvement in school building. Its more constructive functions should be recognised.

The Architects and Buildings Branch of the Department of Education and Science was first set up in 1949. Since then it has played a major development role in school building. Not only has it, over the years, scrutinised the plans of all authorities; but through development projects its own architects have co-operated with the architects of local authorities in planning and building schools and other education institutions to meet what have been seen as the needs of any particular moment. A secondary modern school, a grammar school, a rural 'open plan' school, nursery accommodation through adaptations of spare primary accommodation: these are but a few of the long list of projects, each of which has tried to find an answer to a widely felt need. And it should be stressed that what has been produced eventually has been offered only as one answer, not as the answer. The building bulletin which has followed each such project has described in both educational and technical terms the difficulties encountered as well as solutions proposed. The building bulletin on fire prevention in schools represents another type of publication from A and B Branch (as it is commonly known) which has been of immense importance to education authority architects. In the case of this bulletin it can fairly be said that to it must go much of the credit for the generally high safety standards of schools in this country.

Let us now return to the local authority facing up to its building project. In many authorities advanced planning may already have begun ahead of administrative approval. The vital process of briefing the architect, making clear to him the educational needs of the eventual user, may well have had to start much earlier if the separate and critical programmes of the architect and the treasurer are to be met.

Of all the many stages in the process of building a new school (or extending or rehabilitating an existing one) this is the most crucial. A vague or inadequate briefing is usually the sign of inadequate educational thinking. It is the surest recipe for an inadequate school. The educational administrator and the architect should each make his own contribution based on a clear and detailed understanding of the kind of school required. On the part of the architect this understanding goes far beyond the number of spaces to be provided. It calls for an understanding of the use to be made of each space and its relationships with other spaces, and of the nature of the educational experience which is to be offered to the pupil. It calls not only for the understanding of the technical but also the aesthetic ambience which is required. It calls for a knowledge of child development. In some authorities, standard briefs exist which should help the architect to develop an appreciation of the educationist's requirements. Initial briefs should reflect a philosophy of education, a commitment by the professional educator to a concept of the curriculum and the teaching and learning methods by which the aims of the curriculum are to be achieved. Both educationist and architect should be fully conscious of the importance of what they are doing. They are creating an environment which will have a major impact on the educational experiences of generations of children. Time spent on developing these briefs is crucial to the success of any operation. In meeting a planning programme or an occupation date 'corners' may be cut at a number of points; they should never be cut during the initial preparation and further development of any initial brief.

To this point, there has been little visible sign of anything that the layman would recognise as part of building a school. Now surely at last what he might well recognise as 'the real business' of school building – the drawing of plans – can begin. But is the site known and available? In terms of meeting programme dates, and the planned phasing of expenditure that is now critical, the availability of the site is of the utmost importance. The process of acquisition, the transfer of ownership and arrangements for purchase in themselves will take time. But where a site has still to be identified, where planning permissions have still to be obtained, and negotiations have to be begun perhaps with an unwilling vendor, then the eighteen months which normally elapse between the announcement of an allocation and a start on site may well prove to be inadequate.

The importance of forward planning and forward purchasing of sites is likely to be particularly great in the case of schools to be built in or near the centre of major urban areas. There the availability of land will be limited, competition from industry, housing and other public services for what is available will be fierce, and the education building programme may well be held up by the complications of other public programmes such as clearance and redevelopment or major housing improvement schemes. In the extent of their forward planning, authorities have quite clearly varied enormously and it must be recognised that the problem of earmarking and acquiring sites has been easier where what has been involved has been a 'green field site'. In such cases to buy and hold a site for twenty or even thirty years has not been too difficult. To do the same thing in the middle of urban areas has been an entirely different kettle of fish.

When, despite the complications involved, the site has been identified and is in the authority's possession, then the time to elaborate on the initial brief and begin to produce sketch plans has at last arrived. Here again emphasis must be laid upon the value of architect and educationist working together as the first thinking begins to take shape on the drawing board. This is a stage when the advice and ideas of the local authority inspectorate or advisory service will be refined and when the views and experiences of practising teachers should be brought into consideration. The most successful planning is not likely to take place in a situation where, having handed over the brief, the educationist sees no more of the project until a finished sketch plan with an ABB2 plan analysis and outline specification appears on his desk. Exchange of ideas, a joint approach by educationist and architect, may lead not only to the most helpful solution to a problem; they may lead to the recognition of an unforeseen opportunity, a good idea which, working separately, neither educationist nor architect might have spotted. The path which leads between the architect's office and the Education Departments should be one of the best trodden paths in county or city hall.

It is at sketch plan stage that many of the basic design decisions are made. Those which relate to the exterior include the location of the building on site, points and means of access to it for pedestrians and vehicles, means of connection from the proposed building to the services of the public utilities and the orientation of the building. Internally basic decisions have now to be made about the shape of various spaces, their relationships one to another, the circulation flows of children. These are but a few of the many questions which call for consideration at this early stage of design. What seems like the obvious solution to one problem may well rule out the obvious solution to another; compromises will be inevitable at many points. Furthermore, compromises which overcome technical problems may well have a 'knock on' effect on the educational acceptability of the plan. This underlines the need for the involvement at this stage of the educationist.

Recent legislation has increased the governors' responsibilities. Where, therefore, work involves the extension, rehabilitation or straight replacement of an existing school, the governors and staff will rightly expect to be consulted when initial sketch plans have been prepared and at all subsequent stages of the design for a building that is likely to affect the curriculum and running costs of the school. The process is unlikely to be well carried out in haste.

Another path which should be equally well worn is that between architect's office and that of the quantity surveyor – a key person in the whole business of school building.

In terms of realistic, as distinct from inflated, expectations from the client (and even from the job architect) the quantity surveyor's close participation is invaluable. He must prepare a reliable budget figure with cash flow predictions which is sufficient to satisfy the brief and meet the programme. Costs may be established using data based on past experience or cost models previously agreed between the Education and Architect's Departments. Such costs need to be compatible with the value guidelines issued by the DES. The quantity surveyor's contribution must ensure that the scheme provides value for money, balancing initial costs with subsequent on-going costs and achieving a balance of expenditure throughout all elements of the project so that the distribution of resources reflects the needs of the brief (e.g., should more or less be spent on external works to the detriment or benefit of the building?). At least it should hold out the hope that the tenders, when received, will be reasonably close to the cost target which in turn prevents the hasty and often under-considered process of pruning plans at tender stage.

The temptation always exists to overcome technical or educational design difficulties by additional expenditure, so there is much to be said for the regular involvement of the quantity surveyor. What is reinforced at this stage of the design process is the extent to which educational, technical and financial considerations are interlocked, that a plan is an organic whole, rather than a series of loosely articulated parts, so that technical problems may well be financial and educational problems as well and that in many cases they will call for an inter-disciplinary solution. It is the complexity of the decision-making process that makes it imperative that the consequences of any changes suggested at the last minute, no matter how obviously good they appear to be, are very carefully thought through. Without such care, the very reason why a different decision was originally made, with its associated knock on effects, may be overlooked.

When sketch plans are available and initial costings determined, the procedures to be followed are as detailed earlier in this chapter.

Detailed layouts, showing the proposed position of fixed furniture, service points are then prepared. It is important, too, that layouts for the loose furniture are introduced at this stage, to ensure all the necessary furniture and equipment can, in fact, be accommodated. Working drawings can then commence. It is now vital that no further amendments are introduced, since they can prove very expensive in terms of time, fees and goodwill of the contract. Extensions and alterations affect the operation of an existing occupied building and need discussion between heads of establishments and the professional staff engaged on the development of the project. It is essential that the occupants know of the conditions that will prevail during construction and have accepted a method of operation which will be clearly described in the contract documents and allowed for by the contractor when preparing his tender. Stopping the progress of a contract for school examinations, for example, will be expensive if requested *after* the contract has been placed. Likewise, temporary boiler shutdown, alterations to kitchens and similar work should be arranged at periods to cause the minimum of inconvenience to the occupants. From here on, unless significant changes in the plans are proposed, the educationist retreats into the background, leaving progress to architect and quantity surveyor, since this stage of the operation is mainly a technical one. As working drawings develop, quantities are 'taken off' and a bill of quantities takes shape. The job is now moving towards tender stage.

Obviously the aim is to obtain the lowest possible satisfactory tender and to this end there are a number of different tendering procedures. Least sophisticated of all is the invitation of tenders from any contractor prepared to submit one. This leaves the authority open to the situation where a very low tender may be received from a contractor who has not the capacity, either financial or organisational, to carry out the work. It can also lead to large tendering lists which increase the cost of tendering which must eventually be passed on to the client. Probably the most common procedure is the invitation to a list of selected contractors known by the authority's technical officers to have the necessary experience and capacity. It can be argued that this leaves the authority open to the possibility of 'ring' tendering. Probably the most sophisticated, though much the least common, procedure is that of the serial tender. In this case contractors from a selected list can be invited to tender for a stated share of the authority's entire building programme on the basis of a prototype bill of quantities which requires the contractor to quote a rate for items of work most likely to occur within the proposed programme. This system can be particularly useful when the programme is based on the use of a building system. In this case objection may be raised on the ground that too small a group of large contractors may corner the market and that the liquidation of any serial contractor will have serious consequences. A further method adopted is to advertise each project in the technical and local press and to select a restricted list of tenderers from the response. This has the merit of ensuring that tenderers are keen to have the work, but requires detailed examination of the suitability of tenderers for each contract and is costly in time and advertising.

In short, tendering procedures vary; all of them have their critics; and by and large, authorities tend to favour one or the other rather than to 'dabble' in all. Experience seems to indicate that, at any rate where the system building from factory components is to be used, a high level of cost effectiveness is to be gained from the serial method. It should be noted that the National Joint Consultative Committee for Building (18 Mansfield Street, London, W1M 9FG) publishes recommended procedures for the various methods of tendering which is extremely helpful in establishing methods of operation which assist the client and are acceptable to the industry.

Tenders having been received, and the necessary DES procedures followed, the stage is set for the start on site. Every effort is then geared to meet the planned opening date. Here again, much of the work is left to the technical people – contractors, architects, quantity surveyors, building inspectors, and the staff of the public utilities. Staff at the Education Office still have a role to play, however. In some authorities there will be furniture and equipment to order, matching the time scales for delivery with the progress of the building work. In all authorities there is the need to monitor the rate of progress on the project in order to relate this to the timing for proposed staffing and to compare the expenditure to date with the budget figure for the current year. Above all, the Education Committee is still the client, and it is important that the educationist recognises the responsibility that implies. Last minute hitches, sudden needs to agree minor changes and, in the case of extensions and rehabilitations to existing schools, the possible need to arbitrate between the staff of the school and the architect all require an awareness of the current state of the development without any active participation on site. Excellent relationships and good communication between the architect and the educationist continue to be vital to the success of the project.

Given reasonable weather, no unsuspected site problems, no industrial disputes to hold up supplies of materials or to impede the actual building process on site, as the completion date approaches what started out as piles of materials and seemingly unrelated trenches and holes takes on the shape of a school. Before the authority will accept the building from the contractor come the formalities of take-over inspections and the preparation of a schedule of agreed defects and deficiencies which will have to be put right. The 'builders' clean' is followed by the more comprehensive 'clean' by caretaking and cleaning staff. Portable furniture and equipment pour into the building.

In the case of a new school, it is usually about this stage that teaching staff begin to appear, and soon after (and often before the entire building is absolutely complete) the pupils arrive and a school is born.

If this brief and all too superficial survey concentrates attention on county primary and secondary schools and makes no reference to special school or further education building programmes; if it does not treat the special features of voluntary school building, it is only through lack of space. In general it may be said, however, that the principles which underlie the building and furnishing of voluntary schools, of special schools, of colleges of further education, are broadly the same as those which underlie the building of county primary and secondary schools. However, while the principles may be broadly the same, the complexity of the provision and the infrequency of major projects in further education demand of the administrator and architect a willingness to consult, learn and exercise humility which is even greater than it would be in more familiar projects.

A general point may perhaps be made. More than once in this survey attention has been directed to the role of the DES in the education building process. It is worthy of note that as far as school building controls are concerned, over the years since the Second World War the hand of central government has rested more and more gently on the guiding rein. Any anxiety which there could have been about the possibility of central standardisation of schools buildings should by now have evaporated. The controls of the Standards for Schools Premises Regulations, for instance, have become less detailed and, so far as the planning of individual projects has been concerned, decisions have been left to the local authorities. After all it was upon them that the 1944 Act imposed the duty 'to secure that there shall be available for all the area sufficient schools . . . sufficient in number, character and equipment to afford for all pupils opportunities for education offering such variety of instruction and training as may be desirable in view of their differing ages, abilities and aptitudes . . .'. It is a duty which on the whole they have well discharged.

Why 'on the whole'? Like all things born, a new school needs support from the moment it comes into existence. It will age and, as it ages, will more and more need repair and maintenance. One would like to think that the design and specification of new school buildings kept firmly in mind ease and economy of future maintenance. But it is hard to escape the conclusion that financial constraints on capital expenditure cause us to neglect or even create future maintenance problems. In the attempt to make too little money go further than it effectively can we probably reached a stage some years ago where what we have built cheaply we shall maintain at great expense. Acres of leaking flat roofs will perhaps serve as one of the most readily recognised examples. And the problem is compounded by the frequency with which, in a period of restraint on revenue budgets, authority allocations for the maintenance of buildings have been squeezed until deterioration of the fabric of school buildings has reached a stage of galloping consumption.

There are those who hold that the rapid changes in teaching methods and the internal organisation of schools demand that no schools should be designed to last for more than about 20 years. It is a view hardly likely to commend itself to elected members or to treasurers paying for buildings, as most of them are, over a period of 60 years.

Somewhat less obvious perhaps is the effect of neglected maintenance on the ambience of a school. It may, with some justice be claimed that the educational benefits which accrue from a stimulating, colourful decor and from tasteful furnishings are of immense importance. Particularly will this be so in schools serving areas of social deprivation where the school may well be the most attractive and welcoming environment in which a child finds himself. If this be true, it must follow that the neglect of maintenance represents an important reduction in the educational opportunity which a well-maintained building has to offer.

Arrangements for maintenance of buildings vary from authority to authority. In some cases all, or most, of the work is carried out by direct labour organisations; in others work is put out to private contractors. In almost every case the responsibility rests on the authority's chief architect or building services manager and the role of the educational administrator is sometimes seen as being limited to that of intermediary between school and architect – passing on requests for repairs, identifying buildings in special educational need or, as some architects would no doubt claim, complaining perpetually – complaining of declining standards, standards of resource allocation, standards of workmanship, standards of materials used. It should, however, be regarded as something more important, if the limited resources available for maintenance are to be used efficiently. Replacing like with like, for example, is not necessarily in the best interests of the present or future needs of the school and an educationist's knowledge of successful initiatives in one school may enable another to maximise the opportunity for change that some minor maintenance works present.

The development area is one which has always offered considerable challenges to the Education Officer and in this area, as in others, the changes in legislation will require skills of the highest order if needs and resources are to be used effectively. It is also true that it is a field of work which contains the potential for frustration to perhaps a greater degree than most. It will be evident from what has gone before that the rationalisation of building stock is a highly sensitive operation and it is hardly surprising that elected members are most reluctant to be held responsible for closing schools, even when the financial state of the local authority as a whole may be less than healthy. The professional may find it more difficult to accept the crude abuse of the Capital programme for political ends. Just as the closure of a school may well lose a local politician some votes, the opening of a school is regarded as a very attractive option. If a logical order of priorities is to prevail, the Education Officer may have to work very hard indeed to commit his committee in advance to a structured programme with which it is difficult to tamper. If he is not successful in this endeavour, he may well have to face the steady infiltration of low priority projects into the high priority places as politicians carry out their endless manoeuvres for personal advantage.

Just as the order of major projects may be affected by a disregard for logical criteria, so too the officer may find himself under heavy pressure to reduce minor works allocations in order to create space for more new building. New buildings are attractive: a wide range of minor works adaptations is less visible to the public eye and does not so readily reflect to the glory of the particular local member.

The other major area of concern experienced by the Manager is the use of Public Works Departments to carry out maintenance work. Although recent legislation has forced Authorities to be more careful in their use of Direct Works organisations, the commitment of many local authorities to the principle of Direct Works may well work to the disadvantage of the Education service. It is not surprising that a clash frequently emerges between the Council's priorities for the Public Works Department which involve a year-long programme to maximise the use of its staff and other resources and the needs of the Education Department which ideally would prefer to control the services which it is offered. Few Education Officers will be unaware of the problems which are caused by the programming of work in schools at a time which is convenient to the Direct Works organisation but highly inconvenient to the management of the schools. The most glaring example is that of painting programmes which, instead of being carried out during vacations, are undertaken during term time. Although many direct service organisations tend to deliver a good service, the disparity of interest between them and their clients is a fundamental weakness: in that context, the lesser irritations relating to the control of information, accountancy procedures and methods of charging assume a greater potential for irritation. It will be interesting to see how great a role is played in decisions about the future states of schools by head teachers who have experienced years of subordination to the so-called support services operated by local authorities.

The main challenges for the Department of Education and

Science and LEAs over the years to the end of the century will be five-fold – first, a constant monitoring and evaluation of building stock in each LEA area as set out in the 'Study of School Building' paper produced by the Department of Education and Science in 1977; second, the remodelling of old schools and design of new schools to take account of new curriculum developments and interventions by such outside bodies as the Manpower Services Commission (MSC), and the wider community use of educational buildings; third, the furnishing and equipping of educational institutions; fourth, a closer examination of the design of and provision for Further Education (FE) colleges, etc; and finally, overriding all of these, the possible consequences of recent legislation for the rational use of an authority's building stock. Let us examine these challenges one by one.

1. Attempts to evaluate the school building stock must look both at the changes, past and future, that affect its adequacy; and at the economic context in which plans for future capital investment are made. This review must take into account (a) substantial and continuing changes in educational policies, techniques and methods, in the role of the school in society, and in the attitudes and expectations of society itself; (b) educational developments such as the reorganisation of schools on comprehensive lines, the reduction of class sizes, the extension of nursery education, the introduction of increasingly active methods of learning and the growing links between school and community all impose new demands on school buildings; and (c) changes in curriculum.

   In addition account must be taken of society's continually rising expectations for standards of safety, health and amenity of which the Health and Safety at Work etc. Act 1974 is one example.

2. The remodelling of old schools and the design of new schools has to take account of the national curriculum, the introduction of some of the new technologies, the much wider community use of schools and so on. In primary schools built before the Second World War we have been left with a great number of the two or three decker variety (mainly in London and the cities) and of those whose single classrooms approached by long corridors radiate at different angles from the assembly hall and administrative area. As rolls fall so spare

cellular classrooms have been and are being used variously for library/resource centres, TV educational programmes, withdrawal groups of different kinds or just for storage. In some schools some classroom doors debouching on the corridors have been opened and apparatus, equipment, books and carpeting have spilt over into them; where a pair of teachers in adjacent classrooms have agreed to do this together for the same age group, co-operative teaching and (incidentally) in-service, on the job, training of these teachers begins to take place; the curriculum is enriched and widened and the problems of differing individual abilities approached much more effectively. This sort of experience needs to be explored in remodelling old primary schools, as does the wide experience of open-planning which has developed over the country as a whole in the last twenty years. Teaching methods do change, however, and the opportunity to remodel a school occurs very seldom. The design must therefore allow for flexibility of teaching styles, which may not necessarily reflect those of the teachers currently on the school staff.

Minor works projects to effect remodelling are probably the quickest method LEAs can employ, but care must be taken to ensure that any major maintenance works that have to be included are costed accurately, so that there is no risk that the cost of the capital works appears to exceed the minor works limit. Remodelling of old primary schools will need to take account of the increased use of microcomputers, with their need for mobility within the school and the associated security consequences as well as appropriate facilities for the under-fives and the relevant school building regulations for children of nursery age.

In secondary schools the introduction of the national curriculum, the continuing development of comprehensive education, the greater emphasis on technical and vocational education within the general education context and the greater use of new technology in the shape of microcomputers and other sophisticated equipment all point to the need to re-assess the distribution and use of practical areas. In remodelling schools, the administrator, architect and quantity surveyor, working in close collaboration with teachers and advisers, need to bear in mind changing attitudes to the curriculum and to reflect these in the new design. This is true not only of practical and laboratory areas, but also of provision for the arts – especially the performing arts such as music, dance and drama – and for physical education and recreation.

Remodelling secondary schools certainly should have regard to community use. More and more, certain secondary schools are being designated as community colleges or centres for the use of the whole community. In rural areas especially, and increasingly in urban neighbourhoods, selected primary schools are being designated as community focal points. In most of these cases, in addition to designing or modifying these buildings for community use, independent rooms like community common rooms with refreshment facilities and bars make them available when the rest of the building is in use for school purposes during the day. School rooms will be used increasingly by adults and will be so even more especially if practical and other rooms have been designed with joint adult-school student use in mind.

In county areas, improved facilities over and above what can be provided within school building costs can be achieved by developing joint schemes with district councils. Swimming baths, squash and badminton courts, all-weather floodlit playing areas, even restaurants and exhibition areas have been provided by joint schemes planned well in advance along with an agreed school building project.

Although attractive possibilities for multiple use exist, two caveats must be entered. First, it will be necessary to take account of the inevitable consequences for building, maintenance and depreciation costs. In this connexion, there is often a failure to acknowledge that a school's budget will suffer considerably if its equipment, which is often designed to standards directly related to educational functions for children are heavily used by adults. Second, the increased power given to governing bodies in recent years means that they have greater control over the use of their school's buildings by other users, which can make it more difficult for LEAs to rationalise the use of the buildings in a particular area.

3. The furnishing and equipping of schools and colleges need careful attention since school supplies are a major item of expenditure in the budget of an education authority. As they

have grown in range, complexity and sophistication, so they have increased in price. Attempts over the years since the war to establish cost formulae for the furnishing and equipping of primary, secondary and FE establishments have all failed. Now the costs must be obtained from within the overall building allocation for the LEA. It is relatively easy to decide on a percentage of the capital cost of a primary school to devote to loose furniture, but much more difficult to do this with secondary schools or colleges of FE and Polytechnics. Efforts have been made in the field of school building to obtain better value for money through standardisation and the establishment of building consortia. These were aimed at securing the financial advantages of large-scale manufacture and purchasing. In the field of equipment and supplies the story of recent years has been much the same. Many of the larger authorities, at any rate, have central purchasing machinery operating on behalf of all departments. Often this has been built up on the foundation of an education supplies department. At one stage further along the line, we find consortia of local authorities. Thus, for example, CLEAPSE (Consortium of Local Education Authorities for the Purchase of Scientific Equipment) consists of some 51 authorities who have joined together to test and purchase scientific equipment and to encourage design and development. The Counties Furniture Group (CFG) has set up its own design team and all 47 authorities in full or associate membership can contribute through their officers and advisers new prototypes and designs more sensitive to developing educational needs. Consequently there has been an overall aesthetic and ergonomic approach to furnishings which has gone some way to achieve an overall design and finish – something sadly lacking in the heterogeneous furniture to be seen in most older schools.

The furniture consortia followed in the footsteps of the big school building consortia like SCOLA and CLASP which were established in the early 1960s to cope with the rapid expansion of the school population and of the basic need of school building. Nevertheless much remains to be done between educators, architects and manufacturers before the furnishing of schools and colleges is carried out functionally and aesthetically in a really effective way.

Some individual authorities have moved towards standardisation through the compilation of lists of approved teaching aids from which their schools must select when making purchases, particularly of expensive equipment. This is a step towards securing not only the benefits of bulk buying, but also the monitoring of the quality and suitability of equipment – a necessary precaution in a rapidly growing commercial market. Another common arrangement is the provision centrally by an authority of stocks of some kinds of equipment – records, cassettes, projectors and the like – which can be taken out on loan by schools. One may perhaps wonder how long this practice is likely to be justified given the increasing delicacy of some of the more sophisticated items and hence their vulnerability to damage during transit. The quite alarming costs of postage and transport also suggest that the advantages of such an arrangement are likely to be felt more immediately in urban authorities with large numbers of schools within a radius of a few miles even though central lending services were in some cases at any rate, originally conceived with the need of small and scattered rural schools in mind. Certainly it is in such places that the provision of central stocks of relatively small items has become uneconomic because of changes in the availability and cost of transport at a time when the cost of purchase of such equipment, in relative terms, has fallen and its reliability increased.

4. The design, planning and equipping of FE establishments present many problems of administration and management. Since the war, a vast building programme for AFE and NAFE has been undertaken. Recent legislation confirms the duty of each LEA to secure the provision of adequate further education to meet the needs of its area. FE colleges are now required to accept a greater responsibility for their financial affairs and to respond to the provision for free trade at a time when they are beginning to feel the effects of a drop in the age cohort and are being pressed by Central Government to provide additional management information and become more cost effective. Pressure for places in colleges is heavy and will probably be increasingly so due to demands from industry, from young people seeking additional qualifications to enhance their employability and from the programmes of MSC

to which reference is made in another chapter. Financial and other resources for building and the up-dating and replacement of technical equipment are likely to be limited, and therefore very careful management and assessment of demand by administrators, college principals and other staff will be necessary if the response is to be adequate.

5. The effects of the 1988 Act have yet to be fully felt. The impact of the removal from local authority control of polytechnics and some colleges of higher education is likely to be felt more in the colleges themselves than by the authorities. By contrast, the Act takes a stage further the process of moving responsibility for the running of institutions from the local authorities to the schools and colleges of further education.

Three sets of provisions may be cited to illustrate how the 1988 legislation offers the possibility of the disruption of arrangements for planning and delivering the programme for managing the plant and resources of the Authority, viz., those which relate to City Technology Colleges, grant-maintained schools, and admission limits, respectively. City Technology Colleges if successful will attract considerable numbers of students who would otherwise have been accommodated in maintained secondary schools. At a time when falling rolls have put the viability of many schools in the balance, the additional, though marginal, drain on the pool of potential students could have a critical effect. The movement of schools to grant-maintained status combines the possibility of losing students with that of loss of school plant by the LEA. This could cause the Authority to reconsider its overall provision and detailed arrangements. Within a three-tier system, involving first, middle and high schools, the impact could be particularly severe, especially in authorities which have developed closely integrated pyramid organisations.

The change in the regulations governing admission limits (see also p. 71 above) of itself threatens the stability of declining schools. The additional challenge of grant-maintained schools potentially exacerbates an already difficult situation. To maintain stability and economically effective provision of plant and resources will be administratively more intricate as the new admission procedures and limits come into force.

Taken together, the three provisions adumbrated above offer

the possibility of an improvement for a minority at the expense of disruption of the planning processes designed to bring benefits to the greatest number. It will not be a simple matter for an authority to prevent a narrowing of opportunity for those students in LEA maintained institutions affected by the impact of grant-maintained schools and City Technology Colleges, nor to support schools in particular localities which are already vulnerable to one form or another of drift.

Provisions for local financial management and their interaction with the legislation in the Local Government Act for competitive tendering will significantly affect the role of the Education Officer. Schemes for local financial management are to be prepared for September 1989, for full implementation by 1993. Capital provision for schools is excluded from the arrangements, but expenditure on maintenance will become a dual responsibility. The Secretary of State expects local authorities to delegate responsibility to schools for non-structural maintenance such as painting and the repair of broken windows and doors, while retaining responsibility for structural maintenance. Similarly, schools should have delegated powers in respect of ground maintenance but the Authority should purchase capital items such as tractors. While the general landlord-tenant relationship is offered as a guide within which to develop a scheme, many issues will inevitably arise which will not be simple to resolve.

The devolution of financial management to individual institutions will diminish the flexibility which the LEA has hitherto enjoyed to meet contingencies and crises in the maintenance of the total educational plant. As its role becomes more strategic exercising oversight over schools and colleges managing their own maintenance, LEAs will need to devise procedures to protect institutions against emergencies, inflation and unusual occurrences.

The 1988 Act and associated notes of guidance make clear Government's intention to give schools within schemes of local financial management the opportunity to enjoy as much freedom as possible to choose the means and nature of delivery of services which at present are provided by local authorities. The implications for direct service organisations concerned with building, grounds maintenance, vehicle maintenance, cleaning and catering are intriguing. The reactions of governing bodies to this offer of freedom will be affected by a range of factors: political beliefs, previous experience of local authority services, consideration of potential economies. Similar considerations will apply to consortia which have developed to purchase and deliver school equipment and furniture on a regional basis and beyond. The entire philosophy and practice of local authorities which see themselves as contractors is likely to be modified.

All these changes are going to make it increasingly difficult for local authorities to plan resources and plant in a reliable and effective way. The challenge for the Department of Education and Science will be no less. The relationship of competing demands from grant maintained schools, city technology colleges, independent HE establishments as well as from the LEAs will undoubtedly make it even more difficult for the Department's officers to determine priorities.

In conclusion it will be appreciated from reading this chapter that the actual management of educational plant is becoming more complex and will challenge Education and Architects' Departments of LEAs on a scale perhaps unforeseen in the years since the war. At present the opportunity exists, mainly through minor works, to remodel schools and colleges on a modest scale to keep pace with curriculum change, with the wider community use of schools (especially secondary schools), with the introduction of new technologies, and with the wider responsibilities laid on LEAs for example, with regard to the special educational needs and multi-cultural education. The need for Education Departments to develop long term strategies for remodelling work, at least to the end of the century, will remain and indeed become more important. Certainly, in the light of recent legislation, increases in parental choice and governors' responsibilities and the possibilities of opting out will become administratively more demanding.

5 Finance

Introduction

Some educators gain the impression that the major limitation on educational development is finance. Some who work outside the service believe that he who pays the piper should call the tune. No longer is there a majority view that increasing financial provision for education will lead to a solution of most of the country's problems. On the contrary, there are those who are critical of the nature and costs of some aspects of the education service and seek to absolve themselves from the responsibility of solving problems by blaming education for causing those problems. It is not surprising, therefore, that the costs as well as the aims and processes of education are looked at by more people and much more critically than formerly and that general financial controls now appear to be more numerous and applied with a tighter rein. Paradoxically, however, a greater freedom of choice within limited budgets has developed in a number of areas – the choices open to head teachers, for example. Education is similar to most activities in that finance can be used either as a carrot or a stick. One of the difficulties experienced by an educational administrator is that, to many others, it seems superficially so easy to apply the stick by a small percentage reduction in expenditure or, less frequently, to provide a small percentage carrot.

Figures about expenditure usually convey little information other than their size. Until 1981 Government expenditure plans were detailed at constant prices and it was possible, for example, to calculate the changing cost per pupil over about a ten-year period including the proposed cost for a three-year planned period. Even these figures could not indicate how far falling rolls, curricular changes, national economic problems, changing attitudes to expenditure on education or, in secondary education, the increased proportion of older pupils contributed to the changes in unit costs.

In 1982 the Government switched their financial planning to cash terms, making it even more difficult to make sensible assessments of the likely volume, or indeed quality of services which may be provided.

The most helpful publication on unit costs with calculations relating to actual costs for two years is the annual Handbook of Education Unit Costs prepared by the Financial Information Unit of the DES and published by CIPFA. Also published by CIPFA are annual statistics of estimated unit costs based upon LEAs' budgets for the year ahead.

The decade from 1979 was marked by constant debate about local government finance in general and education finance in particular. The culmination was legislation in 1988 introducing the community charge to replace the domestic rates, requiring competition in certain services, and setting a new statutory framework for the financial management of schools and colleges. More than ever before the administrator needs to devote time and effort to explain the real relationship between finance and service to those who, such as the teachers, spend the money and provide the service and those, such as the elected members and the public, who provide the money. The educational adminstrator will realise, however, teacher that he is, that no teacher can teach well anything that he does not himself fully understand. Even if he would prefer to spend most of his time thinking and talking about education, he must of necessity learn and then talk about its finance.

Expenditure

Control

Central government needs to be able to have a reasonable measure of influence on, some would say control of, expenditure in the local authority education service, which accounts for over 80 per cent of all public expenditure on education, science and arts. The LEA must control education expenditure which, in some areas, is more than two-thirds of its total expenditure. However such controls have to be reconciled with the inescapable reality that a teacher must be able to spend money on books, a college head of department on new equipment, a careers officer on a careers exhibition, a youth leader on club heating, or an educational adminstrator on teachers' salaries or on equipping a new school.

Education expenditure, like all local government expenditure, is authorised by statute or orders and regulations made by Ministers. Such authorisation does not imply uniformity. The first major enquiry into local government finance for 60 years, often referred to as the Layfield Report, in 1976 noted that it is difficult to find elements in the education service that are not open to local variation in interpretation of the statutory requirements – that it is difficult to distinguish between functions which are mandatory on the authority and those which are discretionary. The legal duty 'to secure efficient education to meet the needs of the population' is an example of a duty imposed commonly on all LEAs but whose cost cannot commonly be measured. On the other hand, the cost of mandatory student awards can be readily assessed.

Government decision and advice

The often heard description of education as a national service locally administered leads to the expectation – which is fulfilled – that a considerable proportion of education expenditure is determined by central government. The national prescription of the standards for school buildings is a good example of minimum provision determined centrally, leaving limited local discretion about the actual levels and costs of provision. In addition to making statutes and regulations, government issues circulars which often give advice about levels of service and, partly because of the consultations with local authority associations which normally precede the issue of circulars, advice is treated seriously, although local circumstances, particularly financial limitations, may lead authorities to respond only slowly. Salaries of teachers account for more than half the expenditure of LEAs. The scales of salaries for teachers are unusual in that they are imposed on LEAs by a statutory instrument, so that a very substantial part of an authority's expenditure is to some extent centrally determined.

In 1980 the Government developed a new assessment of expenditure needs usually referred to as GREs (Grant Related Expenditures). The system was intended to be more comprehensible, stable and equitable, encompassing plausible and intelligible factors, excluding so far as possible differences which are the result of local preferences. GREs were said to be an attempt to measure the cost of a common level of service and as such were given a cautious welcome. It soon became clear, however, that the appropriate common level of service was not the prime consideration. It was the fact that the costs in aggregate were to be consistent with the Government's expenditure plans for the year that determined the 'acceptable' level of service. Moreover, the arguments about weighting to be given to the different parts of a service and to the factors affecting the costs of providing a given level of service have continued. What weighting should be given to special needs, and how should the various contributory factors be calculated, for example? Or how should sparsity of population be related to educational costs? Nevertheless, for the first time attempts were made to calculate the costs of providing some level of service and undoubtedly the assessments will improve. Government calculations of GREs for individual services may have considerable influence on actual expenditure on those services in spite of the apparent wish of many who are not concerned with specific services to concentrate on general grants and freedom of local authorities to spend as they wish. A detailed example is that in 1987 and 1988 DES gave indicative allocations to each authority of new 'A' incentive allowances for teachers' salaries based on factors used in the calculation of GREs. The full significance may become apparent as central government assumes greater control of local government finance generally following the introduction of the community charge when it will be more difficult for authorities to depart from expenditure norms by raising taxes locally.

The national process of annual education budgeting is described in the first part of Appendix 1. Assumptions about the maintenance or change of education policies are built into the government's annual announcements about local government finance. However, after the statutory orders have been laid before Parliament to implement the government decisions, the subsequent circular from central government to local authorities invariably contains an observation that the decisions on expenditure on individual services are properly a matter for each local authority. The decisions of authorities vary. Some try to match, as far as possible, percentage changes in government estimates to their own situations, bearing in mind demographic and other factors. Others, particularly those that either receive considerable benefits or suffer disadvantages from changes in the distribution of grant or calculations of GRE or financial targets may well be much more generous or much tougher than government guidelines suggest. In practice, however, government guidelines have always had a considerable influence on most authorities. The influence is not always one way, however. In 1986 government expenditure plans for education for 1987/88 had to be adjusted upwards by over £2 billion to bring them closer to the cumulative total of expenditure by all LEAs. The collective view of the LEAs was that the needs of the service were greater than those implied by government assumptions. Using the freedom to raise taxes (the rates) locally enabled the needs to be met.

The development of the Training Commission has had a very considerable effect on the financing of non-advanced further education. Although not directly part of central government the large central government funds the Commission distributes are in effect seen as specific grants often with linked expenditure controls. More detailed discussion on this development is contained in Chapter 17.

Government action to contain general levels of local government expenditure has an effect on local decisions about education spending. The establishment of the Audit Commission in 1982 has resulted in a number of influential reports on economy, efficiency and effectiveness in specific service areas; the statutory power to 'cap' an authority's level of community charge can effectively limit absolutely the capacity of the authority to spend in a given year; the requirement for competition in services such as meals, cleaning, grounds and vehicle maintenance ensures that expenditure levels are comparable with the private sector.

Inter-authority agreements

A second group of expenditure determinants involves part of the education service where LEAs believe it to be either to their advantage and/or fair to individuals to have nationally accepted standards. LEAs work through either the Association of County Councils (ACC) for non-metropolitan authorities or the Association of Metropolitan Authorities (AMA) or jointly through the Council of Local Education Authorities (CLEA). These organisations negotiate with the DES, teachers' associations and others to produce recommended expenditure policies. Examples are recoupment payments to be made by LEAs to each other for educating one another's pupils or students, some conditions of service, and levels of payment for residential duties in special schools (which seem to be generally accepted by LEAs) and the levels of fees for non-advanced full-time further education courses and grants for discretionary awards (which are not always accepted). The recommendations of the associations are usually adopted by LEAs and expenditure patterns are consequently predetermined in certain areas.

LEA financial planning

Each LEA has its own rule book on finance – often referred to as Financial Regulations – to deal with the mechanics of financial transactions and to ensure the proper safeguarding of public money. The major control exercised by the local authority is its annual approval of estimates of expenditure. Just as no Council can make a decision on an educational matter without a report from its Education Committee (unless, in their opinion, the matter is urgent), equally no financial commitment can be entered into by the Education Committee or its officers except within the limits of estimates approved by the Council. Only the Council can set the level of the community charge or borrow money. As far as revenue expenditure is concerned the final approval is normally given by annually approved estimates. In most authorities capital expenditure is similarly approved annually. Some authorities have additions – rolling programmes of expenditure, for example – or requirements that certain items of expenditure – of a particular type or above a given level –

should receive specific council approval. Whatever the local arrangements may be, the authority to incur expenditure is given ultimately by the Council and the annual review of expenditure and income is usually the focus of the LEA's financial activities.

Some policy changes may have little financial effect but others may have considerably more, especially in the medium and longer terms. For example, a reorganisation of secondary education throughout an authority's area may require a multi-million pound building programme and a well-thought-out plan to provide adequate in-service training for teachers over a number of years. Such changes require long-term financial commitments which constitute inescapable expenditure spread over a number of years. Variations in the levels of annual expenditure cannot be allowed to prejudice such commitments.

The cumulative effect of commitments arising from central government statutory or advisory powers, from local authority and governors' duties, policies and agreements, and from continuing consequences of local policy decisions, is such that a large part of education expenditure is virtually fixed and not subject to variation. The consequences of relatively rapid changes in income – as from government grants – or in expenditure – such as inflation – can be very severe on the few remaining areas of expenditure which can be made subject to rapid change, such as provision of books or discretionary grants.

Assessing local needs

The needs of individual children, of students, of the community vary widely. If it is accepted, as it should be by Education Officers, that the education service exists to satisfy, or to help to satisfy, those needs, then the assessment of those needs and discussion about the methods of satisfying, or helping to satisfy them, is required before there can be any realistic decisions about the education budget. In determining institutional needs general formulae statistically derived from practice and experience may be used to give guidance on teaching and non-teaching staffing levels and on expenditure on items such as books, equipment and out-of-school activities. Assumptions about the spending needs of institutions in a variety of different circumstances must inform the total assessment of the expenditure required. Schools that are remote or with many immigrants or with particular problem children who are deprived, physically or mentally, are obvious variants from the average, as is the college with a high proportion of craft students or the youth club in the difficult inner-city area. It may be equally important, however, to give some special help to the establishment which has just lost a senior member of staff who has allowed some aspect of work to run down. Attention has to be given to staff development, to helping teachers and others the better to reflect changes in knowledge, methods of teaching, the internal organisation of the school, the community in which they live or the national or international scene.

All the above have to be considered before arriving at the total expenditure requirements of each sector of the service, nursery education, primary and secondary education, further education and so on. For schools and for colleges individual budget shares will be determined by a formula, largely pupil or student number driven, approved by the Secretary of State. The formula must be designed to meet as great a variety of local circumstances as possible. Critical decisions have to be taken about funds to be held centrally which may be no more than 10 per cent of the total for schools or 15 per cent for colleges.

Consultation

Discussions about institutional needs will be interwoven with proposals for change, either from central government or from the local authority. Education Officers and advisers will meet groups of employees. Discussions with staff representatives, particularly through the union representatives, may take place. The introduction of formula funding for schools and colleges following the Education Reform Act 1988 requires extensive and regular consultation with governing bodies. In cases of major change and annual consideration of financial priorities, elected members may be involved.

Consultation with governors of a school or college or with members of the local community may prompt or reveal possible voluntary action which can help to solve local problems or create new opportunities, the financial consequences of which need careful consideration. In particular, there will be discussions with governors of aided schools who have certain financial responsibilities for the care of the school fabric and with organisations and committees concerned with activities which the authority supports financially or operates jointly. By no means all the actions which are essential or desirable for any institution or any community will have financial implications, although in practice a high proportion do, and these implications are not necessarily obvious in the early stages of formulations of proposals.

It is inevitable that a good deal of consultation with governors, head teachers and principals will be concerned with the effectiveness of the authority's formula for calculating the budget share for individual schools and colleges and taking full account of the particular needs of the pupils or students involved. Similarly discussions have to take place about the performance indicators to be used to show the efficiency and effectiveness of the spending decisions by governors in relation to the education of the pupils and students for whom they are responsible. To be complete, measures of performance not only have to show that the accounts properly balance but need to address measures of educational output. This is a notoriously difficult task requiring some assessment of the external factors affecting educational performance such as home and school environment.

Consultation with governors on the budget formula also extends to the services to be required from the authority. For example, will the governors be making their own arrangements for cleaning the school, or will they be using the service offered by the authority, whether 'in-house' or through a private contractor?

Consultation about capital expenditure normally takes place in the same way. Building programmes and consequent site and equipment requirements are dealt with in a separate chapter. In addition, however, initial and replacement provision of vehicles – buses or delivery vans, for example – the provision of large items of equipment for new further and higher education courses, capital grants to voluntary organisations, and, in some authorities, replacement of equipment, must receive regular consideration. The decision about whether to finance such expenditure from revenue or loan is not a matter for the Education Committee or the Education Officer.

Discussions about expenditure are normally limited to groups who are particularly concerned. For example, the money needed by the careers service in helping to deal with the unemployed is not likely to be discussed with primary school representatives, a variation of the budget formula to provide more weighting for ancillary help for the under-fives will not be on the agenda for the further education teacher discussions, and the discretionary elements of the Salaries Document will not interest the youth leaders or psychologists. The Education Officer is, however, concerned with the whole of the education service. Sufficient finance will never be available to do all that is put forward from separate institutions or from particular groups of employees. The Education Officer must weigh up the merits of the proposals and the financial, as well as political practicalities and investigate alternative ways of satisfying needs.

He will at various stages discuss proposals with colleagues in other relevant departments as well as with the chairman and, probably, some senior members of the Education Committee. When some order of priorities between all the claims of the education service has been decided by the Education Committee it will be either the chairman of the committee briefed by the officer or the officer himself who will argue the case for education expenditure in competition with expenditure on other services – social services, roads, fire service, for example – or with those who would prefer reductions in expenditure.

Education expenditure

The references so far have been to matters which are, without doubt, educational. The section of Appendix 1 dealing with local estimating procedures gives the headings under which the estimates are usually considered. Some of these headings which were entirely appropriate when the education legislation was enacted in 1944 may now seem to have little to do with education. Maintenance of buildings in which education takes place will probably be accepted as an educational expense. Maintenance of pupils or students is more doubtful.

School meals are sometimes a matter of dispute. No longer does the government fix the charge per meal. Precise nutritional and staffing levels are not prescribed nationally, as was once the case. The 1980 Education Act limited the duty of authorities for the provision of a mid-day meal just to children from families in financial need, and the Social Security Act 1986 limited the power to provide free meals only to children from families qualifying for 'Family Support'. For other pupils there is a power (exercised by most, but not all authorities) to provide a mid-day meal at a charge decided locally, and a duty to provide facilities free of charge for those who bring sandwiches. There are wide variations in local authorities' charging practices and, partly in consequence, in net school meals expenditure. It is generally, but not universally, accepted that the broad oversight of the school meals service, linked as it is with many other pupils' activities at mid-day and on the school site, is properly part of the responsibility of the head teacher. Nevertheless, the provision of mid-day meals and the way in which they are financed can be regarded as a welfare, not educational, matter and the inclusion of school meals expenditure under the 'education' heading is not regarded, by some, as appropriate. Following the Education Reform Act 1988 schemes of financial delegation may provide for school meals expenditure to become the responsibility of school governors, thus allowing some decisions about 'education' and welfare priorities for expenditure to be made at school level.

The second largest item in many LEAs that may be regarded as non-educational expenditure, but one which can be very large in rural areas, is transport of pupils to school. Central government determines the distances above which pupils must be transported free to school. Authorities may have general lower limits and they may allow free transport in special cases, but increasingly they are having to provide free transport where there are considerations of road safety. There have been many long and detailed arguments for changes in the law and proposals to increase the LEAs' discretion but there has been no agreed conclusion. In 1980 the Government attempted to change the law to give LEAs more discretion over this expenditure but the proposal was defeated in the House of Lords.

Clothing and maintenance allowances to help children of poorer parents to benefit from education without hardship have a caring or welfare element and are not simply educational payments when paid in respect of children who are legally compelled to go to school. The justification for maintenance payments after the age of compulsory education, however, is largely educational. The introduction of the Government's Youth

Training Scheme with attendant £25 per week training allowance and the variety of other payments available to those outside the education service illustrates the point well. It has been asserted that young people are being attracted away from school or college because they are financially better off unemployed or undergoing some form of education or training under YTS. Moreover the proportion of children of poorer parents still receiving full-time education after the compulsory school age limit is well below the levels for children of other parents. The main argument for education maintenance allowances is based on the need to encourage, and to avoid discouraging, full-time education. However, shortage of money seems to prevent some LEAs from increasing either the number or value of such awards.

In practice, until the late 1970s, it seemed to matter little that payments which were not narrowly and exclusively educational, and in some cases largely, if not wholly, welfare payments were met out of education budgets. However, it became very important for some LEAs when overall cost limits were applied. Decisions on the availability of finance for education in those LEAs depended to some extent on the finance required for school meals, transport, maintenance allowances and other such payments.

Delegation of powers to spend

The practices of local authorities in authorising expenditure vary considerably. Once the revenue estimates are approved the authorisation to spend within those estimates is normally delegated to the service committee and, through them, to sub-committees and some virement between headings of estimates is common. Considerable delegation to Officers and other staff is normal. Indeed, without substantial delegation services could not function effectively. There may be some items reserved to the Council or to the main committee, although generally these are large items, often of capital expenditure or directly linked to major policy changes.

In the education service there was for many years considerable debate and variety of practice about the delegation of spending powers to individual governing bodies or heads of institutions. The scheme introduced into Hertfordshire in the early 1950s, which gave the head of each educational establishment a bank account into which was paid a general allowance to cover most items of non-staff expenditure and from which the head paid his own bills, did not spread. At the time that the Hertfordshire scheme was introduced authorities generally restricted expenditure rigorously to expenditure headings of the kind indicated in the local authority section of Appendix 1. Gradually, however, it was recognised that virement between headings of estimates was likely to lead to more sensible expenditure, and delegation of authority to spend increased the levels of accountability of individuals for the service provided, rather than for the money spent. Delegation of freedom in staffing matters was slow to develop and in some areas was reversed for non-teaching staff following local government reorganisation in 1974 and an upsurge in those areas of a confusion between corporate management and detailed central control.

The Education Reform Act 1988 has introduced a statutory requirement for financial and staffing delegation to governing bodies of colleges, secondary schools, and primary schools with 200 or more pupils on roll. When fully implemented the legislation provides for the budget share for all schools and colleges to be calculated on a formula basis, and governors of institutions subject to delegation to have power to spend the budget share according to their priorities, subject to advice from the Head or Principal.

The government's aims for delegation to schools say that effective schemes of delegation will:

(a) enable governing bodies and head teachers of schools to plan their use of resources to maximum effect in accordance with their own needs and priorities and

(b) make schools more responsive to their clients – parents, pupils, the local community and employers.

For the Education Officer, widespread delegation of spending powers to governing bodies means concentration on strategic issues of planning the total budget, monitoring performance, and advising governing bodies and heads of institutions. He is central to the authority's responsibilities for deciding the scope of delegation, establishing the formula for resource allocation, and setting out the conditions and requirements within which governing bodies must operate. The formal operation of sanctions may be rare, but monitoring and advice are essential to achieving the best educational value for money, and avoiding the damaging experience for pupils that would occur if matters had become so bad as to warrant invoking the power to withdraw delegation.

Income

The income to a local authority from which education expenditure is met comes from:

1. A general grant from central government towards the cost of services for which that authority is responsible (known as the Revenue Support Grant, or RSG for short).
2. Specific grants to cover the whole or part of the cost of selected activities.
3. The income from the commercial and industrial rate as determined nationally by central government (known as the National Non-Domestic Rate).
4. Fees, rents and other charges for services rendered to individuals or organisations, and, apart from a few minor items of income, from sources such as endowments.
5. The balance, from other sources of revenue of the local authority, largely the income from the community charge.

Revenue Support Grant

RSG (Rate Support Grant prior to 1990) is by far the most complicated of the five sources of income. Each year discussions take place between representatives of the local authority associations and central government. For the education service the main discussions take place between officers in the Expenditure Steering Group (Education) known as ESGE. These are followed by discussions for all local government services (including Education), firstly at officer level, and then between elected members in the Consultative Council on Local Government Finance. After discussing the levels of service, the size of government grant and its method of distribution, central government announces its conclusions about the level of relevant expenditure considered appropriate, the proportion which it is prepared to finance, and the method to be used to distribute the grant to local authorities.

The level of grant has varied considerably over the years. From 1980/81 when it was at 61 per cent of relevant expenditure there was a rapid reduction until 1988/89 when it stood at 46 per cent.

A brief description of the national budgeting process for education is set out in the first part of Appendix 1. The methods of distribution, although intended to be based on an authority's needs on the one hand and resources on the other, have varied considerably and have caused considerable argument and, often, acrimony. On the one hand, counties have argued that their problems, often including increasing population and small, remote villages, require an increasing proportion of finance. On the other, metropolitan districts have argued that their problems, often involving declining populations and inner city problems, require a greater financial allocation. Reference is made to the introduction of Grant Related Expenditure (GRE) assessments as the basis for grant distribution earlier in the chapter.

After the government has decided on the total grant it will give to local authorities, certain deductions are made before the distribution is effected. These deductions are mainly non-educational involving, for example, police and transport. One deduction is however, very much concerned with education. This is the amount which allows the government, after consultation with the local authority associations, to defray expenditure on the provision of services for local authorities and deduct the amount so spent from the total of the grants otherwise payable to local authorities. Those who seek the maximum autonomy for each local authority argue that no deductions should be made before grant is distributed. Each authority should be free to contribute, if it so wishes, to a particular organisation. Others argue that there are certain educational needs which local authorities cannot meet individually and that if LEAs jointly do not make, or help to make, such provision then central government would do so, thus upsetting the balance of power that would follow any increase in the proportion of finance contributed to by central government.

In 1978 this facility was used by agreement to continue to fund, or partly fund:

The Schools Curriculum Development Council (equally with the
DES)
The National Federation for Educational Research
The National Institute for Adult and Continuing Education
and
The Further Education Staff College.

Changes in the list may be made from time to time, but with
the central government responsibilities for the National
Curriculum, and Schools Examination and Assessment Councils
introduced in the Education Reform Act 1988 a major area of
activity which in the past was funded by local government using
this mechanism may finally have been eliminated.

Specific grants

At one time the whole education service was subject to a
percentage grant and the school meals service to a 100 per cent
grant. From 1958, however, various forms of block grant were
introduced and local government argued strongly against most
forms of specific funding. Nevertheless, some special grants
applied, notably 75 per cent grant under Sesction 11 of the Local
Government Act 1966 designed to meet the needs of ethnic
minorities from 'new commonwealth' areas, 100 per cent funding
for prison education, and 90 per cent (subsequently 100 per cent)
grant for expenditure on mandatory awards. Additional careers
officer posts to help with the effects of unemployment were funded
100 per cent by the Department of the Employment. A constant
cry from successive Secretaries of State has been that they have
had no power to spend any money directly on the education
service and that any government decision that development is
needed is frustrated by the Block Grant System which allows
only for additions to the general grant, which can then be spent
– or not spent – by LEAs as they wish. Agreement by government
and the local authority associations about an education priority
cannot ensure that additional grant, provided by additions to
relevant expenditure, is spent on that priority – or even on the
education service.

It can be argued that education is a national service, that it
is unfair to provide widely different opportunities within one
nation and that central government should be able to finance,

or provide inducements to LEAs to finance, what it believes to be necessary improvements. The need to avoid detailed central direction of the education service, and the consequent political danger, can also be argued whilst asserting the reasonableness of people, the influence of the ballot box locally to ensure adequate services, and a willingness to try to respond to reasonable proposals from central government. At a time of increasing resources few seem to wish to see direct government funding with a possible consequent increase of central control. When resources are limited or reducing, the attraction of direct funding is much greater.

In 1977, for example, the Secretary of State talked about, but did not achieve, a specific grant to improve the quality of the education service by increasing the level of spending on in-service education for teachers. By 1984 the Government had introduced percentage grants for certain kinds of in-service training (subsequently to become the LEA Training Grant Scheme) and had funded a major curriculum project – the Technical and Vocational Education Initiative – by specific funding through the Manpower Services Commission. The Education (Grants and Awards) Act 1984 took the process a step further by empowering the Secretary of State to fund specific projects through Education Support Grants, limited initially to ½ per cent, and subsequently one per cent of total education expenditure. The Local Authority Associations argued that this could be the thin edge of the wedge that could eventually lead to a national system of education and that local government autonomy was being undermined. Others argued that what was being proposed was very little different from what was happening already, and to a much larger extent, by the way of Manpower Services Commission funded activities and that possibly the availability of specific grant powers at an earlier date could have had the effect of retaining within the DES and the local government service the training initiatives and developments which the MSC had undertaken.

By 1988 specific grants for the training of teachers and Education Support Grants were well established as an effective means of influencing LEAs in the introduction of government policies. While the Local Authority Associations are consulted annually about priorities for LEATGS and ESGs the agenda is set and finally decided by central government. Specific grants had been used to improve science and maths teaching, to introduce new technology, for the implementation of new mid-day supervision arrangements, and for the change to GCSE examinations. Some old grants were withdrawn to release central finance for grants for the introduction of the Education Reform Act, and local government had of course to pay for those activities no longer subject to grant but which had to be continued.

Not all specific grants come direct from central government. Reference has already been made to Training Commission funding, notably for the extension of TVEI, and for NAFE, but also for a variety of smaller projects. The Education Reform Act has introduced new arrangements for funding higher education courses in LEA colleges requiring specific grant negotiated with the Polytechnics and Colleges Funding Council. A significant number of LEAs have secured grant from the European Social Fund for vocational training courses.

The Education Officer has had to develop new skills of bidding for grant, monitoring performance, and accounting to funding bodies for the outcome.

A new, reverse form of specific grant was introduced in the 1988 Education Reform Act. The governors of any maintained primary or secondary school with more than 300 pupils may apply for Grant Maintained status, and if successful the school becomes independent of the LEA and directly funded by DES. Government recoup the cost of the school from the LEA the amount being determined annually according to the LEA's funding formula and an allowance for overheads.

The national non-domestic rate

Until 1990 over half the income to local government came from the local rate levied on domestic and on commercial and industrial property in the area. The same basic rate was applied to all main categories of property, but there was a system of rate relief for domestic ratepayers. Government had argued for many years that the rating system was unfair. The same household had to pay the same charge whether occupied by one or two or three or four people; many local government voters did not pay rates at all; industry and commerce had to pay substantial charges without significant influence in local elections. The Local Government Finance Act 1988 introduced the community charge to replace domestic rates, and effectively nationalised the commercial and industrial rates by providing for a uniform national rate set initially by central government and adjusted annually for inflation. Transitional arrangements are needed initially to smooth the introduction of a single rate instead of the wide local variations which applied with local discretion. The new system restricts the freedom of authorities to raise revenue and substantially increases the proportion of local authority income subject to central control, from 46 per cent to about 75 per cent.

Charges

Most aspects of school education must be free and charges cannot be applied. The Education Reform Act 1988 re-stated this general principle, distinguishing between school activities which in general (apart from individual music tuition) cannot be subject to charge, and out-of-school activities for which charges may be applied. Such charges which do apply generally cover the cost of the activity and are dealt with at school level rather than appearing as part of the formal income of the authority. The major exception is the charge for school meals. A feature of the financial difficulties of the 1970s and 1980s has been an increasing dependence of many schools on voluntary fund raising to enhance the resources provided by the authority. Some have argued that this is unfair on schools that may not have access to large sums of voluntary money in their locality, and that anyway central and local government should be required to provide the full cost of the needs of the schools and not just a basic minimum. Government, however, have encouraged local voluntary effort, and indeed continued Education Support Grant funding for information technology in schools had been made conditional on LEAs and schools raising voluntary funds from local industry.

Fees, rents and charges for services rendered to individuals and organisations can vary greatly from authority to authority although, for some services, fees may be standardised. The average costs of tuition for pupils of differing ages and for students in further education are calculated and agreed nationally and used by LEAs in paying for those from their area who are educated by other LEAs. Tuition fees for full-time advanced further education courses are determined by the Secretary of State and for full-time non-advanced and part-time vocational courses are recommended by regional or national groupings of local authorities. Most agreements with industry training boards and the representatives of the Training Commission were based on the LEA taking responsibility for the education of those of 18 years of age and under (for whom the LEAs did not usually charge fees); and the employer accepting responsibility for the fees for the over-18s and for any training undertaken by the LEA for those under 18. This was a compromise between those who argue that employers should be responsible for all costs to LEAs for the education and training of their employees and the others who believe that, because employers pay rates, they should not be required to pay fees. However, following the introduction of the Youth Training Scheme in 1983, which included considerable lump sum payments by the Training Commission to employers or managing agents in respect of each trainee, new arrangements were negotiated by the Local Authority Associations with employers and standard charges for trainees were recommended.

Non-vocational classes have been generally recognised as a good leisure time activity but even more, as a contribution to an individual's personal well-being and development. Attitudes of the LEAs towards the financing of these classes as educationally and socially worthwhile did not normally differ greatly. As resources became more limited in the 1970s and later, local authorities slowly developed divergent attitudes, some working towards making non-vocational fees lower and others increasing charges from nominal levels. By the late 1970s some authorities had made non-vocational courses almost self-supporting, although in other areas these courses continued to be heavily subsidised.

The income from charges and fees which are not laid down nationally or regionally is only a small proportion of LEA income. It is nevertheless useful for an LEA to be able to decide, for example, whether or not to subsidise local clubs or individuals. The amounts involved in so doing are small but the free or cheap use of accommodation for a youth club can make all the difference to a club's success or even survival. 'Pump priming' in the form of revenue, and sometimes capital, grants or subsidised charges to voluntary organisations usually leads to input by others of time and money which have many times the value of the LEAs help.

Community charge

After all the estimated income from the above sources is totalled and set against the estimated cost of providing the services for which the LEA is responsible, together with a reserve to meet unforeseen requirements, there remains an anticipated excess of expenditure over income. This difference may be found in part from balances, i.e. the estimated difference between income and expenditure in the previous year. A further contribution to filling the gap may come from relatively small sources of income such as trusts and endowments, but the main contribution will be the community charge levied on the adult population of the area (with a few very limited exceptions). It is the duty of the local authority to determine the level of the charge required to enable it to meet its financial obligations. In deciding on those obligations the authority will take into account not only the needs of its services, but the political judgement of the level of charge that its electors are willing to pay, and any limit on the community charge imposed by central government using powers first introduced in 1984.

Conclusion

This is not the place to discuss the merits of different methods of local government finance, either those which operated in the past or those considered for the future. The Layfield Report, Local Government Finance (Cmd 6453), issued in 1976, was the most thorough enquiry into local government finance for many years, but in spite of the committee's recommendations, no consensus of opinion in favour of major change was forthcoming. Finally, after twelve years of debate and a host of detailed changes to the Rate Support Grant system the government succeeded in passing legislation in 1988 to make the fundamental change introducing the new community charge. Whatever the merits, there is no doubt that the technicalities of the new system will be at least as great, and that financial knowledge and skills on the part of the Education Officer will be just as much at a premium.

There are times when many educators despair of the way in which the service is financed. Educational policies seem to be of secondary importance. No longer is it the universal practice to try to determine policies most likely to benefit the individual or the nation and subsequently to find the money to put them into effect. Occasionally individuals give the impression that they would prefer local government to spend no money at all on parts of the service and relatively little on other parts. Perhaps the problems of administering education would be fewer if the service were financed in a different way, possibly independently of other local government services. However, the history of education finance in this country, which cannot be described even briefly here, offers no simple solutions in spite of the variety of methods of financing used since local authorities assumed wide educational responsibilities in 1902. Moreover, without the financial strength of the educational service, local government as we know it might cease to exist.

6 Statistics and record-keeping

The administrative need for numeracy

The collection and maintenance of records and the preparation of statistical information is essential to administrative planning and the monitoring of performance. To say, however, that an educational administrator must be capable of a numerate approach to his work is not in any way to deny or belittle the qualitative human and educational aspects of his task. There is perhaps nothing more provoking than to be asked when putting forward a proposal, 'Is this suggestion being made on purely administrative grounds or is it made on educational grounds?' That question calls for – and has received – the response that it assumes a quite false dichotomy. Every educationally sound proposal will have resource implications which have to be assessed numerately by the interpretation of available data, as well as by the less objective factors, human and political, that must be taken into account along with legal constraints. Nor must one be lured into the presumption that because a problem can be wholly or partially defined in numerical terms it is capable of a unique or 'right' solution. In practice, a choice of solution must be made – based on the data, information and other factors which are known or can be assembled and interpreted within the time available for the decision-making process, of which an increasing proportion will nowadays be occupied in consultation.

The selection of relevant data and information is as important as its compilation. The school boy's Euclidean model problem – 'given: to prove: proved' may be a useful training in intellectual rigour, but in no way mirrors life's real problems which call for a balancing of the advantages and disadvantages of alternative solutions which are logistically and politically possible. To sort out the relevant data and recognise the gaps in the data available are equally important. Gaps are inevitable not only because of manpower limitations and past omissions in the recording processes but because future developments, yet unknown, will produce fresh data which will amend the best possible forecasts and projections which can yet be made. In such cases the administrator looks for branching options – options capable of evolutionary change as further data becomes available.

Data and information

It is natural to slip quickly into the use of these terms 'data' and 'information' and to adopt the respectable distinction between them, i.e. that 'information' is processed 'data'. Records are, loosely, the stuff that data is produced from and 'statistics' can consist of anything from agglomeration of more or less unprocessed data to a collection of useful and carefully presented information. This distinction between data and information is important: it is not new, though it has more recently been given added strength by the new breed of management experts. It was always there in the days before data processing and computers began to affect our lives so profoundly. The job of political adviser or statesman to a Tudor court was to collect his data and process it before presenting it to his master as 'information'. Of course his master had a shrewd idea of the data selection that had taken place, and his personal knowledge of his adviser's qualities would colour his view of the validity of the processing that had occurred. The adviser, it is true, was disciplined in the knowledge that too overt a departure from rigour or objectivity could have fatal results. If those processes are taken over by expensive electronic machines and the information presented in computer print-outs or visual display, it is unwise to credit it with a spurious validity. With all these electronic processes, there are similar opportunities for error in selection and interpretation.

What records should be kept?

A major question which the Chief Education Officer must answer at an early stage is what records should be kept, what data should his office extract from the records which are available or can be established, and what management information does he wish to formulate from it. There is always a danger that this question will be answered only by the momentum of the administrative process without proper regard to need. It is quite possible to allow records, data and statistical compilation of facts to proliferate, and the first and obvious essential is to ensure that the work undertaken is related to some specific need and is kept in proportion to the priority to be attached to that need.

An attempt is made in the following section to distinguish groups of data and information in relation to the purpose for which they are collected; the overall extent of the data and information with which an Education Department is normally involved is discussed in the last section of this chapter. This data and information may be financial or non-financial. A high proportion of it will be required for management purposes either locally or nationally and many of the records and data will be used for both financial and non-financial information. For example, returns of teaching staff and pupil numbers are used to calculate overall pupil/teacher ratios and the size of teaching groups – non-financial information which relates to the standard of educational provision. This same data, however, coupled with budgetary control processes, will produce information on the average salaries of specific groups of teachers and unit pupil costs. The combination of this non-financial and financial information will influence staffing policies and assist management in the determination of policy options for future years.

Some records and data should be kept processed regularly to meet information needs which are not yet clearly recognised. Balanced judgement is required to avoid wasteful and irritating exercises while at the same time ensuring that future management decisions or decisions as between policy options will not be prejudiced by lack of relevant information. Thus, for example, in 1987 when the LEA Training Grants Scheme was introduced it was necessary for many authorities to define for the first time measures of the output and effectiveness of the INSET provided in order to justify the specific grants. Several authorities resorted to buying in computer packages developed for this very purpose.

The Chief Education Officer will need to keep abreast of the changing requirements for different data in response to changing national concerns. In the 60s and 70s LEA were largely obsessed with the logistical problems of accommodation and teacher supply. In the early 80s their preoccupations were falling rolls and financial constraints. Curricular matters were substantially delegated under central government's own model 'Articles of Government', nominally to governing bodies but in practice to the heads of schools. The latter half of the decade has seen LEAs and others seeking greater influence over the curricula available to pupils, especially in the 14–18 age range. This has led to the need for detailed curricular data to enable not simply the monitoring of change but also the provision of staff directly linked to an authority determined curriculum. At the same time, the Training Commission (at that stage the Manpower Services Commission) has resourced and influenced the introduction of a wider range of courses in many schools under the TVEI. This initiative has brought its own requirements for data collection in relation to the curriculum in order that the LEA, as part of its contract, may secure the funds from the Commission. This continuing interest of others in the curricula of schools is evident in the terms of the 1988 Education Reform Act with the introduction of a National Curriculum, where the LEA's role will be to monitor its detailed provision. The need for developing data collection systems in relation to the curriculum will, as a result, continue to figure high in LEA priorities.

It is also necessary to form a judgement as to whether data needs to be extracted on a continuous year-to-year basis or may be extracted on a 'one-off' basis for a particular task. Judgement is required as to the balance between the administrative effort and expense involved and the likely use to be made of the data. It may be relatively simple to record data on a day-to-day basis and therefore worthwhile doing so, even though reference to it for information purposes is likely to be occasional or some uncertainty exists as to the use to be made of it. There is clearly a special need for review of any practice of this kind from time to time.

The range of material

It is not proposed to attempt to catalogue the wide variety of statistics and records produced in an LEA office. Since the education service is locally administered, they do of course form the data base of virtually all the information published nationally, though a good deal of the data may be processed elsewhere (especially, for example, at the DES and Chartered Institute of Public Finance & Accountancy) before being presented as information. In addition to the last section of this chapter, indicating the range of data and information processes in an education office, Appendix 2 (Sources of Statistics) provides a guide to the information which is available nationally.

It is possible to distinguish broad purposes for which records are maintained and information prepared. These categories are, however, not mutually exclusive, since the results of much of this work will be used for more than one purpose.

1. Many records must be maintained for purposes of day-to-day administration – much of this work being done within the educational institutions themselves, though in such cases a good deal of the information will be needed centrally, both for those parts of the day-to-day administration which are centrally managed, and for other management purposes. Staff, student and pupil records will be required for a whole range of needs related to the management of the institution itself. Staff records are required centrally or at area level for salary assessment and payment, superannuation and absence records, etc. Indeed, the personnel management function within a single large LEA is a major undertaking, extending as it does to the needs of tens of thousands of teaching and non-teaching full-time and part-time staff.

   Where fees are chargeable, e.g. for further education students or boarding pupils, they must be assessed and invoiced. Meals must be paid for and free meals recorded, much of this work being performed at institutional level, subject to LEA financial controls and audit. Records of live births, age groups of pupils in school and under school age, records and forecasts of completion of housing units and of population movements, and records of school accommodation under construction or planned, are required for year-by-year decisions about admissions to schools as well as for decisions relating to the

LEA's capital programme of building, which may run to many millions of pounds per annum.

Data on 'extra-district' pupils or students (a student not properly to be regarded as the responsibility of the ratepayers of the LEA maintaining the institution in which the student learns is 'extra-district') is needed to control the process by which one LEA pays another for services provided on its behalf.

Records of commitments under headings of capital and revenue expenditure must be maintained for budgetary preparation and control.

2. Data is also required for the formulation of policy options. Much of it derives from a process of the records maintained for day-to-day administrative purposes and a great deal of the information which finds its way into the nationally published DES or CIPFA statistics is of this kind. Projections of pupils and student numbers are essential to teaching and non-teaching resource planning and to the formulation of practical options for the organisation of the educational system. The absence of information can pose difficulties, as can its proliferation. Attempts to develop a sound methodology for determining further education teaching and non-teaching costs (especially staffing and equipment costs) per student full-time equivalent and premises costs per student place, represent an endeavour to fill such an information gap which is widely recognised.

3. Information is also required for performance review. Records within the establishments are necessary for the educational and career guidance of pupils, students and parents. Overall records of the qualifications being sought by pupils, students and parents and of their achievements help to monitor the contribution which the educational system makes to the country's economic and social welfare. The need for information for the monitoring of performance arises not only for management purposes, but from political considerations. Expenditure by LEAs on the education service is of the order of £14,000 million annually and the LEAs, being accountable to the public for this expenditure have a duty to demonstrate, so far as is practicable, that their use of this resource is reasonably efficient and productive. It is not possible, as with manufacturing, or marketing, or commercial or service industry, to strike a profit and loss account and assess

performance in this way. But the process of commanding such a share of the nation's resources demands that reasonable public confidence is maintained. This process does not and cannot depend wholly or mainly on statistical data, but such data has its part to play. Public examination results in relation to age group sizes, levels of basic skills attainments, unit costs, staffing ratios, and levels of administrative cost in relation to total expenditure, are examples of areas in which the measurement of performance is important in the political sense as well as in respect of the more direct administrative need. So far as public examination results at 16 and 18 are concerned, LEAs have a statutory duty to ensure that they are published in respect of their maintained schools and the 1988 Education Reform Act establishes procedures for the publication of attainment tests at various ages.

4. A substantial volume of the statistics with which an LEA is concerned is produced as a requirement of central government, but this nevertheless does not, perhaps with minor exceptions, constitute a separate category from those indicated above. There is a great deal of common ground between the DES and LEAs as to their needs for information, and indeed standing arrangements exist for them to review in some detail the information-gathering process both as to the content and methods. Educational policy determination at national and LEA level goes hand-in-hand – there are also standing arrangements for the DES and LEA associations to review policy options or, in these days of 'expenditure-led' decisions, at least to assess and monitor the policy implications of such decisions – so the common ground in their information requirements is based on common need. As indicated at (2) above, the substantial body of information contained in the DES annual statistical publication derives from LEA returns but it would be largely true to say that these returns, though required of LEAs by statute, can be seen by them in practice as a by-product of the LEA's own needs.

Where should responsibility lie?

How should the work of collecting and processing data be organised? It is possible to argue for the creation of a central statistical group within an Education Department or indeed within an LEA. It is likely that most authorities will have given consideration to this matter and in particular will have attempted to assess the degree of common or inter-departmental use of data. If this were substantial, there would be a case for establishing a common 'data-base' on which the management information needs of departments could draw. In practice, it is found that the great majority of the data is required to meet a specific information need of a branch, and is specific to that branch. While, therefore, overlapping needs and functions must be recognised (as in the case, for example, with housing statistics and health statistics relating to live births), it remains generally true that responsibility for most data collection continues within the branch of the department with the major concern in the relevant area. That at least has the merit that the motivation of the staff involved is sharpened by their own management needs, but it is important that the inter-branch and inter-departmental communication referred to later in this chapter are sound so that any data separately collected by an individual department can be incorporated in a common data base where this is appropriate. At least it appears true that even where some centralisation of statistical work has been implemented, much of the work remains in practice with the branches themselves. It is however important that it should be quite clear to the department as a whole where the responsibility for each area of data collection and processing lies and this is especially true of those areas such as basic school population forecasts which are required for a variety of purposes, including budget preparation and determination of staffing policies.

The role of the computer

It is also important that the department has a clear policy on the computerisation of data processing which recognises both its value and limitations. A computerised management information system will not tell management what information is required. Computers, however, now play a major role in an LEA's work. The increasing use of microcomputers throughout departments means that their power is now often distributed away from the mainframe computer of the authority. The LEA's computer manager should possess a general view of the whole of the data collection and processing which is going on within the departments and of their information needs. There is a need for regular discussion of the ways in which he or she can both in the short term assist departments in their task within existing resource limits, and, in the longer term, determine what additional resources of manpower and equipment are required to meet the authority's needs.

Management information needs should be identified at the right level of management. Top management will identify what is required for decisions about policy options. These requirements are made known to middle management, who are themselves fully aware of the day-to-day collecting and processing needs for administrative purposes. The major responsibility for continuous appraisal between departments and the central computing system is thus best discharged at middle management levels. It is top management's responsibility to see that this appraisal process is maintained. That appraisal will need to have regard to the 'time critical' nature of much management information and the desirability of building into it a degree of flexibility which will permit a computerised system to produce more information from the data than may seem immediately necessary. These considerations are not unique to a computerised system. Even in the case of a simple manual return and analysis, the data needs to be assembled and handled in a way which enables a variety of selections and combinations to be made from it.

It is fair to ask whether there are any general considerations which will help to identify the work for which the assistance of the computer service would be sought. If good middle management communication is maintained, the question will be answered progressively from year to year and that communication will also serve to establish the extent to which a 'data base' should be established, a 'data base' being a group of records capable for use by all departments of an authority, as opposed to those held by branches in conventional files for specific purposes. Amongst other considerations which will govern the computerisation of data processing are, firstly, the amount of manipulation of data involved – an ad hoc return relating to a class of technical equipment requiring replacement may be handled manually, but the establishment of an inventory of machine equipment by age and type and its regular up-dating with data linked to supply, maintenance and disposal procedures, could be a candidate for computerisation. A second consideration of some importance is the number of variables involved and the network linkage potential. For example, further education students' records will relate to college statistics and college resource needs, to overall LEA statistics and possibly to invoicing for fees. They also cover a wide variety of full-time and part-time students working at different levels in different learning areas. Limitations of resources will in practice mean that the selection of matters for which computer assistance should be sought will depend generally on their priority and the likely cost effectiveness of the operation.

Examples of data processing for which computer services are currently used are:

1. School population records and forecasts including school leaver projections.
2. Local school accommodation and pupil numbers, records and projections.
3. Further education records and production of related statistics.
4. Further education awards, calculations of parental contributions, issue of grant letters and making of payments, and preparation of statistical management information.
5. Payroll work for staff – and increasingly the extraction of management information, including age and qualification structure of teaching force by subject areas.
6. School meals and catering – meal costs (food and overheads) and menu planning, for optimum cost and quality benefit.
7. Home to school transport route planning.
8. Careers guidance.
9. Secondary school selection procedures, where still in use – quantification of primary school records and assessments, calculating scores, and serial listing by schools and LEA.
10. School timetabling – at least to a first degree of approximation – the need for manual intervention is difficult, if not impossible, to avoid.
11. One-off applications, e.g. reading age or other attainment surveys, and analysis of returns required for special management needs.
12. Library work – cataloguing, ordering and circulation control.

13. Recoupment claims between local authorities.
14. Staff profiles – qualifications and experience – subjects taught and 'level' of teaching.
15. Energy usage and conservation measures for school buildings.
16. The transfer of information from LEAs to schools/colleges (e.g. budget allocations and latest expenditure profiles) and from schools/colleges to LEAs (manpower, pupil number, etc.) required to run schools/colleges operating under schemes of delegated management.

As the development of micro-electronics leads to the availability of comparatively cheap small computers, the degree of sophistication required of the system – especially the flexibility needed in the selection of combination of pieces of information required – is also a factor determining whether the application is best handled by access to a major central computer or by equipment available in the department or branch involved. Where continuous operation of set procedures is required, e.g. at collection and issue points at branch libraries or for staff and teaching space timetabling work within a school, including the storage and print-out or visual display of individual pupil's subject options and timetables, local equipment may be suitable although there is much to be gained from links to a major computer network.

It seems reasonable to assess the major changes following the development of micro-electronic techniques as arising from the fact that applications which could not be considered for a main computer centre for economic reasons can now be developed on micro equipment. This is still most profitable with processess requiring a comparatively low volume of data and it is necessary for other processes to link micro equipment to a major computing facility, with its capacity to store a massive data base to which the micro application needs access. As an example, the data volume required for secondary school accommodation and roll forecasts can be comparatively small. One element is the existing student capacity of the buildings. It is theoretically practicable to assess this from a major data base relating to all school premises and required for the purpose of care and maintenance, energy conservation and estate management. The development of such a data base, however, could set back the initiation of the roll/accommodation forecast application for some years, and an interim exercise using existing departmental-based assessments of existing student capacity on micro equipment could well be feasible. As hitherto, the crucial question will be whether a computerised system, centrally based or otherwise, will justify its cost in terms of the value of the information produced. In any case the objective should be to provide facilities in education offices for access to management information from the central system and there should be facilities to withdraw files of information from that system and insert files into it from the separate smaller computers when necessary.

Computers – what does the administrator need to know?

The senior manager's main need may well be one of attitude and background rather than technical knowledge. He needs to be aware of the potential of computer-assisted processes and to be sufficiently receptive to their adoption as to be able to assess or secure an assessment of their cost and efficacy, and to give the right degree of priority to investment costs. The techniques themselves will mainly be handled at middle management level and it is the middle level managers who, through their structured relationships with the computer management of the LEA, will initially identify most development possibilities. Nevertheless, top management must have sufficient knowledge to display a healthy curiosity which can trigger off fruitful lines of enquiry, as well as respond sympathetically and with knowledge to representation by middle management. For example, how much time do staff handling school accommodation problems spend in retrieval of information? At what point will it be fruitful and economic to provide selected staff with visual display units (requiring on-line facilities) to present such information and to train them to handle it? In other fields, e.g. major awards for students at universities and polytechnics, wherever the essential records are on a computer system, facilities for visual display of vital information (in this case, individual student's assessments) are always technically practicable.

In general, the need of senior managers is not for training in skills which, since they will not be practised, will quickly be forgotten. Nor is there a need for in-depth knowledge of computer technology, which is the province of the computer professional and which may be overtaken by continuing development. In-service training should be designed to generate awareness, and this implies obtaining sufficient knowledge of the fundamental principles of current computer development. For example, communication networks (e.g. the desirability or otherwise of linking colleges or area offices to a central system or to each other); data base facilities (the ability of several users to have access to a common pool of data) on-line information retrieval (how quickly is the information needed, and how up-to-date should it be?). The use of such a network could extend not only to the passing of stored information from one institution to another but to a more general interchange of messages through electronic mail in lieu of correspondence. This awareness can be achieved by periodic computer presentations at management seminars. Computer literature can be helpful, but it has drawbacks, such as its technical nature, the use of jargon and the inability to question or discuss its findings.

An example – primary schools accommodation and rolls

Earlier in this chapter it is pointed out that a simple heading in the list of areas of work covered by data preparation and processing in an education office may deceptively mask a fairly complex area of work.

Heading 4 ('Premises – accommodation and rolls') of the final section of this chapter may be selected as such an example, this being an area in which there are clear advantages to be gained from computerisation of the system. The problem may be stated as the need to keep under review the accommodation and pupil rolls of some hundreds of primary schools within the LEA (secondary schools present a somewhat different problem requiring a different approach) with a view to assessing:

(a) the needs of schools for additional accommodation;
(b) the need for the provision of new schools;
(c) schools from which temporary accommodation may be transferred;
(d) staffing and accommodation needs which would be generated by alternative policies on class sizes and alternative staffing policies.

The input into this programme should include:

(a) details of the existing accommodation (this may in practice be derived from a central data base used for other departmental purposes);

(b) accommodation under construction or planned to start in an approved capital programme (with completion dates), including the effect of new schools to be opened in the area;

(c) an analysis of present school roll by age groups and class sizes;

(d) the year groups of children under school age already in the area and expected to seek entry to the school;

(e) planned future housing completions by size of dwelling unit – both local authority and private schemes;

(f) estimates of initial and subsequent 'school product' of these dwellings;

(g) historic and projected figures for net migration into or out of the school's catchment area; and

(h) the local practice in respect of the admission of children under statutory school age.

The computer programme can be designed to give a clear school-by-school print-out of the relevant management information and if carefully devised can give valuable information about the resource implications of different policy options. As so often with computerised systems, its introduction inevitably involves a new and carefully thought through discipline in the assembly and input of the information, ensures that problems common to large numbers of institutions are dealt with equitably and, subject to what is said below about interpretation, assures management that incipient difficulties which could be overlooked in a less regulated manual system are brought to light despite the scale of the exercises.

Decision-making

Management information systems, however sophisticated, are not a substitute for good management. It has already been pointed out that it is necessary to pose the right questions, to ensure that the data is available and to process the data soundly. A word now needs to be said about the interpretations of the resulting information and about decision-making. It is commonly said that you can prove anything by statistics. This is of course quite untrue, but you can deceive yourself inadvertently by the manner of presentation. You can also go seriously astray by false logic in the process itself or by failing to take into account the degree of accuracy of the original data. Faulty local secondary school roll projections, for example, led in the immediate postwar years to at least one school that was redundant almost before it was completed. In fact the short-term (six to seven years) projection of future secondary school rolls should, in theory, be relatively simple, since the children are already in the primary schools. No secondary school can, however, be matched with a precise set of primary schools and the effect of parental choice and of family movements, especially in newly developed housing estates, must be carefully and fully assessed. The impact on this of the Education Reform Act provisions for enhancing the ability of parents to fill schools to their physical capacity is still unclear but will certainly make planning by the LEA more hazardous.

It is also important to distinguish between long-term and short-term needs. It is a matter of historic fact, for example, and can also be demonstrated by a simple mathematical model, that a housing development carried out quickly – over a period of a few years – will show a short- to medium-term demand for primary school places, which is far in excess of the steady longer term need. The same development with the same family pattern of initial occupancy spread over a longer period will show a reduced discrepancy between medium-term and long-term needs. For example, a large estate developed in two years can, with a certain family pattern of initial occupancy, show a short-term need which is double the long-term need. The same estate and family structure spread over an eight-year construction period could produce a short- to medium-term need no more than about 25 per cent of the longer term numbers.

Statistics, data and information constitute essential management tools which like all tools should be used with skill and care. They will not do the job themselves. Good systems will both facilitate the general administration of an office, alert management to incipient problems and, within their own limitations, quantify them. The manager should know these limitations and in particular the degree of accuracy of the original data. In the primary school accommodation survey described above, for example, the data is known to be of variable accuracy and objectivity. The records of accommodation call for judgements as to the pupil capacity of buildings of different types. Projections of housing completions are notoriously subject to marked change because of planning and other technical difficulties, political and economic conditions and market fluctuations. Reliable figures for migration and children under school age are easy to come by. The responsible administrator will not commit himself to substantial capital expenditure on the strength of an uncritical look at a computer print-out. Before this step he will cross-check the strength of the data and the validity of the conclusion. With the lead time involved from the programme to the contract stage of building, he will need to update those conclusions from time to time, however irritating this may be to his architect colleagues. It may even be necessary, exceptionally, to write off abortive work and fees and pull out of a proposal at a late stage, if that is the sensible long-term decision.

In this example, as in many others, we live in a real world where the exercise of free will and the interplay of views of individuals and organisations dictate that decisions must be flexible and adaptable to changing circumstances. Firmness of purpose as to policy must not be confused with rigidity of thinking as to means. The late Frank Barraclough, a man not easily to be deflected from a policy aim once firmly grasped, and one who regarded the pre-determination of the 'abscissae and ordinates' of a problem as basic to its solution, would nevertheless place his hand on his heart and say to his young men, 'Whatever you think you've proved, and however much you may be convinced that the facts add up – if it feels wrong here – don't do it!'

Records, data and statistics maintained regularly or as required by LEA

Note: This list cannot be exhaustive and the categories inevitably overlap. The volume of information extracted from the data varies considerably. For example, the further education student records form the basis of virtually the whole volume of the DES annual statistics. The list is intended to serve as a guide to the range of the data prepared and maintained in an education office.

1. *Teaching staff*
Establishments and numbers (full-time equivalent) in post, by total LEA, by area (if applicable), by schools or institutions, by type or grade of posts.
Age and training needs qualification structure.
Average salary levels, incremental 'drift'.
Probationary teachers, numbers and records.
Volume of attendance at in-service training and induction courses.
Leave of absence records for sick pay, etc.
Use of supply teachers.

2. *Pupil and student numbers*
Live births and total population figures for area and sub-areas (actual and projected).
Actual and projected school rolls, classified in age, for total LEA (for areas) and for individual schools.
Further education student population (classified by age, numbers and full-time equivalent) by mode of study, by courses pursued (levels and objectives) and by types of institution.
Pupils and students 'belonging to' other LEAs or to no LEA (for recoupment and pooling purposes).
Pupils with statements of special need: numbers and types of statement and types of placement (e.g. day and boarding, maintained, non-maintained and independent schools).
School attendance, non-attendance and exclusions.

3. *Schools and institutions and their management*
Number and types of schools, colleges and other institutions.
Size of registration and teaching groups.
Pupil/teacher ratios in schools and student/staff ratios in colleges.
Teacher staff establishments and numbers of teachers in post by school.
Proportion of AFE/NAFE total institutional costs in colleges.
College and course information – enrolment, objectives and attainments.

Examination attainments of school pupils.

Integrated courses, linked courses and industrial training courses.

Staff usage in colleges – actual and potential contact teaching hours and relief for non-teaching duties.

College/school interrelationship for 16–19 year olds; distribution and size of 'A' level courses.

Appointment, resignations and records of managing and governing bodies.

4. *Premises*

Accommodation and rolls – records and forecasts by LEA, by area and institution.

Building programmes – performance and monitoring.

Building maintenance, floor areas and cleaning costs.

5. *Youth and community and careers*

Numbers, types and usage of institutes, centres, camps and community centres.

Staffing establishments and posts filled.

Income and expenditure of institutions operating on net budgetary basis.

Participation records, youth and adult activities – centres – award schemes – adult literacy.

Employment statistics – vacancies – unemployment figures – average earnings.

Actual and projected numbers of school leavers.

Employment and further education destinations of school leavers.

Usage of Youth Training Scheme Programme.

6. *Awards and welfare*

Financial data – numbers by type of award and unit cost to LEA.

Educational data – types of institution and course and student objectives.

Records required for pooling purposes and claims on DES for statutory awards.

Free meals records for schools and colleges.

Provision of clothing and school uniform.

7. *General administrative*

Manpower statistics.

Staffing establishments and numbers in post.

Payroll records and statistics.

Catering – school and college turnover and take-up.

Kitchen accommodation and usage.

Staffing and food unit costs for school meals.

Institutional catering costs – profit and loss.

Ground maintenance costs and data.

7 Personnel management and development

Introduction

Fourteen years have elapsed since the reorganisation of local government. It is therefore appropriate to review changes which have occurred in that period, opening as it did with a mixture of anxiety and enthusiasm within the new Local Education Authorities, many much different from their predecessors, and all with different teams of education officers and advisers.

The structure for personnel management and development in the majority of new authorities was based upon their interpretation of the report of the Bains Committee. That report drew attention to the highly labour-intensive nature of local government and emphasised that the major way to improve its efficiency was through the more effective use of human resources. It considered that local government lagged behind industry in the recognition and development of personnel management.

In those early days of the new authorities there was a general tendency to establish a personnel department led by a chief officer or assistant chief officer, with direct access to the Chief Executive, whose specialist personnel knowledge would, it was believed, be accepted and acted upon by all departments. Education Departments, as the largest employers of staff within the local authorities, frequently felt threatened by the new centralist arrangements. In catering, grounds maintenance and cleaning they were often the largest operators in their area. They believed that their specialist officers had considerable experience and expertise in the management of large numbers of staff in specific service areas which supported the work of the schools and colleges for which they were also responsible. Furthermore, their personnel management experience had covered highly qualified professional staff in higher education, schools and colleges, together with educational psychologists, inspectors and advisers, education officers, careers officers and education welfare officers, plus many other kinds of staff such as technicians, nursery nurses and drivers. They were experienced too in the management of large numbers of part-time employees. Managers in the education service therefore had confidence in their ability to manage large numbers of staff in diverse areas of activity with a wide range of negotiating bodies and a variety of conditions of service.

It was hardly surprising therefore that there was a degree of resentment within education departments at what they saw as a usurping of their responsibility by a central department and a risk, as they saw it, that the total operation of the service might be threatened by insensitive and inexperienced handling of individual groups of staff in a highly complex service. Of particular concern was the transfer of responsibility for teachers, in a small number of authorities, from the Education Department and the Education Committee to the Personnel Department and the Manpower Committee or its equivalent. Education officers were reinforced in their view at the time by the 1977 SEO statement on the role of the Education Officer: 'Chief Education Officers are high calibre managers of very large human enterprises who have, as a central function, giving leadership to the authority's education service, including the staffs of its establishments; they give advice and support to all staff, teaching and non-teaching, in the performance of their duties . . . and contribute to their professional development or vocational training and generally promote their effectiveness'.

The reality of the situation however was somewhat different. A number of statutory enactments, introduced at or before local government reorganisation, had had significant influence upon the personnel management by Education Departments of their large staffs. In applying that legislation they were increasingly dependent upon the expertise and guidance provided by central personnel departments who, quite properly, were concerned to ensure that the Council, as an employer, treated all employees equitably. This legislation included, for example, the Redundancy Payments Act (1965), Contracts of Employment Act (1972), Trade Unions and Labour Relations Act (1974), Health and Safety at Work Act (1974) and Rehabilitation of Offenders Act (1974), followed in close order after 1974 by the Employment

Protection Act (1975), Sex Discrimination Act (1975), Race Relations Act (1976), Employment Protection (Consolidation) Act (1978), Employment Act (1980) and Employment Act (1982). Allied to this legislation was the emergence of a growing number of codes of practice at national level for local application, particularly in relation to equal opportunities and race relations and health and safety at work. There also emerged locally determined codes of practice in relation for example to equal opportunities, redeployment and early retirement for teachers. At the same time there was an increasing demand on the part of teacher associations for more precisely defined conditions of service based upon the Burgundy and Silver Books and for local negotiation of conditions of service in both schools and further education colleges.

Consistent with the legislation, there emerged complex procedures leading to industrial tribunals for employees having a grievance in relation to the termination of their employment or their failure to secure a post. Education officers and advisers found themselves increasingly involved in a world which was unfamiliar to them and within which they had to learn new skills, assisted by specialist colleagues in central departments, notably personnel and clerks.

A further significant factor has been the emergence of better trained and more active trade union representatives for both teachers and non-teachers. Education Officers cannot negotiate with non-teaching staff in their department in isolation since, particularly in the case of manual workers and APT and C staff, the issues involved may impact upon the conditions of service of similar staff employed by a number of other Council departments. In short, Education Officers have had to learn, if they did not know it already, that they do not operate in a vacuum but need to have regard to the overall staffing policies of the Council as employer. Furthermore, the production of quarterly figures for the manpower watch, identifying categories of employee and comparisons of the number employed year on year, has presented a form of accountability for the education service which has not always been comfortable for Chief Education Officers and their committees. The formula for calculating the full-time equivalence of part-time employees has worked to the disadvantage of Education Departments and the seasonal appointment of staff, particularly part-timers in the adult education service, has tended to inflate the figures and give rise to headlines about 'massive' staff increases which are far from reality: Education Officers have had to come to terms with increased public scrutiny of staffing levels in the education service.

The mid-80s

The establishment in most authorities in the early years following local government reorganisation of formal bodies for consultation and negotiation by Teacher Associations where they did not already exist has given Education Officers new experiences in the delicate process of local consultation and negotiation.

Practice has varied from authority to authority particularly so far as the involvement of elected members is concerned but the fact that these bodies exist presents a forum for teacher association representatives and officers to share a jointly formulated agenda on matters of interest to both parties. At the same time, many senior managers in Education Departments are part of a generic interdepartmental team of managers meeting with representatives of manual and APT and C staff in similar bodies established by the Council for its employees in all services. The separate approach required for teaching staff on the one hand and manual and clerical staff on the other has not always been easy for Education Officers, nor indeed for Personnel Officers, to come to terms with. The salary and conditions of service position of professional staff in the education service, for whom, generally speaking, the Education Departments have been responsible, compared with those for clerical and manual workers, for whom generally speaking, central departments have been responsible, has given Education Departments a degree of independence in relation to teachers that they have not enjoyed in relation to other categories of staff. This has sometimes given rise to interdepartmental difficulties arising from different treatment in terms of conditions of service between the two categories of employee.

Falling rolls have presented a whole new set of challenges for Education Department managers. Most authorities were obliged in the late 70s to negotiate with their Teacher Associations schemes for the management and deployment of the teaching force, initially in the primary schools and latterly in the secondary schools as a substantial reduction in the birth rate worked its way through the system. Redeployment of teachers has become an art form highly developed by education practitioners. Other devices for the effective management of a reducing teacher force have included retraining, particularly through one year secondments, and premature retirement with or without compensation. It is significant that a good number of authorities do not have similar procedures for non-teaching staff although those staff are increasingly vulnerable as the secondary school population reaches its trough.

The Houghton and Clegg awards for teachers and the link between Soulbury salaries and head teacher salaries had a profound effect upon the relativities within the service between professional Education Officers on the one hand, and advisers and head teachers on the other. Local Education Authorities have, in the past, frequently been unsympathetic to arguments advanced by Chief Education Officers that the relativities which were established in 1974 need to be maintained to secure the recruitment of young, high quality, experienced teachers into Education Departments. Compression of the span of salaries did not always assist Education Officers in the complex negotiations and consultations which they were undertaking with Teacher Associations, nor in their work with advisory and head teacher colleagues.

The weak relationship within the former Burnham Committee between salaries and conditions of service had remained an area of complexity and vagueness for many years. The culmination of this unsatisfactory state of affairs was the damaging teachers' dispute of 1986 and 1987 leading to the Secretary of State's decision to intervene. This has raised major issues for Teacher Associations and officers of LEAs in terms of the validity and future scope of local negotiation of conditions of service. One feature of the dispute was teachers' readiness to take unprecedented industrial action in support of their claim. It was perhaps a new experience for Education Officers to find themselves in a position in which there was virtually nothing that they could do by way of effective negotiation to alleviate the impact of teachers' industrial action upon the schools, whilst, at the same time, facing demands from the public and elected members to do something to end the disruption of children's education. The implementation by the Secretary of State of new conditions of service for teachers, together with some long overdue court judgements about the professional duties of teachers has eliminated a great many doubts, and LEAs are now clear about the major components of a teacher's professional duties and what action they can take in respect of individuals or groups of teachers who choose to refuse to carry out those duties.

Education Officers have had to prepare strategies for the management of the education service and personnel within it in a period of constrained resources but high expectations by staff and clients. The greater part of an Education Committee's budget is devoted to staff, both teaching and non-teaching. The demographic effects on the education service have created a need to reduce teacher and non-teacher numbers. Much staff reduction has been achieved on a year-on-year basis rather than in a planned and progressive way.

The pressure on manpower in Local Authorities has had its effects on central departments too. Increasingly, the tendency has been to shrink the size of central personnel departments to provide an advisory service rather than a full personnel service. Responsibility for personnel management has been passed back to some Education Departments often without the accompanying additional support staff to do the job. This of course is at a time when there is unprecedented activity in personnel matters relating to teachers and non-teachers.

The future

The 1987 pay award for teachers, with its restructuring proposals, has created for Education Officers and head teachers a complex three- or four-year programme of structural development within schools. This requires skilled supervision and management following careful consultation or negotiation at authority and school level if the Secretary of State's targets are to be met and financial limits are not to be exceeded. The 1987 Manual Workers' pay award carried with it substantial implications for Education Department personnel managers, the effects of which will take some time to appreciate and implement but will certainly increase the costs to LEAs

The requirement of the Local Government Act 1988 that a number of local authority maintained services should be put out to competitive tendering during the course of 1989 to 1991 presents particularly significant challenges for education managers who cannot, in this regard, operate in isolation from other departments. The volume of personnel management will decrease, in some sectors significantly, if contracts are won by the private sector. LEAs now have to consider how the personnel function is to be undertaken where contracts are won by Direct Labour Organisations. What is clear is that the Direct Labour Organisations' staff will form part of the Education Department or County Council's staffing depending upon arrangements determined within the local authority. No doubt different models will emerge but it is clear that the DLO could either provide its own personnel management structure or purchase from the Education Department the personal service it requires. It is perhaps too early to see what the implications might be of individual schools contracting out their own services under arrangements for the Local Management of Schools following the Education Act 1988.

Councils, or their Education Departments, depending upon local arrangements, will have to address the need to provide staffing structures for the contractor side where their DLO is successful in securing contracts and, whether all or some of their services are contracted out to the private sector, they will have to develop an organisation to fulfil the client roles of service specification, contract preparation and supervision of the contract. This raises important issues for the organisation of an Education Department and the role which its personnel section plays in the process.

Some of the clauses in the Education Act, for example in relation to local management of schools and employment of staff, plus the establishment of grant maintained status, may well serve to shift the emphasis within Education Department personnel sections from the management of staff and indeed possibly the negotiation of conditions of service to an advisory and guidance role equivalent in relation to head teachers and governors to that played by central personnel departments in relation to Education Departments.

The Act moves much of the responsibility for the appointment, management and disciplining or dismissal of teachers firmly to school level. Those authorities which do not devolve responsibility for local management to schools with less than

200 on roll will continue to fulfil the functions which are currently their responsibility for those schools. At the same time, however, head teachers, principals and governing bodies will be looking to the LEA for advice, guidance and support in exercising their responsibilities under the Local Management of Schools Scheme. Education Departments' personnel and finance sections will have an important responsibility to produce guidelines and detailed documents of advice on employment and conditions of service legislation and good practice to assist heads, principals and governors to fulfil their functions at local level. There could be significant implications for the size and structure of Education Department personnel sections in the future as a result of this decentralisation. Local authority staff, notably Education Officers and advisers who have day-to-day contact with schools and colleges and clerks to governors, where they are local government employees, will need greater expertise in these important matters if they are to give advice promptly and correctly when it is required at school and college level. There will need to be a re-evaluation of training requirements for senior staff in schools and Education Departments, and of the role of Education Department personnel staff.

Local authorities have been called upon by the Secretary of State to indicate in their schemes of local management of schools, the training programmes which they propose for teaching and non-teaching staff, governors and their own staff, to ensure that the scheme is implemented efficiently. For this, detailed consultation with Teacher Associations, governors and others involved is required to ensure that the programmes are relevant and purposeful.

Staff development

1. Teachers

LEAs' responsibility for the training of their staff has always been an important aspect of their personnel management role. It is fair to say that in the case of most authorities far greater emphasis has been placed on training and retraining of teachers than it has on training and retraining of other categories of staff. The budget for professional staff training usually far exceeds that for non-teachers. The changes in the grant-related in-service training programme have influenced the structure, delivery and priorities of LEAs' arrangements for in-service education and training, and will have the effect of equalising expenditure between authorities. This will benefit authorities who have not been able, in the past, to give as much attention to this important area of their work as others. The virtual elimination, following removal of access to the 'pool' for the purpose, of one year full-time secondments of teachers has not helped to assist the management of the reduction of the teacher force and other solutions are having to be found by education managers. As rolls began to rise again in the primary schools in many parts of the country, the pressures of contraction gave way to problems of recruitment including the need to retrain secondary teachers for primary work. Similar retraining needs may well emerge in the secondary schools in the late 90s in various parts of the country. Carefully planned staff development programmes including retraining to overcome curriculum mismatch amongst secondary teachers as rolls fall and to implement the National Curriculum, will certainly be required.

Training programmes for shortage subject areas have been evolved nationally and locally in an attempt to combat an increasingly serious problem. Competition from industry for scarce skills has continued to present problems for LEAs and their managers.

The introduction of an entitlement national curriculum for all pupils in all schools has added to the need for Government and LEAs to focus on long-term recruitment into and training within the teaching profession. The demand for an increased share of graduate physicists, chemists, mathematicians and modern linguists has been addressed by Government through the TASC (Teaching as a (Second) Career) Group. Incentive payments to certain shortage subject area graduates who enter a PGCE course has provided an initial attraction, although insufficient of those entering the course have actually gone on into teaching. General problems of recruitment into teaching, in part related to salaries, but also in part to the status and public image of the profession, along with particular problems in specific shortage areas, are being added to by two other factors. Firstly, there is a generally accepted view that pupil/teacher ratios in school will need to be improved to take account of the time teachers must spend on systematic periodic assessment of pupils throughout their primary and secondary careers, the maintenance of records of achievement for pupils, and the appraisal of teachers themselves. The other factor is that this need for improved recruitment into the teaching profession comes at the very time when there is a trough in the numbers of young people in the school leaving age groups. All employers, therefore, will be recruiting from a declining market, and the pressure on the graduate market is going to be particularly severe. The Secretary of State's proposal for licensed teachers is one measure which may assist the recruitment of teachers in the future, but urgent consideration also has to be given to the nature and quality of the on-the-job training provided both by LEAs and teacher training institutions if sufficient people of the right calibre are to be attracted and retained within the education service.

LEAs have a long way to go to meet the recommendations of the James Report on the induction and early in-service training of teachers. The introduction of grant related in-service training for teachers, greater specification of national priorities and the opportunity for LEAs to add their own local priorities has been helpful. In many authorities, there is increased emphasis on school-based curriculum review and the formulation of staff development policies as a means of achieving curriculum development with school focused in-service training to support that process. Many schools have designated professional tutors who will fulfil a most important staff development function, not only for newly qualified teachers, but also for teachers in mid-career. The increased call on teachers' time for school focused INSET in school hours has created major problems, particularly in the context of the determination of a teacher's directed time commitment of 1265 hours per annum. The shortage of teachers has led too to difficulties in many parts of the country in securing supply teachers to cover the absence of teachers from their classes on in-service training or a variety of other legitimate activities associated with their professional function in the school or college. Several authorities are giving consideration to alternative ways of providing resources for supply cover, particularly by the allocation of full-time, permanent posts to individual schools or groups of schools to enable them to manage the cover for absent teachers and at the same time to provide effective teaching for the students. The evaluation of such arrangements is particularly urgent in view of the need to resolve the matter satisfactorily for schools operating under local management arrangements.

The provision in the 1986 No. 2 Act for the Secretary of State to introduce a process of appraisal for teachers represents a further personnel management area for professional staffs in LEAs whether they are school or education office based. The process is at a relatively early stage in those schools and colleges where it has been introduced. Work through Education Support Grants in a number of authorities and the research undertaken in Suffolk, will be valuable to the profession in addressing the issue of the introduction of appraisal for teachers and has no doubt influenced the Secretary of State's thinking about the form of appraisal which he would wish to see introduced.

Good appraisal systems, to have the confidence of the staff involved, must have clear outcomes in terms of organisational and individual development and must be consistently and painstakingly operated. Anything less will be seen as a cosmetic exercise. Pressure on teacher time is a factor which needs to be resolved if appraisal systems in the schools and colleges are to be effective.

2.   *Education Officers and advisers*

A wealth of training opportunity is now available to Education Officers and advisers. The involvement of large consultancy organisations in this field is of relatively recent date and is threatening to swamp the existing structures which have the confidence of Education Officers. The Management Development Committee of the Society of Education Officers has created a clear structure of staff and management development for Education Officers both at regional and national level. Introductory courses for new entrants to the profession, the 'main phase' course for experienced officers mounted in association with Sheffield Polytechnic, the advanced course for more experienced officers organised in association with INLOGOV and courses organised by the Society working jointly with the Local Government Training Board and the GRUBB institute are all highly valued by participants and Chief Education Officers. The opportunity for colleagues from different authorities to meet together away from their offices, and to share experiences under the guidance of experienced trainers and senior managers from Education Departments has proved successful in meeting the staff development needs of individual officers. The format is also used effectively to train staff in specific techniques or specialisms, an increasing need in these days of rapid change. Regional meetings of the Society of Education Officers and a large number of conferences and training opportunities provided by consultancies and agencies outside the education service contribute significantly to the great need for further training and information giving opportunities for managers in the education service.

There are many areas in which joint training between senior management staff in schools and Education Departments is necessary at the present time. A number of authorities find ways of organising joint senior management training for heads, advisers and Education Officers, often in association with the more experienced consultancy groups. If Education Officers are to fulfil the important tasks presented by current and future legislation, continued attention will need to be given to the range, quality, accessibility and cost of relevant training opportunities in the future.

3. *Manual, clerical and technician staff*

The general concept of development for non-teaching staff and support staff is equally vital, not only to ensure that staff are kept fully up-to-date on the effect of new legislation on their work and the introduction of new technology and systems of work, but also for updating and developing their personal and occupational skills. Local Authorities have provided courses over the years in a whole range of activities, notably health and safety courses and induction courses for new employees and, in the case of manual workers, courses for supervisors. School meals, caretaking and cleaning and grounds maintenance staff generally have training opportunities to develop the skills required to carry out their work efficiently. Administrative and clerical staff in Local Authorities usually have access to in-house and on-the-job training with opportunity for day release for qualification training. In many authorities however, insufficient opportunity exists for institution-based clerical and administrative staff to pursue similar training opportunities. The efficient operation of schools in the changed circumstances following the implementation of the Education Reform Act will require high level performance of such staff. Further attention needs to be given to identifying the continuing training needs of such staff and the best means of responding to them.

Conclusion

Senior staff in Education Authorities have achieved much in developing their personnel policies and practice since local government reorganisation. Mechanisms are in place for effective consultation and negotiation with staff of the service although seldom in one forum. Procedures to deal with legislation introduced in the last fourteen years which impacts upon LEAs in their personnel management role, are soundly established and generally working well. Good working relationships have been built between education departments and central departments to ensure a consistent delivery of service to staff and through them to clients and there is clarity about the respective roles of central departments and education departments. Staff development programmes are well articulated, carefully planned and delivered and participation rates are increasing. More emphasis however, needs to be given to joint staff development programmes for Education Officers, head teachers and advisers and there must be an improvement in provision for non-teaching staff who are institutionally based. Above all, education managers have demonstrated their ability to respond positively and effectively in a variety of ways to local manifestations of national problems in a period of increasingly rapid change. The service is in good shape to adapt its operations to cope with the particularly significant changes which are likely to impact upon its role as a result of the Education Reform Act.

8 Curriculum and course control

'A very remarkable omission occurs in the new code just issued by the Board of Education. It is the omission of curricula. The Board is wisely leaving the framing of the course of instruction in the elementary schools to the Local Authorities and to the teachers.' So ran the *Morning Post* editorial on 22 May 1926. The 1926 Code said simply that 'the secular instruction in a school or centre must be in accordance with a suitable curriculum and syllabus framed with due regard to the organisation and circumstances of the school or schools concerned.' Circular 1375 announced that the grant regulations for secondary schools would no longer include a list of subjects because there was consensus about what should be taught. It was, they might have said, a consensus maintained, and to be maintained until the School Certificate gave way to single subject GCE in 1950, by the examination boards practice of setting grouped subject examinations. But 'it is', said the Circular, 'and has long been open to an authority to vary the curriculum'.

For the next sixty years central government followed the same hands off approach towards the school curriculum. As recently as March 1985, the White Paper 'Better Schools' said roundly, 'the Government does not propose to introduce legislation affecting the powers of the Secretaries of State in relation to the curriculum'. Only three years later the Education Reform Act was to give the Secretary of State far greater powers over what is taught than any previous minister had ever had. The main purpose of this chapter is to explain this extraordinary bouleversement.

Who should be educated? What should they learn? Who should decide what should be taught and what be learned in the schools? And how can the schools' success be judged? These are the kinds of question which may legitimately be asked about a public education system.

In England and Wales the answers in 1988 are muzzy and unclear. This is because the 1944 Education Act was concerned more with general principles than detail. 'Secondary education for all' was a flag under which many were happy to sail without enquiring closely about either the destination or conditions on board. The Act's drafters could assume a high level of common understanding and shared commitment among teachers, parents, and legislators. Only religious education excited discussion or dispute, so the benefits of devolving statutory responsibility for secular instruction to local authorities and de facto control to individual teachers seemed self evident. The Department, said Minister George Tomlinson proudly in his introduction to the Ministry's 1950 Report, 'has been zealous for the freedom of schools and teachers'. There was therefore no chapter on educational method and the curriculum. 'Minister', he said, 'knows nowt about t'curriculum.'

Curiously, the word 'curriculum' itself appears only once in the 1944 Act, in part of clause 23 which has to do with a Local Education Authority's power to compel attendance at classes held outside the school premises. It was to become clear later that neither local authorities nor their school governors knew significantly more than the Minister about the curriculum being delivered in schools. Under the 1944 model articles of government for secondary schools, the governors are responsible for the 'general direction of the conduct and curriculum of the school'. But 'there was little evidence', said George Baron and David Howell in a research paper quoted in the Taylor Reports, 'to show that . . . in 1965–69 . . . the standard provision in the articles was taken seriously.'

For their part, local authorities were accountable for providing efficient education. In practice a convention had grown that curriculum was the teachers' domain, a secret garden. From the 1950s to the 1970s, most authorities were probably like Inner London, of whom Robin Auld said in his report on the William Tyndale School,

> . . . 'the Authority has no policy:
>   (i) as to the standards of attainment at which its primary schools should aim; or

(ii) as to the aims and objectives of the primary education being provided in its schools, save the very general aim of providing the best possible opportunities to be given to the children to acquire the basic skills and social attainments so that at the age of 11 they can transfer to secondary schools equipped to do so; or

(iii) as to the methods of teaching to be adopted in its schools.

My purpose in recording this lack of policy is not to criticize the Authority – whose approach, I understand, is typical of most local authorities in the country – but to demonstrate the difficulties for the Inspectorate in the diagnostic and advisory function that it has.'

A broad measure of consensus about relative responsibilities persisted for two or three decades. Central government, local education authorities, and teachers, were partners in the education service. This 'partnership' was strained in 1962 when the Ministry of Education established an internal Curriculum Study Group. Sir William Alexander for the LEAs and Sir Ronald Gould for the teachers saw this as a major threat to English liberties. From the subsequent debate came an ingenious proposal to make the partnership a standing feature of English, and Welsh, education. A Schools Council for the Curriculum and Examinations was established in 1964, with membership and powers reflecting the idea of partnership. Each partner would contribute funds and expertise, according to ability, to meet the schools' curricular needs.

But harmony lasted no longer than the golden sixties. Publication in 1969 of the first Black Paper marked the beginning of a decade of challenge. In October 1976, in tentative remarks at Ruskin College, Labour Prime Minister Callaghan lent the weight of his office to this challenge, which culminated in the election in 1979 of a Conservative government whose ministers openly criticised the performance of maintained schools. From the late 1970s, this criticism was more than matched by the mounting range and pace of central intervention in curriculum matters.

Robin Auld's public account of the way things really were, prompted the DES to seek systematic information about school curriculum. In Circular 14/77 LEAs were asked to describe their arrangements for the school curriculum. The DES published its analysis of their replies in 1979.

The Circular posed 50 questions about the information authorities had about the curriculum offered by their schools, the authorities' arrangements for developing policy, what these policies were, and the extent to which provision and policy were in accord. The Circular assumed that authorities had accurate information about what was happening in their schools, and explicit curricular policies. The first requires simple and accurate ways of conveying curricular information, which was not readily available; and as Auld suggested, the second was doubtful.

Most authorities had few explicit policies relating to curricular matters. Their implied policy was to leave curriculum to the schools, and to support changes by providing accommodation, equipment, teachers, advisers and other resources. The provision of a major resource such as language laboratories, the adoption of Nuffield Science, or the creation of a field centre, would require council approval. But in large and small matters the most common practice was to provide a resource, and thus imply a policy, rather than declare a general policy.

At the centre, this way of running schools no longer seemed acceptable. In October 1981 Circular 6/81 drew local authorities' attention to the way in which the Secretary of State thought they and their school governors ought to exercise their responsibilities for the school curriculum. In a few brief paragraphs the circular overturned the conventions which had underpinned curricular arrangements for the previous thirty years. Local authorities were expected to review their curricular policies and practice in the light of what was said in *The School Curriculum*, and individual schools to set their aims out in writing. The steps taken in response to the circular were to be reviewed in about two years' time.

Two years later Circular 8/83 asked LEAs for a report on the progress they had made in drawing up their policies, and the part played in this by heads and other teachers, parents, governors, and others, together with a statement as to how the policy was being put into effect and how far resources matched the policy, with a summary of the steps being taken to ensure that the curriculum was planned as a whole and was related to what happens outside school. A summary of LEA replies was published in 1986.

The Department also launched, nursed and fostered a national debate about the school curriculum. In July 1977 a Green Paper, *Education in Schools* (Cmnd 6869), suggested that the time had come to establish generally accepted principles for the composition of the secondary curriculum for all pupils, and to decide whether all pupils should have a protected or core element in their curriculum. The Green Paper broke new ground in saying that 'schools must have aims against which to judge the effectiveness of their work', and then suggesting eight possible aims.

A somewhat sharper DES statement followed the first survey of LEA policy and practice. *A Framework for the School Curriculum*, published in January 1980, seemed a sterile offering to many who were relieved the following year by *The School Curriculum*. This called 'not for a change in the statutory framework of the education service but for a reappraisal of how each partner in the service should now discharge those responsibilities assigned to him by law'. 'Neither the Government nor the local authorities', it said, 'should specify in detail what the schools should teach. This is for the schools themselves to determine.'

The Department kept on refining its own thinking about the curriculum as a whole in a series of statements. Of these Curriculum 11/16 (1983), the Secretary of State's speech to the North of England Conference (Sheffield 1984), *The Organisation and Content of the 5/16 Curriculum* (September 1984), and *Better Schools* (Cmnd 9469 March 1985), are the milestones. The purposes of school education set out in *Better Schools* provide a basis for assessing the reforms now in train. They were:

1. to help pupils to develop lively enquiring minds, the ability to question and argue rationally and to apply themselves to tasks, and physical skills;
2. to help pupils to acquire understanding, knowledge and skills relevant to adult life and employment in a fast-changing world;
3. to help pupils to use language and number effectively;
4. to help pupils to develop personal moral values, respect for religious values, and tolerance of other races, religions, and ways of life;
5. to help pupils to understand the world in which they live, and the interdependence of individuals, groups and nations;
6. to help pupils to appreciate human achievements and aspirations.'

The report went on to discuss how these aims might be achieved through the curriculum. The primary curriculum, for example, would emphasise competence in the use of language and in mathematics, introduce pupils to science, lay the foundations of understanding in religious education, history and geography, and the nature and values of British society, introduce pupils to a range of activities in the arts, provide opportunities for craft and practical work, provide moral education, physical education and health education, introduce pupils to the nature and use of new technology, and give pupils some insights into the adult world, including how people earn their living.

Apart from these papers on the whole curriculum, the Department published also a constant stream of papers on individual subjects and specific aspects of the curriculum. These included *Schools and Working Life* (1980), *Science Education in Schools* (1982), *Foreign Languages in the School* (1983), *Science 5/16: a Statement of Policy* (1985), *Economic Awareness* (1985), *Foreign Languages in the School Curriculum: a Draft Statement of Policy* (1986), and *Working Together*, a report on careers education (1987). The Secretary of State gave set speeches on such topics as the importance of history, and of geography.

While the Department developed its own increasingly clear view of what the curriculum should be, from the same base in Elizabeth House, Her Majesty's Inspectorate presented their own assessments of curricular practice and desiderata. *A View of The Curriculum* (1980), and *The Curriculum 5/16* (1985) gave overviews of the whole curriculum, supported by more detailed analyses of individual subjects in two series of papers, *Matters for Discussing* and *Curriculum Matters*, which covered most widely studied subjects.

This bombardment by paper, through survey, discussion and exhortation, was like HMS Warrior, the ultimate deterrent when launched in 1860 but obsolete within a decade. Government found more powerful instruments to establish effective control over what is taught and learned in schools.

Unlike their predecessors, who seem to have relished their role, ministers and their senior civil servants increasingly found the management of influence an irksome constraint when there seemed to be real work waiting. Fred Mulley spoke for many of the new men when he complained that the only thing he could actually do was to authorise the demolition of war time air raid shelters. Central government might allocate billions of pounds to education but the Secretary of State seemed to have not a single pound to spend on schools. He took one small step forward in 1980, when Section 21 of the Education No. 2 Act gave him power to make grants for the teaching of Welsh, or 'the teaching in that language of other subjects'. About £500,000, a very large sum in relation to expenditure on curriculum development in Wales, was available for such grants in 1980–81 alone.

Central government's determination to effect decisive changes in the country's education system led it, like Canning, to call new worlds into being to redress the balance of the old. Since the Department of Education and Science's power to give specific grants was limited, the Department of Industry created an Industry Education Unit which sponsored a network of Science and Technology Regional Organisations, and a number of curriculum developments to promote understanding and commitment to technology and the 'wealth producing' industries. The Department also funded a Micros in Schools programme which subsidised the purchase of microcomputers by first secondary, then primary and special schools. In 1980 the Department of Education and Science funded a complementary programme, whose main aim was to promote the study and use of microelectronics in schools.

More threatening to LEAs was the Government's use of the Manpower Services Commission, a rich and powerful satrap of the Department of Employment. Like many other Western states, when confronted with unprecedented turbulence in the economy and the labour market, the Government turned to its department of employment rather than its department of education to develop new forms of vocational preparation and training. This led to the dramatic rise of the MSC described in Chapter 17.

An even more startling innovation followed. In November 1982 the Prime Minister herself announced that the Manpower Services Commission would be responsible for funding and managing a Technical and Vocational Education Initiative for fourteen-to eighteen-year-olds. Its purpose was 'to explore and test methods of organising, managing and resourcing general, technical and vocational education; and to explore and test the kinds of programmes, curricula and learning methods required for success'. It was thought at first that the MSC might even establish its own schools if local education authorities proved unwilling to co-operate in pilot projects. Most authorities found, however, that the proposals were broadly in line with their own perceptions of the need for a curriculum more concerned with practical capability. Sixty eight quickly prepared proposals for five-year pilot projects, and on 25 March 1983 fourteen were selected to run projects starting in September 1983. Sufficiently encouraged by this response, the Government announced in June that it had asked MSC to extend the scheme. By 1984 there were 62 pilot projects, and by 1988 every LEA was taking part.

Each of the pilot projects was confined to a small cohort of pupils in a limited number of schools, and the Training Commission, as MSC is now called, is now discussing with LEAs their detailed submissions for extending TVEI to every school.

In educational content, TVEI projects vary greatly, reflecting the local economy and the character of the schools. In terms of curriculum management, they all involve LEAs in submitting draft proposals, amending these to meet Training Commission requirements, signing a contract to deliver what has been agreed, and keeping records to show that the LEA has done what was agreed.

Another significant proposal was also announced in June 1983. The Queen's Speech opening the new parliament said 'legislation will be introduced to allow grants to be paid to local education authorities in England and Wales for innovations and improvements in the curriculum'. 'The proposal will allow the holder of my office', the Secretary of State (Sir Keith Joseph) said, 'to exercise greater influence at the margin over improvements in the curriculum and other innovations in various parts of the education service'.

The scheme was approved under the Education (Grants and Awards) Act 1984, and launched in 1985–86. Education Support Grants already encompass a wide range of development projects, including mid-day supervision and training for governors, as well as mathematics, science, the spoken word, foreign languages, social responsibility and many others. To obtain grants local authorities must prepare detailed submissions and keep careful records of their expenditure and the outcomes of their projects. They must also contribute 30 per cent of the cost of projects, in order to qualify for grant, the cost of which is met by withholding up to one per cent of the funds which would previously have been included in the general grant to local authorities. With reduced support grants, and the threat of rate capping, LEAs have increasingly to choose between externally funded developments such as these, or none.

Education Support Grants were introduced just in time to help another major innovation, the General Certificate of Secondary Education, with courses beginning in 1986 and the first certificates awarded in 1988. Grants were offered to every local education authority to meet part of the cost of equipment, books and materials for these new courses.

It has long been held that external examinations are the price we British pay for having no agreed school curriculum. To have two systems of external examination, the General Certificate, and the Certificate of Secondary Education had long seemed too high a price. The case for merging the two systems was argued and investigated throughout the 1970s. The suggestion seemed to threaten the supposedly high standards maintained by GCE, but central government was persuaded when it became clear that government could set up co-ordinating machinery and insist on national criteria for the new examination. The Secondary Examinations Council was set up in 1983, approval for the GCSE announced in 1984, and approval of National Criteria in 1985. These dealt with the format, content, and presentation of syllabuses, groups of subjects, external moderation, and assessment. Many of the alleged faults of the previous dual system, the number of examining bodies, the bewildering variety of syllabuses and subject titles, the difficulty of comparing standards, and the lack of a market price for many of the courses followed and certificates awarded, would all be swept away. A reformed examination system would be the first instrument for creating order and establishing rigour in the upper secondary curriculum.

Both TVEI and ESG schemes include funds for employing leaders, co-ordinators, and advisory teachers, whose function is as much to train teachers as to develop the curriculum or produce new teaching materials. There is indeed no clear divide between curriculum and staff development. They are two faces of the same coin, as MSC soon found in launching TVEI. In March 1985 MSC was invited to extend its writ from curriculum to staff development, in a pilot scheme called Technically Related Inservice Training. This scheme was intended to remedy the shortage of teachers in some key areas like CDT, technology, information technology, micro-electronics, business studies and physical science, and to develop teachers' knowledge of management, the world of work, and teaching and learning styles. TRIST was little more than a trailer for the much more extensive Grant Related Inservice Training Scheme (GRIST), launched in 1987 under sections 50 and 63 of the Education No. 2 Act 1986. This authorises the Secretary of State to make grants for the further training of qualified teachers, for training as teachers, others who are employed as teachers, and for the further training of youth and community staff, educational psychologists, and LEA inspectors and advisers. Within cash limits predetermined for each LEA, the Secretary of State will meet 70 per cent of other costs, provided that he approves an authority's proposals. As with TVEI and ESG, the scheme gives central government a powerful instrument for controlling what is taught and learned in schools and colleges.

The centre's barrage of enquiries, surveys, and reports had weakened the confidence of possible opponents, and their skilful use of grants and contracts had undermined the outer walls. It was time now to take the secret garden. For this the centre deployed its most powerful instrument, the legislature itself. The Education (No. 2) Act 1986 was the first twentieth century act of parliament to deal extensively with the curriculum.

The Act's declared purpose was to clarify the relative responsibilities of LEAs, governors and head teachers. Local authorities must determine and keep under review their policy in relation to the secular curriculum, make and keep up to date a written statement of their policy, provide governors and heads with copies of that statement, and publish it more widely as they think appropriate.

Governors are required, in their turn, to consider their authority's statement, and how far it should be modified in response to their views about the aims of the curriculum in their own school. They have also to decide whether sex education should form part of the curriculum, and if so to make a written statement about its content and organisation. In exercising these powers governors must consider any representations made by people connected with the community served by the school, and any representations made by the local chief of police.

Head teachers must also have regard to representations from these quarters, in exercising their own responsibilities. They must ensure that the school puts into effect the authority's and the governors' policies, except when the governors' policy on sex education is incompatible with a public examination syllabus. Heads must also have copies of the policy statements available at all reasonable times for people wishing to inspect them.

Finally, the Secretary of State is to make regulations saying how governors are to inform parents of the syllabuses and other aspects of the education provided for their children.

The Act went well beyond thus clarifying various levels of responsibility for the formal curriculum. It began also to define the aims and nature of the hidden curriculum. Subject to any views expressed by their governors, head teachers are to determine measures to promote self discipline and proper regard for authority, to encourage good behaviour, to secure acceptable standards of behaviour, and to regulate pupils' conduct. Corporal punishment is no longer one of the permissible measures for securing good behaviour, but exclusion is.

The head alone has power to exclude a pupil. When a pupil is excluded for more than five days in any term, or at a time which affects the pupils' opportunity of entering an external examination, the parents may appeal for reinstatement. Either governors or local authority may direct a head to reinstate a pupil. Both governors and parents may appeal beyond the authority to an independent panel whose decision is binding.

Time will show whether this formal and hierarchical system really helps the disturbed, disruptive youngsters who often play leading parts in the mini dramas which precipitate exclusion.

A late amendment to the bill ensured that the Education Act reflected the concern of some who feared political indoctrination in schools. Local authorities, governors and heads must all forbid partisan political activities by junior pupils and the promotion of partisan political views in teaching any subject. Whenever political issues arise at school or in any extra curricular activity, pupils must be offered a balanced presentation of opposing views.

Another late amendment made local authorities, governors and heads jointly responsible also for ensuring that any sex education is given in ways which encourage pupils to have due regard to moral considerations and the value of family life.

In its concern for these aspects of personal and social education, Parliament had penetrated the secret garden. This whiff of legislative action was music to the new Secretary of State, Mr Kenneth Baker, who succeeded Sir Keith Joseph in May 1986. He would lead the centre's onslaught on the curriculum redoubt.

A year later, at the 1987 General Election, the Conservatives maintained their handsome majority. The Queen's Speech confirmed the government's long heralded decision to take further measures to reform education. Perhaps it was Mr Baker himself who adroitly christened these measures 'The Great Education Reform Bill', a title with shades both of 1832 and of bygone greatness, and a title all too easily abbreviated as GERBIL, which reminded most people of a cuddly mouselike pet. As the summer holidays approached and came, the Department of Education and Science published details of the proposed bill in a series of consultation papers, harbingers of an early autumn.

The Consultation Paper on the National Curriculum, published on 20 July with a request for comments by 30 September, claimed that there was now widespread support for the aims of education set out in *Better Schools*. Important advances had been made during the previous decade, but 'some improvement is not enough. We must raise standards consistently and at least as quickly as they are rising in competitor countries'. The government wished 'to ensure for all pupils in maintained schools a curriculum which equips them with the knowledge, skills and understanding that they need for adult life and employment'. A national curriculum backed by clear assessment arrangements will help to raise standards of attainment by ensuring that all pupils study a broad and balanced curriculum, '. . . setting clear objectives for what children . . . should be able to achieve, . . . ensuring that all pupils have access to broadly the same good and relevant curriculum . . ., and checking on progress towards these objectives and performance'. In addition, such a curriculum would enable children to move from one area of the country to another without disruption, help progression between primary and secondary schools, help to secure continuity and coherence, and enable schools both to evaluate their performance and be more accountable to parents, the local authorities, and the Secretary of State.

The Education Reform Act embodies these proposals. As part of its curriculum every maintained school must provide a basic curriculum to be known as the National Curriculum. This consists of religious education, the three core subjects of mathematics, english and science, and seven foundation subjects, history, geography, technology, music, art, and, for pupils over eleven, a foreign language. Welsh is a core subject in Welsh speaking schools in Wales, and a foundation subject in other schools in Wales.

The Secretary of State is required to establish the National Curriculum as soon as is reasonably practicable (taking first the core subjects and then the other foundation subjects). He may also specify in relation to each subject such attainment targets, such programmes of study and such assessment arrangements, as he considers appropriate for each of four key stages in a child's education, from 5 to 7, 7 to 11, 11 to 14, and 14 to 16.

LEAs, governing bodies, and head teachers, each have a statutory duty to secure that the National Curriculum as it exists at the beginning of any school year is implemented in that year. Local authorities must also make arrangements for dealing with any complaints about the delivery of the National Curriculum in their schools.

The Act attempts also to cover certain other eventualities. Among these are for example a proviso that no course leading to an external examination may be followed unless it has been approved by the Secretary of State or a designated body, and another empowering the Secretary of State to extend the provision of this curriculum chapter to students of 16 to 19 in schools or colleges of further education.

The grounds for exemption from these curricular requirement are also identified. The curriculum may be modified for children with special needs, provided their statements so direct, and the Secretary of State may direct that the curriculum be modified in particular schools to enable research and development to be carried out.

Crowning the new edifice of curriculum control and management will be a National Curriculum Council, a Curriculum Council for Wales and a Schools Examinations and Assessment Council. Members of these bodies will be appointed by the Secretary of State. Their main function will be to keep, respectively, the curriculum in maintained schools, and examinations and assessment, under review, to advise the Secretary of State, to carry out programmes of research and development if so requested by the Secretary of State, and to publish relevant information. They must furnish the Secretary of State with such reports and other information as he requires, and must comply with any directions that he gives.

In response both to the consultation paper and the Education

Reform Bill, critics levelled three main charges against the curricular proposals. First, that the Act concentrates too many powers on the holder of one office. This concentration is thought to be constitutionally and politically dangerous, and managerially ill-suited to the developmental needs of a large and necessarily dispersed system in a rapidly changing world. Second, that the National Curriculum as described is rigid and out of date. Even Mr Baker's immediate predecessor, Lord Joseph, has described its imposition as a straitjacket on schools and teachers. The list of subjects is thought to be inappropriate in the education of young children, and too like the list specified in the 1904 Secondary School Regulations to meet today's needs. There is for example no reference to economic awareness, careers education or TVEI, to health education or home economics, to environmental education or the arts other than music and art. Some of these fears about the National Curriculum have been allayed by ministerial concessions. Whereas the consultation paper implied that the National Curriculum including religious education might take 90 per cent of the time, Ministers later talked of 70 per cent, and the Act includes a clause saying that ministers may not prescribe that any particular periods of time or provision should be made for the teaching of any programme of study. Ministers have also referred increasingly to the importance of developing other aspects of the curriculum such as multicultural education, health education, economic awareness and information technology as cross curricular themes. Perhaps the most attractive feature of the National Curriculum is, after all, the gaps it leaves, gaps which LEAs could fill with subtlety and vision.

There is much still to play for too, in working out the details of attainment targets, programme of study, and assessment arrangements, the third area of concern. As the consultation papers went to press in 1987 the Secretary of State established a Task Group on Assessment and Testing, and National Curriculum Working Groups on Science and Mathematics. The Task Group was asked to advise on the practical consideration governing assessment within the National Curriculum, the Working Groups on the knowledge, skills, understanding and aptitudes which pupils of different abilities and maturity should have attained and be able to demonstrate at 7, 11, 14, and 16, and on programme of study which would be consistent with those targets.

The three groups all succeeded in reporting before the end of 1987. The Task Group won plaudits for their report. They said that any system of assessment should satisfy four criteria: the assessment results should be based on objective criteria, and should provide a basis for decision about pupils' further learning needs; the assessment grades should be capable of comparison across classes and schools, so the assessment should be moderated; and the assessment should relate to expected routes of educational development, giving some continuity to a pupil's assessment at different ages. The Group also considered in some detail how a system of assessment might be implemented. They thought preparing and testing new assessment methods, training teachers, and allowing the pupils to benefit from experience of the new curriculum, pointed to a period of at least five years between promulgation of the relevant attainment targets and general adoption of the new assessment system.

The Task Group also kept in close touch with the subject working groups. In their interim report the Science Group identified knowledge and concepts, skills and attitudes, which the study of science should promote, and related these to major themes, programmes of study, and attainment targets. They emphasised that assessment should encourage continuity and progression. The Mathematics Group reported somewhat more tentatively, and both the chairman and another leading member resigned soon after.

In April 1988 a third subject working group, for English, was appointed immediately after publication of the Kingman Report on English.

The reports of the Task Groups and the Science Group have been welcomed by many teachers, advisers and education officers. At first many had feared that the machinery of targets, programmes and tests would lead teachers to focus narrowly on achieving externally defined targets. These two reports offer a broader vision of assessment as part of the creative process of teaching and learning. But the Secretary of State has still to declare his own hand, and there is some evidence of other counsellors who would like him to adopt simpler, cruder instruments than those the Task Group has recommended. The Act gives him the power to decide, so much depends on his wisdom.

In the system of dispersed management which characterised education in England and Wales from the 1940s or even the 1920s to the 1980s, local authorities had room for curricular initiatives: establishing a field studies centre, promoting local educational broadcasting, appointing an adviser in a new area, funding Nuffield science, launching a local project, creating a study group: the possibilities were legion, and the potential energy boundless. The new look LEAs of the 90s will have a more clearly defined managerial role.

They must secure delivery of the National Curriculum, they must monitor and evaluate the new system, they must establish machinery for dealing with complaints and arrange for information to be published, they must ensure that teachers are trained to undertake their new responsibilities for offering the National Curriculum and assessing pupils. These are formidable tasks. Whether they differ significantly in nature and scope from the tasks undertaken by area managers in, say, the Training Commission or Social Security, is rather less clear.

These managerial developments in education from 5 to 16 have been matched in education beyond 16. Government has deployed a similar armoury to bring about significant improvements in the quality of training and levels of skill in Britain's work force. Its chief instrument has been the Manpower Services Commission whose work is described in Chapter 17. The Commission developed new forms of training and education for the unemployed, and bought educational services from local authority colleges and elsewhere as part of these programmes. In 1984 government invited the Commission to assume the more threatening task of negotiating contracts for and funding a quarter of all the work-related non-advanced further education undertaken by local authority colleges. To secure funds, whose cost is met by diversion from rate support grant, authorities must submit annually, an annual programme and a three-year development plan for all their work-related non-advanced further education. The centre has devised a simple means of keeping a close watch on virtually all vocational and professional further education.

Locally, the LEA has an important strategic role, confirmed by the 1988 Education Reform Act, in planning and coordinating the provision of further education to meet the Commission's requirements. But its boundaries are clearly marked, by the

Commission's responsibilities on one side, and the autonomy awarded to colleges under the 1988 Act.

In addition to using a new agency, grants and contracts, and the legislature, to establish control over education beyond 16, government has also stepped in to regulate the mass of courses and qualifications which characterise further education. In March 1985 government announced a Review of Vocational Qualifications. Its aims were set out in the White Paper *Education and Training for Young People* (April 1985).

The Review Group reported a year later, and its proposals accepted in the White Paper *Working Together – Education and Training* (Cmnd 9823 July 1986). The National Council for Vocational Qualification was established in October. The Council has devised a framework for vocational qualifications based on four levels of qualifications and defined areas of competence.

The Council believe it should not specify what types of assessment are to be used. What are appropriate will depend on the nature of the elements of competence to be assessed, but various types and methods of assessment will almost certainly be needed to assess all the elements of competence needed in employment. The Council will not create its own qualifications, but its aim is to bring all existing vocational qualifications within its framework by 1991.

In further education as in schools the role of local education authorities is to be one of efficient branch management within a national system.

Part 3 Educational administration practice

9 Practical management of a Local Educational Authority's system

Books do not fully reflect life and this will inevitably be clear to anyone who reads this book and who is engaged in educational administration. A major reason for this is, of course, that educational administration concerns people, and people's behaviour will perversely not follow the neat and logical layout of a book.

The Local Education Authority

One of the first and most obvious ways in which this fact will manifest itself to the newcomer to educational administration is through the existence of the democratic organisation – the Local Education Authority – which the educational administrator serves. The authority consists of members elected by the people living in the area for which it provides education, and the administration of education in the area is essentially a joint venture in which both the elected members who constitute the authority and the officers who serve the authority play vital parts.

The Education Committee

Those local councils which are LEAs have by law to set up an Education Committee and in practice the Council will delegate most of its educational functions to it, with the exception of basic policy decisions such as the final approval of its budget. The sub-committee structure under the Education Committee can vary considerably from one authority to another. There is likely however, to be a sub-committee dealing with finance and general matters. There will almost certainly, too, be at least one sub-committee dealing with schools and in some areas there will be two or three sub-committees dealing with different types of schools such as primary schools, secondary schools and special schools. There will be also at least one sub-committee dealing with further education, although again in some areas there will be other sub-committees in the general further education field, either working to the further education sub-committee or directly to the Education Committee; these may include sub-committees for youth and community work, adult education and recreation. Most authorities will have a careers sub-committee, although in some cases careers work will be handled by one or possibly two of the other sub-committees. Finally, where the Education Committee is responsible for libraries and museums, there will certainly be another sub-committee dealing with them.

Not all the members of the Education Committee will be elected members. There will be a group of 'other members' who are not councillors, appointed under the provisions of the 1944 Education Act. There will be, in the words of the Act, 'persons of experience in education and persons acquainted with the educational conditions prevailing in the area for which the committee acts'. These Added members will include representatives of the teachers, the Churches, and Institutions of Higher Education such as the local University. They will also include persons co-opted by the elected members to reflect, for example, the needs of industry and commerce. But these 'other members' will, in accordance with the Act, always be in a minority on the Education Committee, and they have usually seen the danger of voting in the committee in support of the party with a minority on the council in order to out-vote the majority party: this has only happened on one or two rare occasions. It can indeed be expected that the 'other members' will not vote in one particular direction or the other as a collective body but will make, as was clearly intended by the 1944 Education Act, independent contributions to the affairs of the Education Committee.

The work of the Education Committee, and in consequence of the Chief Education Officer and the other officers who serve it, is extremely wide in both scope and variety. It ranges from the provision of pre-school education to the strategic planning of further and higher education in its area. The work will also vary in nature – from, for example, large-scale catering through the school meals service to the education and training of professional people. There is variety, too, in the type of work, which will cover both routine administrative and clerical procedures such as the drawing up of contracts of various kinds, the payment of wages and the making of transport arrangements, and work of a highly creative kind such as the development and introduction of more effective methods of teaching. The committee and the administration serving it must deal with this scope and variety of work and enable the routine to be dealt with effectively at the same time as ensuring that the creativity is not stifled.

The Education Committee is clearly the committee to which the educational administrator will mainly work. The word 'mainly' is important because other committees of the Council can have a considerable significance for him. He may, for example, find, particularly if he is or becomes a Chief or Deputy Chief Education Officer, that he has to defend his committee's proposals on finance at the Council's finance committee or his committee's personnel proposals at the Council's personnel committee. Or he may have to outline what the Education Committee is proposing to do at technical committees dealing with such matters as the purchase of land.

It will soon become very apparent to the Education Officer, as he undergoes these experiences, that he is dealing with people who have to be convinced of a particular case and that, if they are not so convinced, a cherished policy may never come to fruition. This fact is just as true in respect of the officer's relationship with the Education Committee itself and its sub-committees. If the Education Committee is not convinced of the rightness of any proposal put forward, such a proposal will not be implemented. The converse is of course also true in that members of committee – with their particular educational and political views – will naturally have their own cherished proposals based on those views, on which the Education Officer will have a duty to advise. He may see considerable professional disadvantages to the education service in some of these proposals but it will be up to him to convince the members of his committee of the dangers latent in such proposals and of the validity of his own professional viewpoint; but if he fails to do so the proposals will be implemented and it will be his duty to put them into effect. Administration is – like politics – the art of the possible.

The Department of Education and Science

A point that always interests those studying the educational system in England is the relationship between the LEA and the Secretary of State for Education and Science (who is the member of the central government responsible for education) and his Department. It has always been difficult to describe this relationship precisely. Under the Education Act 1944 the Secretary of State had the duty 'to secure the effective execution by local authorities under his control and direction of the national policy for providing a varied and comprehensive educational service in every area'. These words, however, give a misleading impression. Although the Secretary of State has very substantial powers indeed under the legislation (in particular, he can determine that an authority has acted unreasonably), the LEA is on the other hand a properly elected democratic body in its own right and in practice exercises very substantial powers. Under the 1988 Act it will determine the money to be placed at the disposal of each of its schools and will lay down guidelines governing the way in which it may be spent. It will continue to provide directly for building matters and will provide services in support of the school governors whilst retaining to itself important functions of inspection and evaluation, possesses a great deal of educational initiative on matters such as work on the curriculum. Nor does the often quoted phrase about the service being a national service locally administered wholly describe the situation if 'administered' is thought to mean simply the carrying out of policies nationally decided (perhaps the difficulty here is that at the time the phrase was minted the word 'administration' had a rather wider connotation than it has at present and was intended to include the creativity and policy-making which are very much a feature of local authority work).

What tends to happen in practice is that on broad policy matters central government takes action through legislation: it decides, for example, the age at which children must start school and it decides when they are allowed to leave school. At times Government has extended its decision-making powers and the

1988 Act has recently given very substantial additional powers to the Secretary of State, for example, enabling him to determine the admission limits for schools, calling for his approval to local authorities' schemes of delegation to governing bodies, and most importantly, giving him power to determine the pattern of a national curriculum and instruments for testing and assessment. In 1980 it decided that there should be parents and teachers on school governing bodies and that there should be statutory committees to deal with appeals from parents about choice of schools.

Not only has the 1988 Education Act substantially shifted powers to the Department of Education and Science on the one hand and school governing bodies on the other, but other legislative changes have substantially changed relationships between local and central authority. Changes in the financing of local government introduced not by the Secretary of State for Education and Science but by the Secretary of State for the Environment have over the years introduced systems of block grants, of government targets, and of financial penalties for local authorities which exceed those targets. Such changes have inevitably affected the Education Service as the highest spender in local government. Equally the rise of the Manpower Services Commission and the interest shown by the Department of Trade and Industry in promoting the use of technology in the curriculum have had a substantial effect upon the way in which the service is provided locally.

There are, too, decisions made by the DES which will affect in purely administrative terms the running of the education department of the local authority. The DES will, for example, call for certain records on teachers; it will ask for certain statistics to be kept; it will ask for returns to be made on which national information can be given on such matters as the ratio of teachers to pupils. Other departments of State can have a similar influence when they have a relationship with the LEA. The Department of Employment has such an influence, for example, in respect of the careers service for which it is responsible nationally but for which LEAs are responsible in their areas.

The Education Officer will clearly come into regular contact with officers of the DES. There are no regional offices of the department and therefore the contact that exists will be with officers in London, particularly those described as 'territorial officers' who deal with day-to-day problems arising in respect of the particular authority that the Education Officer serves. There is a tradition of good relationships between officers of the department and officers of the authorities which has withstood the strains that might have been expected to occur when the central government is under the control of a party of one political complexion and the LEA is under the control of a party of a different political complexion. Undoubtedly, the direct contact with the department itself and the lack of any necessity to go through a regional office have contributed to this. But what has also undoubtedly contributed has been the fact that the LEA has its own democratic base and has an extremely free hand in many of its operations, as described above.

Most of the contacts between the DES's officers and the officers of the LEA will in practice be on such matters as the size and composition of building programmes, the closure of schools and the individual cases in which the pupil or parents or students have appealed against the decision of the authority in the hope that the Secretary of State will decide that the authority has acted unreasonably.

The Education Officer will also meet from time to time Her Majesty's Inspectors of Schools who are working in the area of his authority; they are not, of course, employees of the authority but are on the strength of the DES. Chief Education Officers tend to value in particular the opportunity to talk over with the member of HM Inspectorate who acts, as it were, as liaison officer in the field between the DES and the authority. Home truths can often be effectively delivered along these particular lines of communication in a way that is not always possible through the normal and more formal channels.

Those Education Officers who find themselves playing some role on the national scene will find that they have the opportunity to meet senior officers of the DES in varying contexts. This may be through the Society of Education Officers or as a result of being placed on a committee or working party as a representative of the Association of County Councils, the Association of Metropolitan Authorities or the Council of Local Education Authorities. Indeed, the contacts may not simply be with officers of the DES but with officers of other departments such as the Department of Employment and the Department of Industry, which now have a stake and influence in the field of education.

In recent years there has been, in particular, a considerable growth in relationships with officers of the Manpower Services Commission which funds, through specific grants, many courses and projects in LEA colleges and schools. All these contacts of course increase markedly the possibilities open to the Education Officer to influence national developments and, although this influence will tend to be exerted mainly by Chief Education Officers, it is by no means solely confined to them. Any Education Officer who makes himself an expert in one part of the educational world will soon begin to realise how far this knowledge (tactfully used, of course), can affect national issues.

The making of policy

The question of the making of policy requires special consideration. There are many illusions about policy-making, some of them unfortunately spread by textbooks on government. What is certain is that policy-making very rarely comes from people sitting round a table, having thoughts and deciding that they will have 'a policy' – whether those people are members of a committee or senior officers in a management team. The actual genesis of a policy is usually quite different. In a sense, of course, policy-making is taking place all the time. A comparatively junior officer who is dealing in a particular way with a particular type of problem that keeps coming on to his desk will be creating 'policy' of a kind. He may, for example, be interpreting certain types of road as dangerous, thus justifying exceptional arrangements for free transport: he may be creating 'case law' in dealing with discretionary awards: he may be deciding that a particular kind of social or home circumstance justify boarding education. Usually, however, by policy-making is meant major policy-making and many major policies owe their birth to one individual with an idea – often responding to a real situation – which is then talked over with colleagues, members and officers, and developed in due course by very many others.

The introduction of a three-tier form of school organisation for pupils aged from 5 to 18 is an excellent example of what can happen. The issue was effectively raised by Sir Alec Clegg, then Chief Education Officer for the West Riding, who – with the support of his members – began to question why all plans for school reorganisation should be based on the assumption that children changed from primary education to secondary education at the age of 11 and why, if another age, or indeed a school spanning the older children of primary school age and the younger children of secondary school age, would be more convenient in the West Riding situation, different arrangements should not be made. The main objection raised was the legal one and this produced the response that, if a law was not based on sound principles, the law should be changed – as indeed in due course it was. Similarly the growth of schemes concentrating provision for students over the age of 16 in sixth form or tertiary colleges owes much to the initiative of individual LEAs. The extension called for by the 1988 Act of delegation of financial responsibility to governing bodies owes much to recent initiatives in Cambridgeshire, whilst Croydon has been to the fore in extending the use of testing and assessment.

There are many examples of new educational policies which owe their genesis to the members and staff of LEAs. Before the Second World War there were the village colleges of Cambridgeshire. Immediately after the Second World War there were the new ideas in school building pioneered by Hertfordshire and on building cost analysis by the North Riding. More recent examples are the work done by Leicestershire on community schools; the possibilities shown by the County and District Councils in Nottinghamshire of providing buildings which served both as schools and as centres for leisure-time activities for their areas; the successful development on a massive scale of higher education provision by Manchester and Bradford and other authorities; the forging of links with overseas countries by authorities such as Leicestershire and Merton; and the new ideas about governing bodies that came from Sheffield. Authorities have taken the initiative too, in curriculum development, as Leeds and Somerset did in French, Kent and Birmingham in mathematics and ILEA and Essex in computer work. Many of the suggestions in the Warnock Report on Special Education, incorporated in the 1981 Education Act, for more integration of the handicapped in the work of ordinary schools clearly rest on work done on the initiative of individual authorities in such matters as partially hearing units and access for the disabled.

The introduction of the Education and Support Grant system has enabled the Secretary of State to indicate his priorities for developmental work. Nonetheless the initiative in seeing those developments through still rests very largely with local authorities. For example, groups of authorities have pioneered the development of the use of appraisal amongst teachers, the 'clustering' of primary schools and new approaches to the education of children in inner city areas.

Credit should also be given in the sphere of educational policy-making to the work undertaken by voluntary bodies, which have often carried out developments and experiments in advance of action taken by the DES and LEAs and which can exert pressures on statutory bodies to initiate policies.

There is of course a long tradition of work by many voluntary bodies in the fields of Youth Service and Adult Education and also in the arts, in recreation and in sport. Other areas in which there has been, and continues to be, a significant contribution from voluntary bodies are pre-school education and special education.

An example of what can happen is the extended debate which took place between the voluntary organisations concerned with children with severe learning difficulties and the statutory bodies during the years before 1970. Prior to that time these children were deemed to be unsuitable for education and the local health authorities were responsible for making provision for them. The work of the various voluntary bodies brought into the open the inequities of classifying children as ineducable: this led ultimately to the Education (Handicapped Children) Act 1970 which gave these children the same rights to education as all other children and consequently made it a condition that staff employed to teach them should be suitably qualified. Since this legislation was introduced co-operation between LEAs and the voluntary agencies concerned has grown considerably; in many areas regular meetings are held between officers of the voluntary organisations and the LEAs to discuss ways and means of improving the educational facilities for these children in school and after leaving school.

The political dimension

It is of course idle to neglect the political dimension in educational affairs. Politics in education is not a simple matter of one political party having a straightforward set of policies which are shared at national and local level. In recent years the emergence of the 'hung' Council has added to the officer's difficulty. Where there is no clear political majority it is difficult to have clear statements of medium- and long-term policy objectives and the skills of political sensitivity of the officer are at a particular premium. The supporters of a party locally may well take a different view from that adopted by their national colleagues because they feel that the latter do not understand the particular circumstances on the ground. Local Conservatives, for example, have at times taken a much stronger line on the need for an effective local authority presence in higher education, because they have seen the value of it in practice, than have some of their national colleagues.

Again, there may well be deep divisions of opinion within the party which has the political majority on the council and its committees, and indeed the larger that majority the more obvious the differences of opinion may be and the more loudly they may be expressed. The officer must not, of course, 'play politics', but the officer who is unaware of these political differences will find the going very hard indeed. This will be because he will be forgetting the essential fact that he serves a democratic organisation – the Council – and that members of that Council have been elected by the people living in its area and the members therefore possess a real democratic base. There are, however, other golden rules to assist the officer as he moves along this twisting and bramble-infested path: honesty matters; the law matters; self-respect matters.

The Education Officer and the public

Members of the Council and the Education Committee will, of course influence the work of the officer through committees. But their activity is by no means limited to the Council and the committee. The elected members represent constituents and their constituents will approach them on a whole range of problems.

Similarly, Members of Parliament will be approached by their constituents on matters affecting education. Almost all these constituency problems will eventually find themselves on the desk of an officer in the Education Department who will soon find that there are two forms of priority – one priority given by the importance of the business, the other priority given by the individual who has in fact raised the business. All correspondence should naturally be replied to quickly and effectively; there is no future in overloaded in-trays and pending trays. But to put a ministerial letter at the bottom of even a small pile is, on the whole, a bad move.

There will, too, be pressure exerted on the officers directly by members of the public. This particular pressure has grown enormously in recent years as the citizen has been increasingly reminded of his rights and of all the possibilities that exist of appeals to the Secretary of State, to the new Appeal Committees created by the 1980 Education Act, to the Ombudsman, to Members of Parliament, to members of the Council, and so on. The officer in the Education Department will soon note that this pressure can at times be exercised by the very people who attack any growth in the number of local government officers and who do not seem to realise that Ombudsmen and appeals procedures and publicity of every kind given to the citizen's rights to use these procedures will involve either the appointment of additional officers to operate them or other work not being done or not being done satisfactorily. If the officer finds this kind of situation irksome he has probably made a mistake, however, in coming into education administration at all.

The Education Officer is of course a public servant. This does not in fact mean that he is employed by an individual member of the public, although he will meet from time to time those who suffer from this particular delusion. Members of the public do very properly enjoy rights. They should always be treated courteously, whatever discourtesies are offered in return. Their letters should always be promptly acknowledged, although at times a full answer may have to be sent later when the many pages and points of the original letter have been digested and investigated. They also have the right to have their cases fully and properly considered. What it is impossible to achieve are such things as the immediate presence of a senior member of the Education Department at the other end of the telephone when a member of the public demands to be put in touch with him or her. The officer's general duty of serving the public by being present at, for example, a meeting of the Education Committee, may have to override the individual requirements of the member of the public on the telephone, although naturally every effort must be made for an officer who will know the case to ring back as soon as possible. One is only too well aware that this paragraph does not fully transmit the flavour of the actual situation when a raging voice is on the telephone which will talk to no one but the Chief Education Officer, or when an individual has declared his intention to pitch his tent in the foyer of County or City Hall until his particular grievance has been met.

Although the Education Officer is a public servant and should be civil, he is certainly not a civil servant. The main difference is that he is subject to immediate accountability in a way that the civil servant cannot be. Parliament is a democratic body, of course, just as the county and district councils are democratic bodies. But inevitably the Education Officer will find this relationship to his Council very much closer and more continuing than can possibly be the case between a civil servant and Parliament. Similarly, although the Secretary of State and his Ministers are elected Members of Parliament and the chairmen of the Education Committee and of its sub-committees are elected councillors, their roles are inevitably different. Chairmen will have considerable powers, for example, to raise policy issues and to deal with matters between meetings of committees. And the effectiveness of the Education Committee in the context of the Council is greatly helped by effective chairmen. But chairmen will not have the type of power enjoyed by a Secretary of State. In a local authority matters of policy and many individual cases will go to the Education Committee or one of its sub-committees. Parliament simply cannot operate in this way and the Secretary of State, or one of the Ministers in the DES, will engage in a wide range of decision-making which, rightly or wrongly – and apart from any legal considerations – would simply not be acceptable to a locally elected Council.

Other departments of the Local Education Authority

The Education Officer will also find that he is involved in another and very different set of personal and professional relationships. These relationships are with other departments of the LEA. Clearly the relationshp will be a close and continuing one with the Chief Executive of the Council (an officer who exists in the great majority of authorities and who is the senior officer in the Council's service), with the Treasurer, the Architect, the Solicitor and, where such an officer exists, the Supplies Officer. This does not mean to say that the Education Officer should not himself be acquainted with problems of finance, of buildings, of site and of law, and the relationship should never be between the ignorant Education Officer and the informed specialist. But the days have now gone when the Education Officer could be expected to know all the complexities and ramifications of, for example, the law in so far as it affects the education service. A glance at recently reported cases of dismissals and of Health and Safety at Work problems will show that this is so. On the other hand it should be remembered that the existence of specialist departments depends on those departments which provide the service to the public and not vice versa.

There are other departments of the LEA with which the Education Officer will have to deal in addition to those departments which are giving a supporting service to the Education Department. These are departments which are providing services themselves. Perhaps the most obvious of them is the Social Services Department where there is an overlap between the welfare services rightly performed by the Education Department and the welfare services rightly performed by the Social Services Department; a clear example here is, of course, truancy and its possible relationship to other social problems of the family of the child concerned. With other departments of the authority the link may not be so obvious but it is still there. An Education Officer dealing with buildings will have to negotiate with officers of the planning and roads department over access to schools or with specialists from the fire department over fire escapes and fire prevention measures. The police too will be involved not only in well-publicised legal cases involving staff employed in the education service but also in the same type of social problems which affect the social services department and the education department as well as ensuring that the Chief Constable is able to discharge his role in relation to the curriculum.

One change that has occurred in recent years is the formalisation of some of the inter-departmental relationships referred to and the establishment of a management team. Such a team will consist of all or some of the Chief Officers of the authority – for example the Treasurer, the Secretary, the Surveyor, the Planner, the Director of Social Services, the Education Officer – meeting regularly under the chairmanship of the Chief Executive to discuss matters affecting the local authority they serve. The management team will often be supported by other teams of deputies and specialist officers. As always, however, it is not the machinery that really matters but how people operate the machinery. The early stories of management teams meeting endlessly and keeping Chief Officers away from the problems of their departments have now given way to widespread evidence that management teams can bring Chief Officers together to understand each other's problems and, more particularly, to plan to achieve wider objectives which transcend traditional departmental boundaries. In any event, however, a formal structure of a management team should never be allowed to displace, indeed it cannot displace, the constant inter-departmental consultation that occurs and, indeed, has always occurred in local government, particularly between those members of staff dealing with money, buildings and supplies and pupil welfare.

The organisation and staff of the Education Department of a local authority

Given the range of relationships with Members of Parliament and members of Councils, with the public, with parents, with students and with other members of staff of the authority, and given the range of the education service itself, the problems to be faced by an Education Officer will be multifarious and will become more so as he or she receives promotion until at chief or deputy chief officer level life will tend to become a kaleidoscope of issues and problems, with one issue or problem after another rapidly appearing before him. His mind must indeed be able to move easily from the closure of a school to the complaint of a disgruntled parent, from problems concerning the teaching of mathematics to the arrangements for a youth orchestra concert, from the development of a nursery school to a complex university award case, from an issue concerning the design of a special school to a question relating to school meals, from a disciplinary case involving a teacher to a general report on a school or college, from a discussion on youth employment and careers for school leavers to the establishment of a youth club. He may then have to attend a meeting of a group of members or of senior officers or of a more formal sub-committee or committee. On a busy day he may have these problems intertwined with perhaps the problem of teachers working 'to rule' or a more old-fashioned strike of manual workers. There will, of course, be some time available in the evening or at weekends for long and more concentrated pieces of work, provided, of course, that the evening or weekend is not already committed to a school function or a governors' meeting, or to speaking at or attending a conference or course. Even at a more junior level, however, than chief or deputy, the Education Officer will meet a range of problems which will involve people, buildings and materials – and even buildings and materials will wear the human face of an architect or a supplies officer. This complexity of problems necessitates a system of allocation of work and delegation. This will take place both within the central education department and in the field.

Education Departments are, of course, organised in different ways depending on such factors as the size of the authority and its geographical nature and on preferences for one kind of structure to another. In the great majority of authorities, however, there will be a degree of specialisation under the Chief Education Officer and the Deputy Chief Education Officer. Indeed, in some authorities where there is more than one deputy the specialisation begins at deputy level. In all the structures, however, there will be a tendency to have two or three major branches covering schools and further education, with the former possibly subdivided into sections dealing with primary, secondary and/or middle schools and special schools and the latter into sections dealing with colleges of further and/or higher education of various kinds, adult education, the training of teachers and the youth service. Most authorities will have a section devoted to matters to do with finance and personnel and statistical information. These functions have taken on more significance in recent years. The careers service is likely to have its own branch or section and there may well be in addition specialist sections for staffing, awards, supplies and school meals.

Of major importance will be the authority's own inspectorate and advisory service on whom the Education Officer, and indeed the authority, will depend so much not only for essential advice on the curriculum but for detailed inspection of and information about colleges and schools and the teachers in them, particularly as HMIs have concentrated increasingly on more surveys of a national or regional kind, valuable as these are, and less on inspections of individual schools. The advisory service also has the responsibility for ensuring that a full programme of in-service training for teachers is provided.

The 1988 Education Act brings the need for local education authorities to review their administrative arrangements. Many authorities already have a system of area or divisional offices under the control of an area or divisional education officer who will be given the authority to exercise a number of functions on behalf of the Chief Education Officer. With the development of schemes for the local management of schools the delegated functions at area level will decreasingly be involved with detailed administration as they assume more general functions in support of the school governing bodies. It becomes more important for the education authority, through its local links, to maintain good relationships with the chairmen of governing bodies and to ensure that the school is offered support and professional services on, for example, personnel matters, property services and financial advice. Very often advisory services will be centred at the local level as advisers increasingly relate to nominated schools. The grouping of schools to meet the needs of the Technical and Vocational Education Initiative in many authorities will provide a convenient pattern to which local administrative arrangements may be added.

A further area of administrative change will be that required by legislation requiring councils to put out to competitive tender a range of services including the school meals service, cleaning and grounds maintenance. Organisational changes are required to separate the client functions from the running of direct service organisations which will compete with contractors for the provision of such services. It is, therefore, now clear that the 1988 Education Act, largely through measures relating to the local management of schools, will require a review of the administrative arrangements traditionally provided. It is likely that more devolved systems will develop in the early 1990s.

The well-organised education department will have clearly annunciated aims. Its Chief Education Officer will have a responsibility with his committee for articulating those aims sufficiently clearly for his department to have clear targets to aim at. Each officer will understand clearly what his duties and responsibilities are and for which of those targets he is personally responsible. In many local authorities such a formal scheme of assignment of duties and responsibilities is seen as the basis of appraisal systems which will on the one hand ensure that individual efforts are harnessed to the overall goals of the education service and on the other enable him to be helped to measure his performance against those goals. A critically important part of this process is the counselling of individual officers about their career development and how their performance might improve. The training of staff is assuming even more crucial importance as the process of change now quickens.

The training of staff

The complexity of educational administration not only makes it necessary to devolve and delegate; it makes it increasingly important that staff should be trained. One can no longer assume that it will be possible for an Education Officer, whether he has been recruited from teaching or whether he has been promoted internally within the Education Department from a more junior post, to be able to pick up the general nature and all the detail of his job as he goes along. At the very least he should have some form of induction training, preferably at an early stage, within the wider context of the authority as a whole. He should be encouraged, too, to attend longer courses so that he can see his work and, indeed, in some cases the work of the authority, against the background of what is happening elsewhere. And of course it is imperative that he attends at least some courses with a more purely educational content so that he does not become out of touch with educational developments and ideas. It will not be easy in present circumstances for an officer to receive long periods of full-time training and re-training but short one-day courses and conferences, and indeed professional meetings arranged by bodies such as the Society of Education Officers in themselves do a very great deal to help in the continued training not simply of junior staff but of the more senior experienced officers too.

As he becomes more senior the Education Officer should indeed be able to contribute himself to the general pattern of training, by what he can offer on courses at national or regional level on the basis of his own work and experience. Indeed, the newcomer to educational administration will soon discover that the general development of education in this country still comes mainly from the grass roots. It has never been a question of wisdom being handed down to authorities and colleges and schools from the DES although the department will often take steps to ensure that knowledge of new ideas and successful practices in education is widely spread. And the Education Officer, through his contacts with HM Inspectors of Schools or with officers of the DES or through the Society of Education Officers, can make his own opportunities to pass on information about the better practices and the new ideas of which he is personally aware.

There is, finally, one thing that the Education Officer should always remember in this world of pressures and problems and work, and that is that he is not simply an administrator but an educational administrator. It is important for committee work and paper work to be dealt with quickly and properly and for correct administrative procedures to be known and used. But the Education Officer first and foremost must know what is going on, educationally, in the colleges and schools with which he deals. He should remember that there can be no such thing as a well-run office if that office is dealing with badly-run schools. Similarly, there is nothing that can take the place of educational vision and educational initiative. All the administration – organisation, rules, regulations, management, communication, consultation, public relations and the rest – only exists in order that the students in the colleges and the pupils in the schools can receive an education which makes them better, more

knowledgeable, more capable and more developed individuals
and wiser, better informed and more effective citizens.

10 Office organisation

Introduction

The origins of most education offices lie in the more important
of the School Boards. In general, School Boards in the cities
and urban areas were stronger and more centralised than those
in country areas where a more decentralised model developed
because of the greater distances, the lower population densities
and the social climate. Education offices nowadays, metropolitan
and county, tend to reflect this different inheritance.

Within this broad classification, however, every office is
different. In the first place, although education is a national
service locally administered, Education Committees do not have
identical responsibilities. Some, mainly among the county
authorities, are responsible for the library service. The other
differences date mainly from the reorganisation of 1974. In a
few authorities, for example, responsibility for the youth service,
or for directions as to the use of school premises outside school
hours, or the education welfare service, has been allocated to
another committee. Otherwise, differences in responsibilities
largely reflect such differences in provision as in the numbers
of special schools and establishments of further education, and
in the development of such features of the service as nursery
education, adult education and the youth service, which have
been more dependent on local initiative.

Apart from these differences, education offices have been
affected by the trend during the last generation to transfer certain
functions from the education office. Twenty-five years ago it was
not unusual for an education office to include an architect's
branch, repairs branch, and to have responsibility for the clerking
of the Education Committee and its sub-committees. This is now

rare; the architects have gone to the Director of Architecture, the repairs branch to the Director of Works, and the clerking to the Secretary. The same period has seen the transfer of financial functions, to a varying degree, from the education office to the Treasurer's and also the development of the Establishment (or Management Services) Department with responsibility for numbers, gradings and conditions of service of all personnel apart from teaching staff. In other words, the corporate entity of many education offices a generation ago has been eroded by the development of other departments and, in recent years, by the application of theories of corporate management that became particularly influential in the upheaval of reorganisation in 1974. Overall, the result of this trend has curtailed the scope of the education office and brought it into a closer relationship with other departments of the Council.

Each authority has its own version of corporate management. Education offices have therefore been differently affected but they have been uniformly wary. What is beyond dispute is that the education service requires the efficient co-operation of virtually every other department, embracing a rich variety of professionals in other fields. Good personal and working relationships between departments are consequently of prime importance.

The size of the authority largely determines the volume of work, the size of the office and in turn its organisation. The larger the office, the greater its capability for specialisation. This is most evident in the number of professional staff, administrative and advisory, and in the range of their specialisms. The professional and more senior administrative staff in the smaller office tend to have a wider spectrum of responsibilities. Offsetting this, however, the smaller office has fewer establishments to manage, and recording, communication and co-ordination requirements are less demanding.

The optimum population size of the authority for the education service was considered prior to reorganisation. H.M. Inspectors suggested a minimum of 400,000 and the Royal Commission a minimum of 250,000 but 17 authorities emerged in 1974 with smaller populations than 250,000. Although the population of the authority is a constraint on the organisation of the office, local circumstances are clearly influential because there are significant differences in the staffing levels of comparable authorities. Only a few categories of staff fall within the purview of national guidelines on numbers and gradings. The inspectorate has previously benefited from an agreed relationship to the Burnham salaries agreement and the Taylor recommendation of a ratio of one inspector to 20,000 population. The basic scale for educational psychologists is determined nationally and the ratio of 1:25,000 recommended by Warnock will become accepted. The basic grades for Education Welfare Officers and Careers Advisory Officers are determined nationally. The salary scale of the Director of Education is related to the authority's population. The numbers and gradings of other staff are determined by the individual authority.

Every office has a personality. They all have the same aims and purposes, they operate within the same constraints of national policies, legislation and regulations as well as an extensive range of national and regional agreements, they are staffed by officers who are comparable in most respects, and they have a similar institutional context. With so much in common, a broad family resemblance in their personalities is not unexpected. Yet their personalities also differ significantly and this can only be explained by a personal factor in their history.

The individuals who over the years have given the office personality its distinctive features are the senior members, notably the chairmen, the senior officers, and in particular the Director of Education.[1] No doubt some offices have been more fortunate than others in this respect but this in itself is significant. The members' contribution is local but outstanding officers have given a distinctive stamp, not only to their own offices but also, through the officers they trained, to other offices throughout the country. This dynastic factor is a live if elusive influence in many offices. The influence of the members though even more elusive, is certainly no less important, and perhaps especially in defining the relationship between members and officer which is of crucial importance for the service as well as for the office.

In short, although there is much that they have in common, education offices are also different from each other. Furthermore, these differences are not just variations of structure and organisation; there is also a distinctive corporate personality that enhances or limits because it expresses the qualities and values that permeate what the office does and its style of operation.

The structure

The division of work

The establishment chart is a crudely simplified sketch map of the office. Figure 10.1 summarises the establishment chart[2] to illustrate a conventional pattern of organisation to which many education offices approximate.

The Director, Deputy, Chief Inspector, Senior and Assistant Education Officers constitute the senior management team. In their own authority, or elsewhere, the administrative officers have generally served in more than one branch of the service so that, although they may have specialised, they have a broad background of administrative experience.

These officers have generally had no formal training or preparation for their tasks. They generally have good academic qualifications, relevant and successful administrative experience, and most have spent some years as teachers before entering administration. They have learned on the job and been prepared for their duties by their experience in the education service. Increasingly, however, Education Officers are receiving various forms of management training through, for example, the training programmes of the SEO and LGTB. They also have in common a professional commitment to the education service and to the principle that the touchstone of policy is the needs of the service. This can give the Education Department on occasion a somewhat separatist stance in town or county hall, and requires from the Chairman, the Committee and the Director a sophisticated loyalty, to the Council on the one hand and to the service on the other, that can be a searching test of their capacities.

The relationship of these senior officers is essentially collegial; they have different ranks and duties but they discuss and transact business as colleagues, and it is the quality of the contribution rather than its source that counts. The Chief Inspector has special status as interpreter and spokesman of the needs of the service because this is his *raison d'etre* but the heads of the 'teaching' branches (schools and further education in the notional model illustrated) also have a distinctive sanction because of their service responsibilities. Finance, administration and building are more narrowly functional in their concerns and the Director and

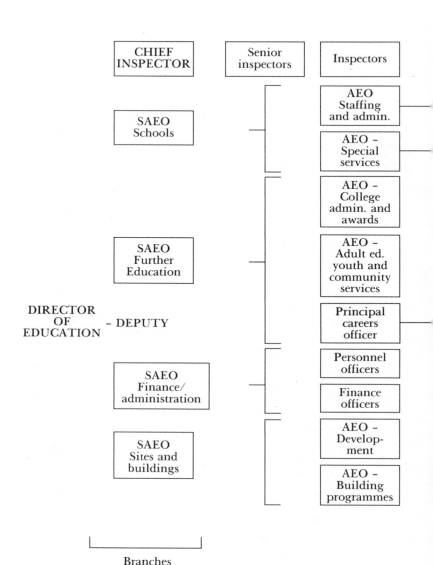

Fig. 10.1 Establishment Chart

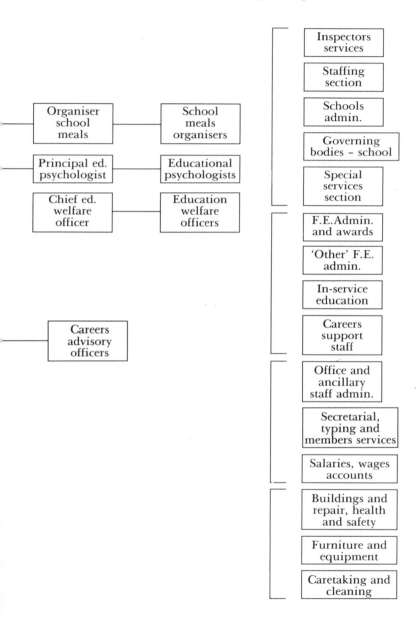

Deputy have wider terms of reference – sometimes more difficult to reconcile – than any of their colleagues.

The meetings of the senior management team are not usually very formal. The agenda is not likely to be more than a list of topics for discussion, and the papers circulated restricted to those requiring general agreement. The meetings also provide opportunity for informal communication, an essential component of the information system.

General characteristics of the branches

Topographically, the principal feature is the branch structure. Each branch combines professional, administrative, clerical and specialist elements but their relative emphasis varies according to the duties of the branch and this in turn governs the structure of the branch. Thus the inspectorate is predominantly professional, with narrow salary differentials, slight administrative support and a clerical unit consisting of a few clerks and secretaries. On the other hand, the sites and buildings branch has only a slight professional presence and is predominantly administrative, clerical and specialist in composition. Whereas the inspectorate has a shallow structure, because its functions are mainly professional, the sites and buildings branch has a deep structure and is bureaucratic in character because its objectives are tangible, ranging from a new building to a minor repair job. The finance/administration branch broadly corresponds in character with the sites and buildings branch. It too has tangible objectives – the payment of wages and salaries, the scrutiny of accounts and their payment and the maintenance of financial procedures and records.

The schools and further education branches are midway in character between the sites and buildings and finance branches on the one hand and the inspectorate on the other. The senior posts in the schools and further education branches fuse professional and administrative components. In recent years, these senior officers have been given additional support by professional assistants, usually graduates with teaching experience but novices in administrative experience. These officers provide a layer of professional/administrative staff at middle management level. Each of these branches characteristically has a strong administrative and clerical structure. At the professional/administrative levels the salary differential is relatively narrow, though not usually as close as the inspectorate's, but their structure is deep and essentially bureaucratic in design and operation.

The hierarchic principle

In all its detail, the establishment chart shows every member of staff, each with specific duties and appropriate salary scale, and the staff as a whole structured as a hierarchy with each officer responsible for a subordinate and each responsible to a supervisor. This is 'line' organisation, based in principle on the division of labour and a comprehensive allocation of responsibilities (matched by the salary structure) which together ensure that work is done in an orderly, accountable, efficient and satisfactory manner.

The hierarchic principle is certainly conspicuous in the organisation of the office. The invariable feature of the structure is the senior post, the Director of Education. This post is a statutory requirement. Prior to 1974, the appointment itself was subject to the Secretary of State's approval[3] but this is no longer required.

In most offices, there is then a Deputy, though in some there are two or even three deputies. The Bains Report, whose recommendations considerably influenced reorganisation of local government in 1974, did not favour deputies but most authorities ignored its advice in this respect. The establishment chart admittedly presents a weak visual case for the Deputy because a triangle with a double apex looks unnatural.

Taken separately, not all of the arguments for a Deputy are wholly convincing but adding them up leaves no room for doubt. The Chief Officer requires at least one other administrative colleague who is wholly committed to an overall view of the service. This perspective qualifies the Deputy to exercise a co-ordinating role which would otherwise fall entirely on the Chief Officer. The Deputy is also available as an alternate who can represent the Director and the service as a whole and who can be plainly seen as an alternate. A good Deputy has an important 'chief of staff' role, interpreting general policy initiatives from the Chief Officer or the committee and ensuring that they are carried out, if necessary by establishing machinery and procedures for dealing with major developments or issues that cannot be satisfactorily allocated to an individual branch or concern several branches. Also important is his interrogative role in the preparation of new policies, and indeed an effective Deputy commonly has a consultant role with the heads of branches for developments generally. He therefore supplements the Chief Officer on the one hand and the heads of branches on the other. The Deputy also has an appellate function. The 'line' principle assumes that responsibility and authority are coterminous – but responsibility normally exceeds authority at every level in the office – 'passing the buck' may be weak and deplorable on occasion but there are circumstances in which it is correct to refer issues to a superior and for the heads of branches it is the Deputy who serves this purpose.

Fulfilling these functions, the Deputy frees the Director for his duties, makes a valuable contribution across the board and, incidentally, develops his capacity to review, a most necessary and effective exercise of authority that sometimes receives less attention than it should have.

Next to the Deputy are the Senior Assistant Education Officers who are the heads of the branches among which the work of the office is divided. The work of a branch has two main aspects.

There is first of all the day-to-day administrative work for which it is responsible. The 'line' principle is manifest in the organisation of this work. But it is important to remember that many officers, at all levels, communicate not only with their immediate colleagues but with a variety of other people inside the office and outside. These communications are functional and authoritative and not always subject to supervision. Many of these communications require an understanding of issues, policies and regulations that may be complex or sensitive or both. These activities exemplify the limitations of the 'line' principle. There is always a risk when responsibility is unsupervised but surprisingly little goes wrong because of the degree to which officers are professionally and administratively literate. Standards vary but great efforts are made to ensure that all officers understand the purpose and significance of what they do and how they do it. A further safeguard is that each officer is part of a complex network and these 'sideways' relationships with their reciprocal dependence have a corrective mechanism that supplements the line discipline. Failure to advertise a teaching vacancy promptly, for example, is more likely to be corrected by an alert inspector or an aggrieved head than by the responsible officer's immediate senior.

The second aspect of the work of the branch is the business of improvement involving changes of one sort or another. The stimulus may be new policies, criticism, the lessons of experience, new technology, the findings of reviews, new legislation, needs that are new or newly perceived and the requirements of a service that is itself developing and changing. It is beyond argument, although it is not always fully appreciated, that an office can be a liberating or a limiting influence on the committee and the service as a whole; the office has regulative functions but these should not limit the potential of the service and there is an inherent commitment in a healthy office to liberate potential. A service that runs more smoothly, perhaps because repairs are undertaken more efficiently or because equipment is more satisfactorily maintained and therefore more reliable, will free attention and energies in schools for their primary objective which is to educate. New techniques such as cook/freeze meals production may improve quality and free resources. The office has stimulated and orchestrated the sustained effort that has been devoted to school design, curriculum development, in-service training, special educational needs, conditions of service, careers education and counselling – a very short selection of developments from the crowded and formidable agenda of development that the office has tackled in addition to its maintenance role.

The quality of the senior officers who lead the branch is critical for the successful management of change and development and they must of course have correspondingly strong support otherwise achievement will fall short of potential. Furthermore, the pace and range of change and the developing aspirations of both teachers and non-teaching staff have led to a further onerous commitment for the senior officers. No development or change of any significance is nowadays launched without consultation. Working parties that include teachers' representatives, *ad hoc* consultative meetings, and joint consultative meetings feature prominently in the diaries of the senior officers. This practice has been described as co-optative bureaucracy, a contradiction in terms that perhaps suggests the difficulties that are sometimes encountered in this dimension. Failure to consult may forfeit the co-operation necessary for success; on the other hand consultation may exact compromise as the price of agreement. The need to consult and its advantages are unchallengeable but it makes more searching demands on leadership.

Because of all this, the heads of branches and their senior colleagues daily face the problem of allocating their attention efficiently between the two imperatives of stability and change. It is not surprising that the office clock ticks too quickly.

Of all the branches, the inspectorate has the greatest potential to develop the service and improve standards and it is a serious handicap for the office and the schools if there are weaknesses in this branch. As the head of this branch, the Chief Inspector therefore carries very great responsibility. He and his colleagues virtually control teacher certification and advise on all teaching appointments; there is nothing that bears more directly on the quality of the education service than the discrimination and influence they exercise in this respect. Furthermore, they make a key contribution in local curricular development and pedagogic practice within the authority. Indeed, they have a positive duty to influence everything that has a direct or indirect bearing on classroom efficiency. The Chief Inspector is therefore the representative of the needs and interests of the classrooms; he must know what they are, be able to interpret them to administrative colleagues, and to influence policy and practice to satisfy and promote them. The authority of this contribution, as in the development role of the heads of branches, is its professional sanction rather than bureaucratic status. Status is not an infallible guide to the distribution of authority at the senior levels.

Environmental influence

The dominant environmental features of the education office were undoubtedly the maintained establishments, notably schools and colleges, and the Education Committee. The office organisation and the office attitude have therefore a strong institutional focus. So indeed does the conventional sub-committee structure – schools, further education, buildings and finance. Usually, therefore, there is a strong correspondence between the structure of the service, the organisation of the office and the committee structure. Explicit or not, the philosophy behind this is that the main purpose is to promote institutional efficiency. On this view, the function of the office is to advise the committee to adopt general policies and to provide adequate resources which will enable the individual establishments to provide an efficient education service. It is a view that has far-reaching implications because it allocates to the office an administrative role committing it to meeting the needs of the establishments. The senior officers of a branch are therefore agents for institutional needs and competitors for resources and, although this competition is kept within narrow limits because of the small proportion of discretionary expenditure in the budget, energetic officers champion the sectors of the service for which they are responsible and which, in this sense, they represent. Given strong sub-committees, the status of the chairman being very significant, these sector interests receive political support.

This interpretation points to the importance of the senior structure of the office and the officers occupying these posts. A single schools branch, compared with separate branches for primary, secondary and special schools, will make certain decisions within itself, whereas where there are separate branches some of these decisions will be made outside it, and may therefore be different.

It is not self-evident that the correct role for the office is to serve the needs of the establishments. The Education Committee, with professional advice that it must listen to, though it doesn't have to follow it, is concerned primarily with policy. An office could therefore be structured on the principle that policy formulation has priority. Logically, this principle leads to the designation of certain officers as policy makers, with others responsible for implementing the policies, and perhaps another team for monitoring the efficiency of the policies in operation. It is broadly this view that has been adopted by the Sheffield Office[4] and there is some evidence that it may be gaining currency elsewhere. In Sheffield, the Deputy co-ordinates the policy makers, a senior assistant Education Officer co-ordinates the executants, and the senior adviser co-ordinates the feed-back. This redeployment was associated with a reorganisation that replaced the conventional branch organisation by branches based on a policy/function principle.[5] This new office, in which SAEOs tackle problem areas (e.g. 16–19 education) that extend beyond a single conventional branch, aims to give an overall view to other officers in addition to Director and Deputy, to give the advisers job satisfaction and to use the available specialists more efficiently.

Whatever the merits of the matrix system, the conventional office structure is probably under increasing pressure because its environment has changed radically in recent years. The 'staff' as distinct from the 'line' principle has been strengthened, for example, by more complex labour legislation which tends to argue the advantage of consolidating 'establishment' functions, usually widely dispersed through the branches in the conventional office. The development of the service is another pressure for change; it is obviously more difficult to draw a clear demarcation between secondary and further education, and the Youth Training Scheme generated closer relationships between the careers advisory service and further education.

Perhaps a more fundamental change than either of these developments is the emergence of policy issues which are politically controversial and which challenge what have been key traditional assumptions. The Alexandrine doctrine of the separation of power[6] under which the DES determines broad policy, the Education Committee applies it, decides local initiatives within that framework and allocates resources, and the individual establishment undertakes responsibility for the curriculum and providing the service, was a good enough analysis so far as it went for its own day and age. Even if it wasn't the whole truth, it was tenable in a context of consensus. But that consensual environment has gone. In the first place, the service has been politicised because a great deal that was tacit is now articulated and controversial. Secondly, the DES and the education committees, as well as the public are increasingly concerned with the quality of the service and less inclined to leave this responsibility entirely to the professionals in the individual establishment. Thirdly, the 1988 Act has given legislative force to both the foregoing. In all these respects, and these are interrelated, education committees are facing new challenges and demands and so, inevitably, are the officers. The disruption of the consensus is complicated by the financial strain on the Alexandrine partnership. With vested service interests, powerful lobbies, political controversy, economic adversity and cracks in public confidence that the service gives value for money, it seems doubtful whether offices geared chiefly to advise on broad policy and the allocation of resources will prove adequate. The office must now develop a greater professional contribution to the individual establishment; thus its own professional capacity must be increased.

Responsibility and accountability

The responsibility of the office exceeds its authority and this is a fact of life for officers that they must learn to live with. The well-being and efficiency of an educational establishment depends partly, for example, on the standard of building maintenance and on the adequacy of its ancillary staff. Yet the former is usually the responsibility of the Director of Works and the latter is determined largely by the Management Services Officer although both are financed from the Education Committee's estimates. Even more significant, the establishment of the education office itself, apart from certain limited categories of staff, is in many authorities determined by the Establishment Committee without reference to the Education Committee. Most fundamental of all, the rate support grant mechanism does not guarantee finance for the needs of the education service. This imperfect match of responsibility and authority causes tensions and strains, and can divert considerable energies in the office and in the service into the struggle for resources.

The relationships between the education office and other departments are therefore of considerable importance. The Education Officers have not only to communicate clearly the needs of the service but also to educate officers in other departments into an understanding of them.

This mis-match of responsibility and authority is also evident in the relationship of the office and the service. The statutory duty of the Education Committee is to provide an efficient education service to meet the needs of the population of its area. The Education Committee, with the office as its principal agent, is therefore responsible for the quality of the service in its area and in the last resort the public expects it to fulfil this obligation. In practice, however, the quality of the service depends on individual establishments maintained (some not by the LEA) with a high degree of corporate independence and staffed by professionals with considerable individual independence. Independence at both levels is to a great extent, required by the 1988 Act, and jealousy safeguarded by the teachers' associations.

The main contribution that the office can make to professional quality in the schools is through its influence on appointments. The importance of good appointments, especially to headships, is beyond question. Formally, however, these are selected by the laity, elected members or governing bodies, or a combination of both. The influence of the office is exercised through advice, mainly from the inspectors, although appointment procedures are important too.

The office contributes to the quality of the service in a variety of other ways. That the general contribution of the office is a liberating rather than a limiting influence has already been noted but the office is likely to be influential in other respects too. It is interesting that although schools and committed teachers have developed over the years a rich and varied pattern of activities for games and athletics, the development of a comparable network for cultivating musical talent has largely depended on office initiative. It is in fact in the development of supplementary services such as reading centres, teams of peripatetic specialists to meet the needs of slow learners or ethnic minorities, resource centres, curriculum development guides, that offices have made a very valuable contribution enhanced substantially by Grant Related In-Service Training.

It is generally agreed, however, that a greater contribution could be made to the quality of the service by developing and systematising induction and in-service training programmes. The inspectorate is primarily responsible for developing this provision but it is clear that its success will depend on a professional commitment in the individual school in the form of a partnership with the inspectorate.

The most difficult challenge to the office is to improve schools that are downright bad. These are known but a curtain of discretion and silence is drawn around them though from time to time such a school is exposed to public gaze. The office does what it can, quietly and discreetly; the inspectors visit and advise, in-service training may be encouraged, visits arranged to see good practice, and any opportunities offered by new appointments developed to the full. This is virtually the repertoire of the office organisation for dealing with this problem with the governors and it does not amount to a wholly credible policy.

Some extension of the professional/administrative role of the office seems necessary if the statutory responsibility of the Education Committee is to be a reality. The view of Mr. Peter Fulton, author of the minority report in a New Partnership for our Schools, known as the Taylor Report, are apposite in this connection. As an elected member aware of the responsibilities of the Education Committee, his conclusion is that the office has a key role to play in securing schools of quality. He rejects the notion that the office has merely to get its administration right and that the school can be left with its governing body and professional advisers to get itself right. Whether or not they fully accept the Fulton thesis, there are those who consider that the office should develop the professional contribution it can make to the quality for the individual school.

The requirements of the 1986 and 1988 Acts strongly indicate that in the near future greater demands will be placed on the professional and advisory staff of the office.

Conflict

The office consists of selected persons organised to achieve certain purposes efficiently and economically and, since it is not a voluntary society, the individual activities of its members are regulated to produce the harmony of purpose and action requisite for success in its objectives. It would be impractical for the staff to begin their day deciding how to allocate the work, and the office is organised to distribute the work load rationally and predictably. The job description prescribes each individual's contribution and each individual co-operates with other colleagues. Most staff are located within sections, the basic unit of co-operation, with more senior staff co-ordinating the sections within each branch, the SAEO being expected to manage his branch. The more self-contained the work of each section the better and the less the risk of conflict.

The risk of conflict, reduced by efficient organisation of the office, is further reduced by the loyalties and *esprit de corps* that membership of an organisation generates. These attitudes are generated in various ways. In the first place, work is a social activity and the personal relationships that develop can be, and fortunately mostly are, a valuable lubricant; an officer whose personal relationships with his colleagues are poor is a liability and that this is always well known within the office indicates what an important contribution good personal relations make to efficiency. There is of course a common interest in efficiency anyway, if for no other reason than to avoid the stress, anxiety and often the additional work that inefficiency usually produces.

Beyond these personal attitudes, clearly much more complex than this brief discussion suggests, the formal hierarchy with its various sanctions – convention and habit, seniority and, more formally, its disciplinary, appointment and promotion procedures – promotes discipline and co-operation and exercises its authority in the event of disagreement or dispute. Authority is of course a subtle solvent of conflict; the establishment chart illustrates its hierarchical dimension and as usual fails to convey the whole truth. In reality, authority in the office flows in all directions and in doing so enormously extends the 'zone of acquiescence'. If the final collection of mail is known to be at 5.00 p.m., an officer who wants a letter posted later is a suppliant, however senior he may be, and a quarrel with the mail-room is just not on. In a more fundamental sense, however, the task for which co-operation is required has an inherent authority that commands the necessary co-operation, regardless of the status of the officers concerned. In short, the needs of the job generate their own authority and are the most powerful and pervasive mechanism for co-operation. For example, requests from the finance branch for information required for the preparation of the estimates are obviously authoritative and the obligation to reply is automatically accepted. It is of course clearly necessary for the purpose of the request to be known, understood and accepted and this is why so much time and effort are spent at all levels in the office in explanation, persuasion, suggestion and justification – essential activities that are often neglected in assessing the office work-load.

Nevertheless, despite all the effort, understanding and organisation, conflict can occur. Within the office, this normally amounts to nothing more serious that the friction and wrangling characteristic of any large organisation. Anything more serious is likely to be due to a serious weakness in the organisation or to an unsuitable officer and a specific remedy is required depending on the circumstances of the case.

Great efforts are made to obviate conflict between the office and the service, and usually successfully. In many authorities there is a joint consultative committee composed of representatives of the Education Committee and of the teachers' associations and attended by officers. Proposals that are important, potentially controversial, or that might be improved by teachers' advice, are referred to it and agreement can usually be achieved. If there is disagreement, it is unusual to proceed further. In either event, conflict is obviated. In addition to this machinery, a formidable volume of consultation is going on all the time. Major policy initiatives and changes are often considered and thrashed out in working parties staffed by officers and teachers and, sometimes, members. Officers, and especially the inspectorate, are in daily contact with the establishments and maintain regular contact with the teachers' representatives. The informal network of information and feed-back that arises from these activities also provides valuable information.

Participative bureaucracy on this scale has its dangers because it can restrict and even sterilise initiative. But it has considerable advantages too, mainly in improving proposals, promoting co-operation and in obviating conflict.

Conflict is perhaps too harsh a term for the friction that is unavoidable in the operation of a large service. Some of this stems from the nature of the service which is an intricate partnership of pupils, parents, teachers, officers and members within the framework of family, school, governing body, office and Education Committee. There are rules, regulations and sanctions but it is a pardonable exaggeration to say that they are unnecessary when the system works and of little assistance when there is a breakdown. The equilibrium of these relationships in a very small minority of cases, but sufficient to be a substantial claim on office time, is very precarious. Bureaucratic authority has only a limited role in these cases and the office must act as mediator and conciliator.

Every branch of the office is constantly engaged in this capacity – the buildings branch expediting an overdue repair that has exhausted a head's patience; the education welfare officers visiting parents whose child's attendance is unsatisfactory; schools branch struggling to deal satisfactorily with disruptive pupils; the inspectors settling a complaint about a teacher; the further education branch corresponding with an aggrieved applicant for an award; a child who has been refused a place at a nursery; a bus pass; a place at the school the parents want; a uniform award; furniture or supplies that have been promised but have not been received; the lollipop lady who has been withdrawn; parked vehicles at the school gates constituting a hazard. The list is endless, not everybody is reasonable, and not everybody who is reasonable is reasonable all the time. But the office must be reasonable because in all this work its bureaucratic discipline is an exacting task-master. The office is at the receiving end and it is seen as its responsibility to reconcile and restore.

There are of course certain duties undertaken by the office that are particularly delicate because of the nature of the work but the organisation and its procedures are suitably geared for the tasks, and conflict is avoided or, at worst, confined to the privacy of the professionals within the bureaucracy. The school psychological and child guidance service is a good example of this. It has nothing but sensitive contact points – the child, the parents, possibly the school, a variety of professionals and administrators in other jurisdictions (the area health service, the social services department and possibly a voluntary agency), officers in the schools branch, the inspector for special education. From time to time there will be genuine and deep disagreement between the protagonists of the different disciplines but there is a common concern for the best interests of the child.

Overlapping or limited jurisdiction is of course a source, if not always of conflict, at least of frustration. It is therefore a healthy instinct for an office to retain, seek or resist – as the case may be – control of the powers believed to be necessary for the efficiency of the service. It is recognised and accepted that changes in the establishment of the office are determined by the Establishment and not by the Education Committee, but however good the personal relationships may be the bondage is frustrating. The Seebohm argument favouring the transfer of the education welfare officers to the social services department is not without merit but only a handful of authorities implemented it and some of those have since reverted. The education service in general is not convinced that it is advisable. If conflicts about jurisdiction amount to no more than bureaucratic imperialism they should have short shrift but the issues at stake are rarely so simple. Problems relating to the exercise of powers may of course arise from external factors. A good example of this is the growing recognition of the superiority of nursery centres combining the advantages of the social services day nursery and the education service nursery school. The main impediment (apart from restrictions on public expenditure) to widespread provision of such centres is the difference in the conditions of the service of the staff concerned rather than any conflict between departments as to the limits of their powers.

The office as a system of information flows

In another perspective, the office may be seen as a system of information flows.

. For example, the birth rate and housing policy determine the demand for school places and the office mechanism must operate to ensure that there is an adequate supply of places. This may have repercussions on the number of establishments or their sizes or both, the number of teachers and other staff employed, the need for furniture, equipment and consumable materials, with corresponding implications for expenditure. Various branches – buildings, schools, inspectorate and finance – and perhaps more than one section in each, play a part in achieving the end result and it must be a collaborative effort. To get it right on the day may well have required a correct initial decision five years previously and a host of interrelated and interdependent decisions afterwards. The basis of the whole operation is information of quality of the right sort on the right desk at the right time. Good intentions, judgement, instructions and action on an inadequate information base are doomed.

The most impressive exercise in quantitative information flow is the preparation of the annual estimates which reconcile resources and needs in money terms and which amount to nothing less than the future of the service, its efficiency and reputation, for at least the next 12 months. Virtually the whole of the office is involved in this work and the quality of the estimates depends on the assembly of a tremendous volume of detailed information presented in a form that guarantees accurate assessments that can be vindicated. The preparation of the budget is the most detailed and comprehensive regular review of the condition of the service and its requirements, and the key to a good budget is reliable information.

The number of information flows is in fact myriad, each with its implications for administrative action and usually requiring a chain reaction. The volume of information that is communicated, usually to stimulate action, is very considerable and it is a great testimony to the office that so much is taken for granted. One activity – catering – illustrates this very forcibly. The biggest catering concern in any area is run by the education office. Over 95,000 school meals are served in Birmingham each day of the term. Demand has to be known; menus planned, collated and translated into supplies that have to be ordered and delivered; unit costs have to be controlled to a fraction of a penny; an establishment of more than 3,500 kitchen staff has to be maintained and paid; kitchens must be maintained and the equipment serviced and replaced; the meal has to be available at a given time so a rapid and efficient response to failure, perhaps late in the morning, must be ready.

A substantial volume of information flows within the education office, the educational establishments and the suppliers. There is also a crucial flow between departments of the Council. Planning proposals and housing developments are the most significant of these for the service as a whole and the sites and buildings branch is normally responsible for liaison on these issues. There is another, and highly sensitive, information flow, directly concerned with the welfare of individuals, in which the schools psychological and child guidance service, the education welfare service, the social services department, the area health authority, individual families, and sometimes the police and the courts, may all be concerned.

Information flows from external sources must also be digested within the office. Those from the DES include papers of every hue, legislation, circulars and administrative memoranda. They often require an immediate response and entail some change of administrative practice. Where a major change of policy is involved (e.g. financial delegation to Governing Bodies) the office can be committed to a tremendous task, nothing less than the transformation of a sector of the service. No less exacting has been the literature issued by MSC and the responses required to it. The last 20 years have been punctuated by the series of reports associated with the name of Crowther, Newsom, Robbins,

Plowden and James, all of which had extensive implications for major sectors of the service and therefore committed the office to strategies and programmes of change of a far-reaching nature. Apart from the DES, there is a constant flow of information from the local authorities' associations and from a host of other agencies. The number of publications by an expanding population of education experts and commentators increases every year and some of them must be read. The irreducible minimum of reading for a senior officer is very formidable and can only be undertaken outside the office – the voluntary contribution in leisure time to the work of the office is an essential feature of the office organisation.

Apart from the organisation and professional torrent of information, there is the flow of political information necessary for the success of the office organisation. This is largely informal since the parties locally are rarely explicit about their objectives beyond their commitment to apply locally the national party policies. It is indeed largely misleading to refer to an information flow in this context. It is the senior officers who need this information and they rely on their own analyses and appraisals, the signals they recognise, what they elicit from committee discussions and the information communicated in conversation, notably with senior members. Surprisingly little of this information is overt, but senior officers are usually well informed and sensitive to it.

This perspective sees the office organisation as a communication network, initiating, receiving, transmitting and interpreting information all of which requires action which is orderly, efficient, economical and timely.

Theory and reality

Descriptions of the office cannot convey what it is like to work in. Its rational structure, the clarity of the chain of command and the detailed delineation of individual responsibility suggest an orchestrated work flow conducted, if not necessarily at a steady beat, then at least at controlled tempos. This is far from reality, if only because the office has certain rhythms in its annual cycle which can impose severe pressure on relatively small groups of officers who cannot be given more than marginal reinforcement because their tasks require experience and expertise.

One consistent rhythm is the inexorable cycle of meetings of the Education Committee and its sub-committees with their deadlines for agendas and all the associated work in preparing, vetting, and approving reports. In the metropolitan districts there is the rhythm of annual elections with their implications for preparing and timetabling proposals that are controversial. Awards of one sort or another provide a continuous flow of work throughout the year but peak markedly between May and September. The preparation of the estimates has tended to become a lengthier exercise and now commonly extends from about July to March with peak activity between November and February. On the other hand, the building programme has in recent years lost its rhythm with the proliferation of special programmes spreading consideration over the year and entailing continuous review and adjustment that handicap efficiency. Work concerning the appointment and promotion of teachers flows through the year but peaks very noticeably in October, February, immediately after Easter and June. Consultation with professional associations swallows more and more time but within the limits of the school terms. Despite their discontinuous pressures, these rhythms are known; familiarity eases adjustment to them.

But there are many more unscheduled committee and sub-committee meetings nowadays than in the not so very distant past and these can dislocate timetables and disturb the flow of work. What must be emphasised, however, is that there is an increasing flow of arbitrary but insistent demands that can obliterate the immediate timetables of more senior officers and levy a very considerable price in interruptions, delays and postponements. In the first place, the media expect an immediate response and there is also an increasing volume of correspondence requiring not only prompt but quality replies. Priority must be given to enquiries from members, MPs and government departments and the public should not be kept waiting. It all amounts to a considerable volume of letters, many requiring a clear and concise explanation of practice of policy that is deceptively easier to read than to write.

Despite the size of the service, and suspicions sometimes in some quarters that the office 'deals in numbers' or is shackled to 'administrative convenience', the characteristic activity of the office is considering individual and group interests and requests, or the welfare of establishments whose needs are vital to the well-being in one way or another of its members. This is not surprising in a service that is labour intensive, has a high proportion of articulate and literate professionals, and is consumer oriented. The office is always in direct contact with a considerable number of pupils, parents, students and their elected and professional representatives. Furthermore, many of the needs at issue are urgent and special cases and as everybody knows, the acid test of a personal service is how personal it really is.

In appraising the extent of these unconvenanted daily pressures, it is salutary to bear in mind that a moderate sized authority of (say) 300,000 population is likely to have almost 200 schools, 50,000 to 60,000 pupils and perhaps 80,000 parents. This is only part of the office public but 200 school offices and thousands of telephones require a vast amount of attention from the office. Perhaps the most graphic example of this open commitment is that some ten years ago Sheffield Education Department was receiving about 55,000 visitors a year, a daily rate of well over 200, some no doubt for very brief interviews conducted by a junior officer, but some requiring the attention of more senior officers and perhaps relatively lengthy discussion. All this adds considerably to the flow of work.

There is of course a certain attraction about office organisation seen in terms of what are commonly regarded as its characteristic activities – policy formulation, decisions, advice, meetings, interviews and correspondence, even the 'papers a couple of secretaries are needed to file' and 'the typewriters (that) never stop'. The basis of these activities, however, are certain skills that the office requires and must possess. The essential skills include the ability to talk to a purpose, to read, to write good letters and reports, flexibility in identifying (c) as the correct choice between alternatives (a) and (b), familiarity with details, memory, fluency in group dynamics, the ability to listen, a point of view, and some imagination. This list is in no sort of order because circumstances dictate the skill(s) required. Even if it is not comprehensive, the skills listed constitute a culture of a sort that is an essential component of the office organisation. They seem pedestrian skills. Good administration and organisation mean that few discussions in the office require above average intelligence but listening is essential and, although it is a common faculty, it is an uncommon skill.

Some such compendium of skills is essential and they must be produced and cultivated at all levels throughout the organisation. It is the behavioural quality of the staff in their daily transactions that supplies a perspective of the office organisation that is at least important as any of the perspectives.

Notes

1. The title may vary, e.g. County Education Officer, Chief Education Officer.
2. The establishment chart sets out the grading designation and relationship of every member of staff. The salary structure is complicated, a variety of scales being applied.
3. In practice, the Secretary of State's approval to the short-list was sought so that approval for the appointment was a formality.
4. See John Mann 'Matrix Management', *Local Government Studies*, June 1973.
5. There are 11 branches: careers, health, psychological, meals, staffing, supplies, financial accounting, management accounting, premises and land, educational establishments, committee and officer services.
6. This analysis of the partnership is associated with Lord Alexander who, as Secretary of the Association of Education Committees, 1946–77, was one of the most influential personalities in the post-war years.

11 Rules, regulations and procedures

Introduction

'There is no reason for it, it is just our policy.' Bureaucracy, the power exercised by an office of public administration, is a proper and necessary function in any civilised community. Over the years, however, the term has acquired a pejorative connotation not least because of those officers who blindly operate rules, regulations and procedures without sufficient thought for the cause or effect of their actions.

The Education Officer, however, is in less danger of becoming a blinkered bureaucrat than some of his colleagues for he is not only an administrator. Certainly he must implement properly the rules of his service, whether of national or local origin, but at the same time he is involved in their creation. He is an 'animateur' who, through his advice, guidance and example, helps to create while he administers. If he is a good Education Officer, he must feel concern for those whose lives he affects, and rules, regulations and procedures will be no more than the necessary tools for putting this into effect.

This chapter falls into three parts. First, it deals with rules and regulations, their nature, origin, strengths and weaknesses. Second, it illustrates some specific procedures which arise out of regulations at national and at local level. Third, it explains where to look for the various rules and regulations.

Rules and regulations

This is not the place for a treatise on legal philosophy. Perhaps it is sufficient to accept Holland's definition that law 'in general is the sum total of those general rules of action as are enforced by a sovereign political authority'. Primitive communities are subjected to laws imposed by consent or by a tribal chief or community. A mature society, however, builds up a system of written rules and regulations by which the daily life of its citizens is ordered.

So it is with the law of education. The base is still the 1944 Education Act which repealed virtually all previous legislation relating to education. The 1944 Act has subsequently been amended or amplified by further Acts.

The Acts are supported, amplified and explained by various documents issued from time to time by the DES. These may be listed as follows:

(a) *Statutory instruments.* Much modern legislation empowers the Secretary of State to make regulations. These are contained in Statutory Instruments which have the force of law. Recent examples are the Education (Special Educational Needs) Regulations 1983 (S.I. 1983/29) and the Education (School Government) Regulations 1987 (S.I. 1987/1359).

(b) *Circulars.* These make announcements often on matters of policy of major importance. They do not have the force of law and many Circulars since 1981 have included a note to this effect. They are numbered serially within the year. Recent examples are:
Circular 3/87 'Providing for Quality: The Pattern of Organisation to age 19'. This sets out guidance for LEAs when they are considering the reorganisation of schools especially in the light of falling rolls.
Circular 11/87 'Sex Education at School'. This gives guidance on the implications of the new framework for the provision of sex education established by the 1986 Education Act.

(c) *Administrative memoranda.* These are the vehicle for announcements of less importance including information designed to ensure the achievement of common minimum standards by local education authorities. In recent years these have been relatively infrequent. An example is Administrative Memorandum 1/86. Modification of Approval Procedures for LEA School and Further Education Building Projects.

(d) *Circular letters.* The DES issue circular letters from time to time offering advice and guidance to supplement existing regulations. Subjects covered include Awards (ACL) and Further Education generally (FECL). There is also a VOL series, addressed to the proprietors of voluntary colleges of education.

The nature and permanence of rules and regulations are important. Some are detailed and precise allowing little or no scope for local initiative. Others provide a more general framework giving greater flexibility and leaving detailed decisions to be made locally to suit particular circumstances. Which model is adopted depends partly on the nature of the subject being regulated and partly on the changing trends towards a more centralised or more decentralised form of government. Smooth administration can also be affected by the rescinding or alteration of regulations following a swing in political power.

Complexity of national regulations is reflected at the local level. It is a truism to say that the size and scope of a service dictates the breadth and complexity of its rules and regulations. A smaller service may need little more than national legislation for its efficient conduct, but the education service, which employs more staff and spends more money than all the other Council departments put together, needs a far more complicated structure and rules to regulate it. The committee structure has been dealt with in earlier chapters. It is this complex pyramid of Committee — Sub-Committee — Governing Body — School of Institution — Parents — Student/Pupils, superimposed on the widely dispersed base of educational institutions — polytechnics — colleges — schools — child guidance service — careers service — meals service — health and dental services which creates the fundamental problem for any personal local government service.

One example will perhaps suffice to show the relationship in practice between national and local rules. Every school must, by law, have a governing body. The composition of a governing body and rules concerning its members and procedures are contained in the Instrument of Government; a definition of the functions of the Governing Body is contained in the Articles of Government. Both documents must comply with specific provisions in the various Education Acts and with any regulations laid down in statutory instruments, especially the Education (School Government) Regulations 1987. There is, however, still some room for local variations although this is now considerably less than hitherto.

The composition of the governing bodies of County and Controlled Schools is set by the 1986 Education Act. (Only very minor changes were made for Aided Schools for which the provisions of the 1980 Education Act still largely apply.) The number of governors and their appointment is strictly related to the number of children on roll and the only local flexibility is for the LEA to decide whether schools with 600 or more children should have 16 or 19 governors. The 1987 Regulations make detailed provision relating to matters such as the election of Chairman and Vice-Chairman, the number of governors required to form a quorum, the confidentiality of governing body proceedings, the withdrawal of governors from meetings in cases where they have a personal or pecuniary interest in a matter under discussion and the disqualification from membership of governing bodies. The LEA does have to decide how to appoint its representatives on governing bodies and will have worked out its procedures about, for example, the role of local county councillors in making nominations and even perhaps whether it wishes to put an age limit on its own representatives.

Beyond the actual constitution of the governing body, there is the question of its functions. These functions are most important, for they involve the relationship between the governing body and the education authority and the powers afforded to each. In recent years subsequent Education Acts have defined relative responsibilities more explicitly. Indeed one of the specific aims of the 1986 Education Act was to define more precisely the role of the Governing Body in relation to the curriculum. This, in turn, has been overtaken by the decision to establish a national curriculum and it will be the duty of both the education authority and the governing body to ensure that it is implemented. The Articles also define responsibility for appointing and dismissing teaching and non-teaching staff, for control of the school buildings, for the conduct of the school and for decisions on the use of resources. The major distinction as far as functions are concerned, will in future be between those schools which have, under the 1988 Education Act, a scheme for local financial management and the smaller schools which are more closely controlled by the education authority.

The education authority, after consultation with governing

bodies and appropriate voluntary bodies such as the Diocesan Boards of Education, has the administrative function of writing the Instrument and Articles of Government. If there is a dispute between the education authority and the governing body of a voluntary school over the formulation of the Instrument and Articles, the Secretary of State for Education and Science has the power to decide. The DES have also issued 'model' Instruments and Articles, for different types of school and, although these are not totally prescriptive, the requirements of the various Acts have little room for local variations.

There are matters on which there needs to be uniformity of practice within the Authority's area. Only in this way can confusion be avoided and a code of practice initiated which is comprehensible to all who are involved. Such lucidity and uniformity are particularly important where the public are involved. A parent seeking financial assistance, advice on admission to schools, on special education, on boarding education and on whether or not the children are entitled to free transport must be given clear guidance on the authority's regulations and on how he may proceed. A prime function of the LEA's rules and regulations is to create procedures which are comprehensible to the people it serves and to ensure fair and equitable treatment to them all. A rule which is capable of manipulation by the unscrupulous is a bad rule.

Within the service itself there are rules and regulations whose aim is to ensure the efficient running of the service. The education service is not only large but its employees embrace a wide range of trades and professions besides teachers. The general conditions of service of these employees will be subject to national or provincial agreement but within this framework there is scope for local decision.

As far as teachers are concerned, a major recent change has been the abolition of the Burnham Committee and the bringing together of negotiations on pay and at least the major conditions of service applying to all teachers. The Teachers' Pay and Conditions Act 1987 empowered the Secretary of State for Education to stipulate, through statutory instruments, the salary scales for teachers and conditions of service. An interim advisory committee has been established to advise the Secretary of State and it is the intention in due course to establish new, more permanent arrangements. There is still some room for discretion and flexibility within the new School Teachers' Pay and Conditions Document. Thus LEAs may allocate scale allowances within certain limits and there is some discretion in fixing the starting salaries of teachers. The national conditions establish, for example, a general list of the duties of teachers and lay down the 'directed' working time in terms of both total hours and number of working days each year. More detailed conditions of service are still required, although these must be consistent with the national conditions. Thus there are some matters e.g. entitlement to sick leave, which are still part of national agreements negotiated with the teachers' organisations by the Council of Local Education Authorities. Other matters are the subject of more local agreements, e.g. on leave of absence.

Regulations concerning non-teaching staff are subject to the same basic concept of national conditions of service, leaving scope for local discretion. For example, there are national salary scales applying to administrative assistants and laboratory technicians but it is for the local authority to decide the salary of particular posts on that scale and the number of posts to establish.

As far as manual staff are concerned, the position is similar although most recently a national framework has been agreed which attempts to apply a broad job evaluation to different types of posts. There are also provincial arrangements, formal or informal, to establish some uniformity of practice.

These arrangements on pay and conditions, especially for non-teaching staff, are likely to be affected significantly by the introduction of competitive tendering for certain services and of local financial management for the larger schools. It seems likely that this will lead to some weakening of national agreements and give individual schools considerable latitude in deciding the salaries of its staff.

We now come to rules and regulations within the education office itself. The Education Officer has perhaps two basic functions: he is first, as has been said above, an 'animateur' who advises on the development of his service and guides those under his supervision; but he is also an administrator who must see that his service runs efficiently. It has been said that most of his administrative functions go to establishing the sort of environment where the right relationship between teacher and taught can be developed. The description of 'oilcan incarnate' is not totally inaccurate, but certainly describes parts of his function. It follows, therefore, that the staff of the education office must be given guidelines within which they must work, for it is through them that the Chief Education Officer co-ordinates the work of his service. For example, instructions will need to be given on the provision of data as requested by central government – attendance statistics, teacher numbers, further education statistics, etc. where information is required in a prescribed form and there must be machinery which ensures that those who are concerned receive information regarding national regulations. Communication is important between the departments of an authority, for example, where the personnel officer may be involved with non-teaching staff, and within the Education Department to ensure that instructions issued reach every person or persons concerned. A DES ruling, for example, on financial arrangements for advanced further education would be of interest to the County (or Borough) Treasurer, the officer in charge of further education, the officer preparing the annual estimates and possibly the principals of further education establishments. Legal interpretations likewise will have a significance beyond the education department (e.g. 1982 House of Lords ruling on ordinary residence requirements for overseas students). There must be procedures in the office which ensure that this information is properly disseminated and action taken by the right person at the right time.

The above deals with rules which call for action, but there are also rules and procedures which are designed to eliminate confusion. For example, it is important for the Chief Education Officer and senior members of his staff to know what is happening in the department as a whole. This is often achieved by an additional copy of all letters being produced, put together each day, and circulated to the director, his deputy (or deputies) and perhaps even third tier officers for information. If this is too cumbersome, then regulations may be circulated among the various departments of the education office, so that practice is uniform throughout the office. There are many minor matters on which guidance is needed within the department. There is often a set form in which complaints may be recorded, there are regulations as to who may sign letters – to the public, to councillors, to Members of Parliament, to the Secretary of State and government departments. Communication with the public is especially important for their view of the department and its efficiency will be influenced by the letters they receive. Guidance to staff on the form of letters and the language to be used, particularly the avoidance of local government jargon, is useful if the proper image of the Education Department is to be presented to the public. Some authorities have found it helpful to issue Handbooks of Guidance for Heads and officers.

The prescriptive regulation, therefore, has been seen to merge into documents which, though not strictly regulations, give advice and information which certainly influence procedures. This is paralleled by the various gradations of DES publications previously mentioned. It is particularly important in the education service in view of the considerable autonomy which is accorded to the individual Head Teacher or Principal. To quote one example, a Head Teacher would not wish to be told how to deal with school uniform or discipline but he would welcome information on recent rulings on the matter.

Finally, the question arises as to how rules and regulations are created at local level. In the first instance, this is one of the functions of the Education Committee which, in accordance with the Standing Orders of the Council, is made generally responsible for the running of the education service. In practice if a regulation on a policy matter needs to be drafted, the Chief Education Officer will submit a report for consideration by the appropriate sub-committee. The draft will be supported by reference to recent legislation and, if appropriate, it will only have been drafted after consultation with appropriate bodies such as teachers' organisations. Arrangements for time off for trade union activities are a case in point. The sub-committee will consider it and, if they approve it, submit it for ratification to the main Education Committee. So much for new regulations, but old regulations also need to be revised from time to time – e.g. the allocation of clerical assistance to schools – and revisions of these are submitted in the same way, on the Chief Education Officer's initiative, to the appropriate committee.

The Chief Education Officer, however, usually has extensive delegated powers which enable him to adopt procedures and operate regulations in his own right. These would include such things as leave of absence, secondment, payment of certain travelling and subsistence expenses, refund of further education fees, minor youth service awards, approval of school journeys and similar matters.

Specific procedures

Certain aspects of the education service call for quite specific procedures in order to fulfil the statutory duties of the LEA. Some of these are dealt with elsewhere, e.g. buildings procedures, financial regulations and procedures for financial assistance to pupils and students, curriculum and course control, consultation procedures and union negotiations.

The 1980s have seen the most significant new legislation in education since the Act of 1944 through the Education Acts of 1980, 1986 and 1988 together with the Act of 1981 which dealt with special education. This chapter would not be complete without specific mention being made of that new legislation although it would perhaps not be appropriate to attempt to summarise all its provisions.

In recent years, starting with the initiative of individual schools, there has been an increasing involvement of parents in decisions affecting their children's education. One of the central themes of the new legislation has been to build upon this and to enshrine in law important regulations on the rights of parents.

Taking the various Acts and related regulations together it is possible to identify the processes to be followed for the benefit of parents of children at primary and secondary schools. First, information has to be made available to parents about the LEA's policies and about individual schools. Parents are then better placed to make informed decisions on their choice of school or at least to state their preferences. Procedures are then required to deal with those stated preferences especially if it is not possible to meet all the requests. Once a child is admitted to a school there are various formal ways in which the parent can be involved in the school. Finally there are procedures to enable a parent to register a complaint about the school.

Information

Section 5 of the 1980 Education Act empowers the Secretary of State to make regulations requiring the LEA (or governors in the case of Aided schools) to publish information about its policies and about individual schools. The requirements are set out in the Education (School Information) Regulations 1981. The LEA has, for example, to publish:

a list of schools in its area;
its policies on the provision of transport;
the arrangements for the provision of meals and milk;
its policies on special educational provision for pupils with special educational needs.

For each school the information required includes:

particulars of the curriculum including subject choices and the manner and context in which sex education is given;
particulars of the arrangements of classes;
policies on homework and pastoral care;
general arrangements for school discipline and any requirements on school uniform;
(for secondary schools) details of public examinations entered and results achieved.

The regulations also stipulate the timing and manner of publication.

Compliance with these regulations is, at one level, a straightforward task of ensuring that the quite specific and detailed requirements have been met. The compilation of the LEA and school brochures, however, require more than that. If they are to fulfil their purpose, they have to be presented in a readable and attractive form and schools, in particular, are increasingly aware of the almost commercial approach which they have to take to such publications if they wish to attract children to their school.

Admission procedures

The starting point, under the 1980 Act, is for the LEA to make known the number of pupils it is intended to admit to each school in each year and on the policy to be followed in deciding admissions.

Arrangements then have to be made to enable a parent to express a preference for the school to which he wishes his child to be admitted. Under Section (3) of the 1980 Act, the LEA has a duty to comply with that preference unless to do so would 'prejudice the provision of efficient education or the efficient use of resources'; or, in a selective system, where compliance would be 'incompatible with selection under the arrangements'; or, in Aided schools, compliance would be incompatible with any arrangements made between the governors and the LEA on admissions.

The number to be admitted is, under the 1980 Act, the number of pupils in the relevant age group admitted in the school year beginning in 1979. However, LEAs were able under Section 15 of the Act to reduce this 'standard number' by up to one fifth. To reduce the admission limit below that level required public notices and the approval of the Secretary of State. Most LEAs found it necessary with falling rolls to adjust the 'standard number' regularly in order to ensure an even distribution of children between schools and so make the most efficient use of teachers and accommodation. The 1988 Education Act has made a significant change in that. It provides that, initially in secondary schools, the admission limits will be the number of children which the school can physically accommodate. This is stated as the number of children who were in the school in 1979 although application can be made to the Secretary of State to vary this provided it can be shown that some change has been made in the school's accommodation since then. As 1979 was the peak year for secondary school numbers this new provision makes it more difficult for the LEA to restrict admissions to some schools in order to maintain viable numbers at others; but the consequence of greater choice is usually a less efficient use of resources.

Even so, not every parent is likely to get his or her choice. Section 7 of the 1980 Education Act requires LEAs and the governors of voluntary schools to make arrangements enabling parents who are dissatisfied with the offer of a particular school place to appeal against the allocation. (This right of appeal does not extend to admissions of pupils to nursery schools.)

Schedule 2 of the Act prescribes the constitution of the appeals committee. It must include members of the authority itself or of any Education Committee of the authority and other people with experience in education, familiarity with local education conditions in the area or who are parents of registered pupils currently at a school.

Schedule 2 of the Act also sets out the procedure for the conduct of the appeals committees, which are subject to the direct supervision of the Council on Tribunals. A code of practice on the constitution and practice of appeals committees has been prepared on behalf of the Local Authority Associations and bodies representative of voluntary schools after discussion and consultations with the Council on Tribunals.

The decision of the appeals committee is binding on the LEA or governors. The Secretary of State, who has no part in the appeals process, may investigate complaints and intervene, if necessary, under Sections 68 or 99 of the 1944 Education Act to determine whether the authority or governors have exercised their powers or performed their duties 'unreasonably'.

Many Education Officers find this whole area of admissions to schools one of the most taxing and demanding of administrative tasks. The various Acts make detailed provision but there are still areas of policy to be made by the LEA. It is for the LEA for example to set a policy on how to decide on who shall be admitted if there are more applicants than places available at any school. It must be clearly stated what factors will be taken into account e.g. distance from the school, medical reasons, sibling connections. Even so not every case will be clear cut and the education officer has to be seen to act fairly and to be able to justify his decision before the appeals committee. Beyond that, the Ombudsman may take an active interest both in the initial decision making and in the proceedings of the Appeals Committees. Finally the High Court may also intervene and test cases, such as R. V. South Glamorgan Appeal Committee ex p Evans (1984), may establish general rules of procedure which must be taken into account.

Parental involvement in schools

There are many ways in which parents may become involved in the school which their children attend. Apart from informal contacts with teachers, there will almost invariably be organised occasions when parents are invited to discuss their children's progress. There will be open days when there will be an opportunity to see the work of the school more generally. Finally, but not least, the large majority of schools will have some form of parents' association which arranges educational and social activities for parents as well as purely fund-raising events.

All these invaluable activities are, however, informal in that they are not obligatory and have no statutory base. The recent Education Acts have established a series of more formal procedures to reflect or encourage greater involvement of parents in their children's school.

Some LEAs had for many years reserved places for parents on their school governing bodies. The 1980 Education Act for the first time made it obligatory for all school governing bodies to have elected parents amongst their membership. County and Controlled schools were to have at least two elected parent governors; Aided schools were to have at least one elected but the foundation governors also had to include at least one parent although appointed rather than elected. The 1986 Education Act increased the parental representation. The total number of governors and the number of elected parent governors relate to the number of children at the school. For the smaller County and Controlled schools with under 100 on roll, there are to be two elected parent governors out of a total of nine governors. For the largest secondary school with 19 governors, five are to be elected parent governors. Somewhat surprisingly, Aided school governing bodies remained unaffected and it is still possible to find such schools with 14 or more governors but only one elected parent.

Elections, of course, have to be carefully organised. The only specific requirement in the 1980 Act is that any contested election shall be conducted by secret ballot. Beyond that it is for the LEA (or the governors in the case of Aided schools) to make all the necessary arrangements for the conduct of the elections. Decisions have to be made on such issues as the polling dates, the qualifying date for electors, validity of votes and it is even for the LEA according to the Act to decide who are the parents of children at the school. Normally, if the procedures have been carefully thought through and clearly explained, the elections will go smoothly. There are times, however, when some elections are hotly contested and unforeseen circumstances arise which will have a material effect on the outcome of the election. In those cases the Education Officer may well be called in to adjudicate. He would do well to learn from such an experience and make sure that for future years that particular loophole is closed.

The 1986 Education Act attempted to go further than giving power to a small group of elected parent governors by involving the whole parent body. The Act requires that the governing body prepares and sends to all parents an annual report. The information to be contained in the report is detailed in the Act. For example:

A summary of the steps taken by the governing body in the discharge of its functions since the last report;
The names of all the governors and who appointed them;
A financial statement as provided by the LEA of the cost of running the school and how any gifts have been applied;
The school's examination results (in the case of secondary schools);
Steps taken to link the school with the community (and with the police).

In answer to the governors' question about how long their report should be, the Act has a classic answer worthy of a place in any anthology of civil service prose – 'to be as brief as is reasonably consistent with the requirements as to its contents'.

The Act then requires that the governors hold an annual meeting of parents. This is to provide the parents with an opportunity to discuss the discharge by the governing body, the head and the LEA of their functions in relation to the school. If there is a quorum present (defined as a number of parents equal to at least twenty per cent of the number of pupils on roll at the school), the parents may pass resolutions which must be formally considered by the appropriate body and a report made at the next annual meeting of parents.

Early experience of these meetings has been that overall the attendance has been very low. Many schools have tried to make the annual meeting attractive by linking it with other more popular events. Even so, a quorum has been relatively rare unless there has been a burning local issue. Attendance may improve as the meetings become better established. Some would contrast this with the very high attendance at those occasions when parents come to discuss the progress of their own children and suggest that parents are generally content to leave the running of the school to the Head and governors.

Probably the most contentious section of the 1988 Education Act is that which enables parents to have an even greater say in the running of their local school. Schools may apply to opt out of LEA control and have grant maintained status with direct funding from central government. Although the Secretary of State for Education and Science has to give final approval, the parents have a major voice in reaching such a decision. If the governing body decides in principle to apply for grant maintained status they must hold a secret ballot of parents. A majority of parents voting (a majority of all parents eligible to vote) must be in favour of the proposal before it can go forward. If the governing body is unwilling to make such application, a group of parents equal to at least twenty per cent of the number of pupils at the school may require the governing body to hold such a ballot of parents.

Complaints

Parents and others have always had opportunities to have complaints investigated. Most will be dealt with and resolved locally through the Head or LEA. If satisfaction is not received in this way, a parent may complain to the Secretary of State for Education who has power to act under Sections 68 and 99 of the 1944 Education Act.

The 1988 Education Act adds to this at least as far as the national curriculum is concerned. Every LEA is required to establish and submit for the approval of the Secretary of State a formal complaints procedure to deal with any complaint that the LEA or governing body has acted or is proposing to act unreasonably to discharge or has failed to discharge its duty in relation to the national curriculum. This also aims to reduce the number of complaints direct to the DES for the Act provides that the Secretary of State may not consider any such complaint unless it has first been considered under the local complaints procedure.

This section has brought together a number of rules and procedures which apply to parents. Some generalisations about the nature of rules might be drawn from them.

Modern legislation is complex and, in most cases, the detailed requirements are contained not in the Act itself but in the regulations which the Act empowers the Secretary of State to make. Even so, there is almost always a need to put those basic regulations into a local framework and to relate them to the local administrative structure which will have to apply them.

If administration is to be efficient, the rules must be clearly expressed and must be seen to be fair and acceptable. Rules can be presented in such a way that they obey the letter of the law but are inaccessible and are likely to deter rather than positively encourage. Some imagination is required if, for example, parents are to be actively helped in knowing about and in using the rights given to them by the legislation.

Framing the rules on a particular topic may also highlight some basic conflicts of aims, e.g. to widen choice but to use resources efficiently. In such cases the issue needs to be explained and the Education Committee requested to declare, within the law, its policy, priorities and general attitude on that matter.

All rules and decisions made within them need to be defensible for undoubtedly those who make bad decisions will be called to account through the various avenues available for making complaints.

Recording of rules and regulations

Reference is made in various documents to the rules and regulations of an authority. Where are these to be found? Practice varies considerably, but the internal handbooks mentioned previously, can be invaluable. Local authority regulations may stem from a variety of sources. Some may originate from agreements reached nationally between the local authority associations and the teachers' organisations, e.g. FE Teachers Conditions of Service, Teachers Sick Pay Regulations, Maternity Leave Provisions. Some are framed to meet legal requirements, e.g. Instruments and Articles of Government for Polytechnics, or Special Schools. Others arise from insurance provisions, e.g. regulations relating to pupil supervision on school journeys and visits; others again relate to situations prevalent many years ago, e.g. Punishment Regulations whose antiquity embarrassed several authorities when court cases caused them to review their instructions with regard to punishment; yet others are recorded in the Minutes of the Education Committee, copies of which may have been circulated to schools.

The need for new regulations arises from the continual and

rapid change not only in education but also in the framework of society. Many authorities have attempted complete codifications: in the face of constant change, however, few are able to maintain a completely up-to-date record.

Constant review, discard and revision is necessary if some articles are not to become obsolete. As pressures grow to limit the costs of educational administration, priorities have to be established and reluctantly Education Officers must arrange for the most urgent matters to receive first attention. As a result, instances occur from time to time where regulations have not been amended to meet changing circumstances and difficulty may arise therefrom. Then regulations are represented as the bureaucrat's delight and evidence of his inefficiency. Rather should such instances be rightly seen as examples of local Education Officers correctly appreciating the nature and function of regulations but being prevented by economic constraints from maintaining them as the apt instruments of policy, which indeed they are.

To assist local authorities in the exchange and availability of information the Education Management Information Exchange was created in 1981. Sponsored by the Department of Education and Science, the National Foundation for Educational Research and the Society of Education Officers, it is designed to provide a range of information services to educational administrators.

Conclusion

It is fitting to end this chapter on the note on which it began. The Education Service is a personal service. It is concerned with people and its value can be measured by the service it provides to the children and other people for whom it exists. Rules, regulations and procedures are essential tools designed to ensure that the minimum requirements set out in national policies are met and appropriately implemented by all LEAs. They ensure, too, that the administrative procedures are fair, effective and clearly understood by those who are directly affected by them. If they fail to be seen as such, then they become mere obstacles. A responsive LEA keeps the need for each tool constantly under review, and ensures that those which are no longer effective are revised, substituted or scrapped.

12 Management at institutional level

Introduction

The scale and variety of institutions provided and managed by LEAs are enormous. There are schools with fewer than ten pupils, and schools with more than 2,000. There are colleges which teach only one subject, and others with full- and part-time students reading everything from the conventional and the useful to the recondite and complex. Some colleges offer basic training for teachers, others set out to meet the continuing needs of those already trained. Institutions prepare students for examinations leading to modest qualifications in GCSE, or to – some would argue not much less modest – doctorates. Centres of one sort provide for the education of under-fives, and of another for the practical or professional or recreational needs of people from the age of 16 to over 60. Everywhere there is educational provision for the most able and the least able, for the very sick and the very fit, for the normal and for the disadvantaged.

All these, whatever their age, their talents or their hopes, expect to be sensibly advised, effectively taught, given proper equipment, safely and attractively housed in buildings which are heated, cleaned and maintained on sites conveniently placed and carefully looked after. Recognising the constraints imposed by finance and by human weakness, and acknowledging a serious responsibility for the nurturing of not inconsiderable assets, management at institutional level is about the attainment of these objectives.

It must be emphasised that this chapter is not about management within institutions, a subject which has attracted a good deal of valuable research and comment from academics and practitioners, and which clearly now becomes a matter of first importance as enlarged responsibilities and accountabilities are passed from local authorities to the governors, heads and staff of individual schools and colleges. No one can doubt that the burdens of management inside institutions have increased, are increasing and are unlikely to be diminished. Some of the old absolutist modes still persist, much as those obscure and autocratic petty German kingdoms survived into the age of liberal democracy, but, for the most part, heads and principals have, in various and resourceful ways, come to terms with legitimate pressures to enhance the work of governors, and take into active partnership assistant teachers, professional associations and parents. They have had to organise the working day and welfare of many more people, dispose of greater sums of money from a range of sources, accept responsibilities of leadership and advice within the local community, and co-operate with a growing number of agencies, some supporting and others with greater powers of direction.

This chapter, then, seeks to explore those areas where the management responsibilities and practices of an authority touch those of the institutions. In the past, the descriptive task has not been a simple one, since practices between authorities, and amongst institutions within authorities have differed greatly. With so many schools and colleges, widely dispersed, with differing histories, and responding to expressed or anticipated needs in individual, sometimes idiosyncratic ways, centralised systems of management have been seen as inappropriate and impractical. So phlegmatic and *laissez-faire* an approach no longer finds favour, and firmer direction is to come from government itself, and from the governing bodies of institutions, whilst the LEAs must resign themselves to a decrease in authority, and seek to extend their influence to balance a loss of power.

For those with the gift of foresight, the direction of change has long been evident in such developments as Education Support Grants, or the establishment of the Technical and Vocational Education Initiative, or the purchase which the Manpower Services Commission now has on non-advanced further education. The 1988 Education Act rejects piecemeal or tentative change. It asserts the importance of central powers for the Secretary of State, matched with substantial devolved powers to schools and colleges, and residual functions for local education authorities, part strategic, part agency, and part monitor-evaluator. None of these last responsibilities are mean or insignificant, but they amount to a re-casting of the LEA role. Whatever the wider implications of that for the future of local government, when set alongside proposals for the privatisation of services or the introduction of community charges, the operational consequences of the Act in a new ordering of relationships between the authority and its institutions are profound.

Schools

County

The commonplace criticisms of an LEA's management of its institutions are blunt, varied, and often contradictory. Schools are judged to be oppressed by over-prescriptive and finicky regulations, and have thus become too dependent on County Hall, lacking innovative zeal and unresponsive to the wishes of parents, the needs of pupils and the claims of industry and commerce. They are prevented from learning the arts of good housekeeping, either because they are over-provided with resources and have no direct accountability, or because they lack powers to determine their own priorities for expenditure. Personnel management is often considered ineffective with its outmoded selection procedures, its reluctance to weed out the incompetent, and its slowness in getting into place worthwhile appraisal systems and staff development policies. The curriculum has been allowed to drift along, changing unevenly and fitfully, corrupted here and there by the extremism and political dogmatising of elected members, and rarely adequate in either social or industrial terms to meet the challenges of the last two decades of the twentieth century.

Something of all this may well be true, though elements of the analysis owe more to imagination than to the evidence. Nevertheless, the remedies for these real or supposed ills are set out in recent legislation, most notably the 1988 Education Act, and the Education Act (No 2) 1986 dealing with school government.

(a) *Curriculum*

The 1988 Act establishes for all registered pupils of compulsory school age in maintained schools a basic curriculum of three core subjects and seven foundation subjects and enables the Secretary of State, with the advice of a National Curriculum Council and a Schools Examinations and Assessment Council, to specify for these subjects attainment targets, programmes of study and assessment arrangements. The special place of religious education, provided for in the 1944 Act, is further safeguarded, and agreed syllabuses, one of the most interesting areas of locally-initiated curriculum development, are to remain.

That apart, however, curriculum change becomes largely a matter of central determination. The National Curriculum Council has a responsibility to consult widely before it gives its advice to the Secretary of State, and the holder of that office may vary provisions of the national curriculum to enable particular schools to experiment or carry out development work. Local Authorities are left with two duties – to ensure that their schools meet the requirements of the national curriculum, and a second to establish machinery to hear complaints that the authority or a governing body are not properly discharging their curriculum responsibilities.

It may be that time and practice will show a liberal harmonisation of the aspirations of government, LEAs, governing bodies and parents in curriculum matters, but a cruder reading leaves authorities in a markedly constrained position. No one can pretend that curriculum work has, in the past, been an area of unbridled freedom. Money, buildings, the initial and in-service training of teachers, the abilities and background of pupils, the demands of examination boards, the sounding board of governors, the influence of HMIs and local advisers have all served to provide limits and opportunities, and much has been achieved by that partnership between the LEA and a range of associated groups within and outside institutions. The Schools Council and the Schools Curriculum Development Committee both stood firmly on the principle that teachers would feel more confident about delivering the curriculum if they had a practical involvement in the shaping of it. LEAs were happy to endorse the principle, and the National Curriculum Council would do well to learn from that experience.

As it is, the LEA task in managing a curriculum in its

schools will now essentially have five parts. It will need to ensure delivery of what is agreed nationally. That will be a time-consuming job – and in danger of being a sterile one – for its advisers. It must, through the schools, provide for the testing of children at ages seven, eleven, fourteen and sixteen, and ensure the publication, as appropriate, of the results of those tests, together with a statement about the environmental factors which may influence results. The follow-up work for the LEA in supporting schools in their efforts to improve pupils' levels of achievement will not be insignificant. Next, the authority will have to recruit the teachers with the right skills and experience, nowhere more difficult than for those subjects, now by law to be taught, whose teacher shortages are endemic.

Equally, since subjects which need laboratories, workshops and practical spaces of all kinds are to be available for all pupils, there will be laid upon LEAs a responsibility to provide buildings and equipment. National capital allocations have for years been less than adequate to meet new developments, and clearly there must be an increase in capital expenditure.

Above all, authorities will have to provide a much enhanced programme of in-service training for its teachers. Some can certainly be arranged in-house by individual institutions to meet their peculiar and local needs, but a central co-ordination of training, as GRIST has shown, is the only really effective and efficient way for an LEA to balance all the many claims on development monies. The task should not be under-estimated or undervalued. Teachers are facing substantial curriculum change, preparing pupils to reach attainment targets and using assessment techniques with which at the moment they may be unfamiliar, and will properly look to their authority for guidance and support in managing that change, and thus helping their professional growth.

(b) *Local management of schools*

A number of LEAs – from Hertfordshire in the 1950s to Cambridgeshire in the 1980s – have developed schemes of financial delegation to schools. The philosophy underpinning such schemes has essentially been that institutions are mature, worthy of trust, but able to determine their own priorities, and can be all the more effective if freed from cumbersome and unnecessary interventions by distant bureaucracies. Such a philosophy now finds extended practical expression in the 1988 Act.

The local authority will determine the overall level of resources to be devoted to schools, and must construct a formula, subject to the approval of the Secretary of State, which equitably allocates those resources between schools. Once allocated, the responsibility for spending money and properly accounting for expenditure rests squarely with the governing body.

However seductively simple all this may seem, an LEA is left with some formidable problems. It remains the employer of teaching and non-teaching staff in its institutions, but is obliged to appoint such staff recommended by the governing body as long as they meet staff qualification requirements. The Chief Education Officer is entitled to attend all selection proceedings, and the selectors must consider his advice. Nevertheless, LEAs have, to all intents and purposes, now lost any discretion they had in appointment matters. Even more contentiously difficult is the impact of LMS on local redeployment policies. There is no gainsaying that such policies have been essential instruments in enabling authorities successfully to respond to changes in pupil numbers. For the future, governing bodies can decline to accept a redeployed teacher and the consequences are evident – further difficulties with reorganisation programmes, increased costs, and unnecessary tensions between an LEA and its teachers associations.

Common sense – a commodity not always in abundant supply – dictates that, as well as creating a budget framework for its institutions, and ensuring that governing bodies observe nationally agreed conditions of service, an LEA will need to produce model codes to help governors frame disciplinary rules and procedures, and grievance procedures, and seek to give guidance on such sensitive issues as sex and race discrimination, time-off for various purposes, health and safety and unfair dismissal – a dense and barbed thicket of personnel matters in which governors will now find themselves entangled. No doubt, most governing bodies will see the sense of using an authority's expertise and experience, and will recognise that co-operation has advantages over confrontation, but an LEA now has to rely on persuasion rather than fiat, an attractive proposition in these demotic days. Yet it remains an affront to good management practice that the authority which employs and pays staff has no real power over their appointment and dismissal, and an increasingly tenuous hold on their pay and conditions of service.

The goods and services element in LMS will also produce its own levels of difficulty. Most schools already have worthwhile experience of handling this part of the budget – books, printing, stationery, telephones – though not uncommonly making use of an LEA's central purchasing system. How much that system, with its many positive benefits to the customer, is now at risk, is a matter for some speculation. More far-reaching will be the effects in the Local Government Act of those clauses concerning competitive tendering, which specify that major services – school cleaning, school meals, caretaking, building repairs and maintenance, and grounds maintenance – are to be put out to contract by the authority. Two principles could thus be at war. On the one hand, financial devolution stands firmly on the ground of giving to schools freedom to determine their own priorities and policies. On the other, an LEA must wish to ensure quality of provision, sensible economies of scale, and some coherence of approach across all its institutions. The problems, then, reveal themselves simply and starkly – a lack of expertise at school level in drawing up contracts; how to guarantee minimum standards; increased volatility in industrial relations; additional costs. Again, the capacity of an authority to manage its provision becomes blurred, uncertain and shrunken.

The most important and intricate task for the LEA is the construction of the formula for the allocation of resources to individual institutions. There is no uniform model. Each authority, reflecting local needs and circumstances, will devise its own – subject to approval by the Secretary of State – but is enjoined to work for simplicity, clarity and predictability in impact, basing the formula on an assessment of schools' objective needs rather than on historic patterns of expenditure. The principal element in that assessment has to be the number of pupils in each school, weighted for age differences, with the subsidiary, but no less critical, elements of the additional costs of children with special needs, and the necessary weighting for small schools.

Matters to be delegated are these – salary costs of staff; day-to-day premises costs; books, equipment, goods and services. Matters excluded are – capital expenditure, debt charges, Education Support Grants, LEA training grants, Section 11 grants, travellers children grants, TVEI, central administration, inspectors and advisers, house-to-school transport. And some other matters will be discretionary, as for example meals, child guidance and education welfare. Finally there is in the regulations a clear recognition that LEAs will themselves wish to initiate new developments, and may therefore hold back provision for such initiatives – and a parish-pump version of the national education support grant system.

A great deal of ink has been spilt by way of commentary on the principles and implementation of LMS (Local Management of Schools). There are, as ever, some problems and opportunities, and at the heart lies a consideration of what ultimately will be the purpose and function of an education authority in terms of its management responsibilities for institutions. On this, it is worth quoting in full a paragraph from the DES guidance document:

> Within the overall requirements of the Act, the LEA will set the framework within which governing bodies will exercise delegated powers. The LEA will set the tone of education through its articulation of its policies for the service, including its curriculum policy, and through its role in co-ordinating national and local specific grant initiatives. It will sustain and support governing bodies with professional advice and guidance on the full range of issues faced by schools. The LEA will continue to have the main responsibility for the professional development of its teachers, including appraisal and in-service training. Its monitoring role will be particularly important. LEA officers and advisers will have a vital part to play in this process, and will report on the performance and achievement of the schools and teachers both to the governing body and the LEA.
>
> LEAs already carry out all these functions to a considerable extent. Schemes of financial delegation will make these

responsibilities explicit and emphasise the need for LEAs to perform them effectively.

All this is, by no means, a trivial list of responsibilities at the margins of educational life, but nevertheless puts LEAs clearly into the field of agency work, and of training, monitoring and evaluating, takes away real executive authority and the capacity, so well explored by most authorities, for imagination, innovation and difference.

(c) *Grant-maintained schools*

A new category of schools has now been called into existence. Any county or voluntary school, with the exception of a primary school which has less than three hundred registered pupils, is eligible for grant-maintained status – put simply, it has the opportunity to opt out of local authority control and be maintained by the Secretary of State. No doubt such a departure springs from the belief that some schools chafe under the malign or bureaucratic or enfeebled dominion of local authorities, and others have the strength, maturity and parental support to ensure that they can successfully manage all their own affairs.

Governors or parents can trigger the request for grant-maintained status and, subject to secret postal ballot to discover what support exists amongst parents, a proposal may then be published by the governing body. The LEA role in this is to have the occasion to object to that proposal. Once the school is established, taking with it the property of the LEA, then the authority has no further position in its affairs of any substance. It will, of course and inevitably, have to pick up all the residual problems – schools within its boundaries which ultimately will develop their own admission policies; the absorption of staff who may decide not to work within such a school; the costs of home-to-school transport; a clumsy machinery for paying, via the Secretary of State, the maintenance grant for these institutions; the dislocations which will be caused by allowing grant-maintained schools, after a period of time, to change their character; the responsibility for educating pupils who may be expelled from these schools; and, perhaps less easy to define, the concerns which will exist about how effectively to provide support services and make available authority expertise should that be sought by a grant-maintained school. Events alone will demonstrate how seductive a proposal this is. What needs no argument is that it will make for very great difficulties when an authority is seeking to reorganise its provision. Grant-maintained schools are not subject to an LEA's reorganisation programmes, and maintained schools, apprehensive of those policies, could well take refuge in applying for the new status, and create long and unhelpful delays. There are as yet – apart from the primary school minimum number – no published criteria of eligibility, and, therefore, no clear signals to deter frivolous or tactical applications.

(d) *Admission limits*

The Secretary of State, in the interests of securing maximum possible parental choice of schools, has determined that no authority shall fix, as the number of pupils it intends to admit to a school in any school year, a number which is less than the relevant standard number, that standard number being the cohort of children admitted to a school in 1979. Constraints on admissions to secure a sensible spread of pupils between schools in an area, or to avoid having to keep in use temporary accommodation, or to reflect that, since 1979, different patterns of use of school buildings have emerged as a result of many valuable curriculum initiatives – none are counted as valid argument. Parental choice is the determinant.

(e) *School governors*

School governing bodies have long been valued elements in the broad and diverse partnership of educational provision, though their place and function in that partnership have not been without critics, who judged such bodies to be unrepresentative, with minimal powers and unclear roles. Just as a former Secretary of State claimed that the only real power he had was to order the demolition of air-raid shelters on school sites, so some governors felt that they splashed about in the shallows of school life, isolated from the tides and currents which swept true change and development along. Of equal concern was the composition of the governing body, packed, it was argued, with political placemen and ineffective local worthies and, therefore, unresponsive and unaccountable. Like all caricatures, some of the lines are drawn true, but such a picture does less than justice to hard-working, concerned men and women who were devoted to the well-being of their school. Power they may not have had, but their influence for good was marked.

The Education (No. 2) Act 1986 now provides for major change. County and controlled school governing bodies will have more places for parents and members of the local community, and a particular emphasis is placed on the need for representation from the business community, their hard-headed realism as consumers of the products of school to be an antidote to the alleged purposelessness and sentimentality of much contemporary teaching and learning. Overall powers are clearly defined – responsibility for the general conduct of the school; the taking of a view on an appropriate curriculum for the school; decisions about the provision of sex education; with the head teacher, the establishment of general principles to inform policies on discipline; control of certain sums of money provided for them by the local authority; involvement in the selection of staff; the provision of information to parents and, in particular, the preparation of an annual report and the holding of an annual meeting with parents to discuss that report.

The 1988 Education Act develops, in substantial ways, a number of these powers. Its declared, and unexceptionable aim is 'to promote higher standards of education in all maintained schools, by strengthening the involvement of parents and the local community, and by raising expectations of what can be achieved'. So, in a sharing of responsibility with the head and the local authority, governors must ensure that requirements of the National Curriculum are met; that courses leading to public examinations are for approved qualifications and follow approved syllabuses; that the law on religious education and collective worship is complied with, and that information about the curriculum and pupils' achievements is available to parents. Admission limits are to be related to the physical capacity of the school, and established initially in relation to the 'standard number' as defined by the 1980 Act. If governors consider that there is room to admit above that number, and thus come into dispute with the local authority, they may seek to raise the limit by appealing to the Secretary of State.

Financial delegation to schools passes considerable new responsibilities to governing bodies. Together with the head teachers, they must manage the school budget as an instrument for the achievement of their educational objectives and priorities, and they must decide on the number of staff at the school, and control recruitment and promotion. Theirs will be the choice of what to spend on extra administrative support, and it will be for them to determine how far to look to the LEA for professional help and advice on financial procedures, staff appointments and employment law.

To help governors to a better understanding of these new duties, and to enhance their ability effectively to discharge them, authorities are to be responsible for offering training. There is nothing new in this. Most LEAs over the years have organised conferences, provided booklets of guidance, encouraged the use of external courses as for example those provided by the Open University, and increasingly entered into a partnership of training with such groups as the National Association of Governors and Managers. The emphasis now is on the scale and deep seriousness of such provision. The simple reality is that since governing bodies are of central importance, then they must be helped to do their work well, and a local authority is best placed by experience to provide that help.

The Act invests a great deal of its hopes for the future in governors, and there are obvious attractions in the concept of involving sensible and interested people in practical ways in the life of a school, allowing them to grow and mature through independence. If there are flickers of doubt or reserve, then they will be over such issues as whether it is naive to think that, with a diminution in the number of politicians on governing bodies, there will be a muting of party political issues; whether, despite the considerable and valuable work to be done, there is a sufficient number of people about, able and willing to give the time that is needed properly to help schools develop their curriculum, personnel and financial policies; whether there really is a constituency of support for the view that education is too important to be left to the educators – certainly, all the evidence of the new annual parents meetings, where turnout appears to be pitifully small, could point to satisfaction rather than discontent.

Higher and further education

Maintained higher education has virtually ceased to be a local education authority responsibility. Institutions with full-time equivalent enrolment numbers for courses of advanced further education exceeding 350, and also exceeding 55 per cent of their total full-time equivalent enrolment number, are now to be conducted by a body corporate. To that body are transferred from the authority property rights and liabilities. A Polytechnics and Colleges Funding Council has been established to administer the available funds for these institutions and for certain higher education courses provided by LEAs. On the Board of Governors of the institutions, representation from the authority is negligible.

None of us can long repine at the freedom now given to polytechnics and those other institutions. Whatever occasional dislocations and differences there have been, the nurture, in finance, advice and defence, given by the LEA has not been inconsiderable, nor has the contribution of these institutions to the vitality and quality of educational provision in an area been stinted. However, their size, influence, range of work and maturity justify their independence, though even that, with so much central control, could prove illusory. The real tragedy would come if polytechnics ceased to value local connections. Those with industry they undoubtedly will retain, but no less fruitful are their links with colleges and schools, with a whole range of INSET programmes, and with much general education activity in their district. LEAs have unique experience in dealing with polytechnic issues, and – at least in the early years of autonomy – those institutions may find it prudent to buy in that expertise.

In further education, colleges, like schools, enjoy new responsibilities, putting some distance between them and their authorities. Governing bodies are reconstituted, so that 50 per cent of their number are 'employment interest' governors, that is businessmen and women and employers. Where colleges have a substantial proportion of non-vocational work, then there is provision, within the 50 per cent, for a small number of co-opted members. The LEA can select and appoint 20 per cent of the governors, and can propose how the remaining 30 per cent of places be filled from categories such as staff and students, neighbouring educational institutions and appropriate local community organisations. The Secretary of State retains a firm grip on how employment interest governors are to be sought. An LEA must, after consultation, draw up a list of nominating bodies – Chambers of Commerce, CBI, Trades Council and the like – and the list must be approved by the Secretary of State.

Governors have great burdens to carry, and the most significant one is the management of the college budget. The authority is responsible for constructing a formula for the distribution of money, and the constituent elements are clearly prescribed by the DES – student numbers, the weight to be attached to programme areas, provision for special education needs, adult education, and the requirements of the Manpower Services Commission. All those considerations must lead to a scheme which ensures maximum freedom for colleges to manage their own affairs, is simple and comprehensible, promotes responsiveness and aids good management. As with the funding of schools, however, LEAs will keep some control of capital, central support services, some staff costs, and amounts for development and contingency. New Articles for governing bodies make clear their responsibilities in the appointment, discipline and dismissal of staff.

To prevent over-much incoherence and inconsistency in the development of further education, LEAs have a duty to prepare, for the Secretary of State's approval, a plan which examines longer-term developments against which the annual plans used for setting college budgets can be measured and paced. The experience which all authorities have in preparing cycles of three year plans for MSC is seen as offering useful models, but obviously the work will be on a wider basis, taking account of higher education in its own and neighbouring institutions, private provision, adult education, and work for the 16–19 year olds in schools. Collaboration with other LEAs in the area is properly seen as inescapable.

Undoubtedly, this duty of detailed forward planning leaves authorities with a critically important management function. The attractions in the policy of delegating tasks to colleges, as indeed to schools, carry with them the dangerous bacillus of fragmentation, and unhelpful idiosyncrasy. A development plan goes some way to avoid this, and, difficult as it is to prepare, given the uncertainties of finance, the well-rehearsed problems of manpower planning, and the attempts at sturdy independence which ambitious colleges will pursue, an authority has in its hands a powerful instrument of its own for shaping and directing further education.

The 1988 Education Act, putting it at its simplest, moves the centre of gravity for much day-to-day management away from County Hall to schools and colleges, and LEAs will need to put a premium on management by co-operation and persuasion, and by demonstrating that the central services it can provide are as effective and competitive as any offered elsewhere. It would be foolish, however, to draw the conclusion that these are wholly new departures, for whatever its pre-eminent position as provider and organiser, an LEA has never possessed a total monopoly, and has worked at partnership. Some examples will suffice.

(i) *Voluntary schools*

The education service of this country owes much to voluntary bodies, largely the Churches, who have built and maintained schools, and trained teachers for them. Their work is sustained through co-operation with the DES and local authorities, and that the partnership is a happy one is due largely to the work of R A Butler and William Temple during the preparation and passing of the 1944 Education Act. Anyone tempted to minimise their achievement should read of the obstructive passions raised when the involvement of the Churches in education was debated on a number of occasions before the First World War.

The 1988 Act further defines the relationship between the partners. How the varying interests are now balanced, the financial responsibilities shared, the nice scale of representation on different types of governing bodies, the differences between aided, controlled and special agreement schools, all are best described in the book *County and Voluntary Schools* by Brooksbank, Revell, Ackstine & Bailey. Reference to it continues to be the salvation of many an apprentice administrator up, for the first time, against a choleric clergyman.

Inevitably management interests in the voluntary institution are more varied and more complicated than in the maintained sector. There are diocesan education committees of clergymen and laymen with responsibilities for the provision and maintenance of their school buildings, and, as important as ever, for developing some clear strategies for overall provision of Church schools in the diocese in the light of falling school population. The importance of their liaison with the local authority cannot be over-estimated since their planning programmes, their bids for grants from central funds, their building plans, the arrangements for admissions to schools, especially at the time of secondary transfer, all operate within a framework still largely determined by the LEA. An important link between the two is the diocesan education officer. Among his principal tasks are the giving of advice to the governors of Church schools about the financial and legal opportunities and constraints in their work, the provision of seminars and courses for teachers, particularly those involved with religious education, and help with the selection of headteachers. Usually, too, he or she serves on the authority's education committee. There are those who would argue the inappropriateness of that placing on the grounds that only people properly chosen in local government elections should serve at that level of committee responsibility, but if partnership means anything at all, it must allow each of the major partners a voice in the framing of policies. It would be naive to pretend there never are tensions and differences, but time and goodwill have brought sensible working arrangements, perhaps because all continue to be in broad agreement on the eirenic purposes of education.

(ii) *Manpower Services Commission*
There is elsewhere in this book a more detailed analysis of the role of MSC. The impact of its work on the management task of an LEA has been considerable, since schools and colleges, for important parts of their work, no longer have to look to the authority for money. One quarter of the funding of work-related non-advanced further education comes from the Commission, on the basis of an agreed development plan prepared by the LEA. Happily there have been no major conflicts. MSC has acknowledged the expertise and professionalism in LEA offices, and authorities have valued the focus on realistic forward planning and better liaison.

   Those qualities and characteristics have been much needed in the introduction and spread of the Technical and Vocational Educational Initiative, perhaps the most significant of all recent curriculum projects. Starting with a small number of pilot projects to give greater vocational emphasis to the curriculum of 14–18 year olds, the Initiative is now being extended to all schools. Schemes are drawn up by the authority, negotiated with its schools, and subjected to further negotiation and scrutiny by the Commission which will then release the necessary funds. Though its start-point was an essentially simple one, the repercussions on teaching method, in-service training, monitoring and assessment and therefore on the whole curriculum for a wider age range have been of major importance. Whether in the out-turn there will be sharp conflict between the cross-curricular philosophy of TVEI and the subject-based proposals of the National Curriculum remains to be seen. The LEA, no longer in sole charge of many activities in its own institutions, will need to ensure the coherence of the work done in its schools and colleges.

(iii) *Specific funding*

The Department of Education and Science, in its search directly to influence activities in LEAs and schools, and to establish some primacy for its own priorities, has developed two powerful instruments. Grant related in-service training has as its declared aims the promotion of the professional development of teachers, the promotion of more systematic and purposeful planning of in-service training, the encouragement of more effective management of the teacher force and other professional groups involved, and the encouragement of training to meet selected needs which are accorded national priority. An authority has, each year, to prepare an INSET plan for submission to the DES, and is then allocated funds accordingly. That plan looks to strike a balance between the declared national priorities, the interests and policies of the LEA, and the needs of the teacher and the school. It can be prepared only on the basis of wide consultation, and can be effective only if there is the most scrupulous evaluation. Both are essential management tasks for the authority.

The other instrument is the Education Support Grant, by which the DES holds back 1 per cent (£135 million in 1989–90) of the amount specified for planned current expenditure on local authority education in the Rate Support Grant to be bid for by LEAs against categories of activity deemed important by the Secretary of State after consultation with the local authority associations. The range of activities is wide, some attracting a 50 per cent grant and others 70 per cent, and although in the scale of things the amounts of money involved are relatively modest, the hold which the scheme gives to government on an LEA's work is a significant one.

In sum, the image of centralist, unregarding LEAs will hardly stand in the face of the evidence that their work can be done only by co-operation – which is not to deny that the involvement of many groups and agencies as paymasters and policy-makers for schools and colleges has potential for confusion. Even the most primitive of text-books on management stress the importance of clear lines of accountability. Present realities, however, are that institutions must look in a number of directions and a prime function of LEAs will be to mediate and harmonize.

Information

Lyndon Johnson remarked that an American president was only as good as his information, and obviously facts are crucially important for decision making. The rapid growth of technology with the capacity to collect, analyse and store information has already had a fundamental and beneficial impact on the work of an education department and its institutions, though it is not the business of education offices, or indeed the DES, to become like the Escorial of Philip II – repositories of information on everything, collected with stupefying industry and arthritic to the point of immobility.

Despite delegation, an LEA will have a continuing need for knowledge of what is happening in schools so to inform its policies on staffing, in-service training, buildings and equipment, as well as its overall development plan. The 1986 legislation provided for the publication of test results and the presentation of an annual report by governors to parents, both adding to the many other sources on which an authority can draw to help it know what is actually going on in its schools. Members of councils serve as governors, and are not slow, formally or informally, to voice their concerns or their pride in the activities of schools. Administrative officers, contrary to much received opinion, regularly visit schools, and are not without experience in judging the health or otherwise of institutions. Authorities have advisers who work with teachers on courses, in classrooms and on working parties; who visit schools individually and in teams, and prepare reports on their findings. Her Majesty's

Inspectors inspect and report on schools, or, less officially, bring to the Chief Education Officer their impressions and assessments of performance. The formal HMI reports are now made public, and authorities are asked to respond to the Secretary of State on how they propose to remedy any weaknesses which the reports have exposed. Whatever initial reservations there may have been, the move can only be welcomed as a contribution to more effective management from a group of highly responsible and discriminating observers. One further contribution of importance is the series of reports by HMI on the effects of local authority expenditure policies on the education service. A number have now been published, and although individual authorities are not named, all can draw conclusions for their own institutions about standards of provision and accessibility to programmes which match student needs.

In similar ways, the reports of the Audit Commission add to the stock of useful commentary, and help to correct some of the more extravagant views found on the wilder shores of public debate about the achievements of education. The search for valid performance indicators, be they for the service as a whole, or institutions or individual pupils is of growing importance. Some of the suggestions so far made are simple to the point of inanity, and a great deal more work remains to be done. Nevertheless the old unsystematic assessments, subjective, uneven and patchy are no longer appropriate, and an LEA will be a less effective manager if it continues to rely on them.

Other institutions

Apart from schools and colleges of all sorts, local authorities support a wide range of less-easily classifiable institutions in response to particular needs – youth clubs, drama centres, music schools, study centres, advisory units, language centres, adolescent centres, and much more. Some, in the management sense, are outposts of larger, more conventional units, and are responsible to those units and staffed by them. Others work in a matrix of different relationships, and though their staffing and budgets are fixed at the centre, and though they must work within the general policies of the authority, they are governed by bodies and constitutions which have been formed to fit comfortably with local circumstances. As good an example as any is the teachers' centre, acting as a focal point for locally-based in-service training, providing library and reprographic facilities, and serving as a meeting place for teachers from different schools with similar interests and responsibilities. The centre is managed by a committee of teachers to whom, in the first instance, the warden or centre leader is responsible. Its activities are inevitably somewhat limited in scale, but the important thing is that authorities have sought actively to involve teachers in devising and carrying out in-service programmes which reflect their own needs, and through that delegation encouraged many lively initiatives.

Conclusions

It may not be straining metaphor too much to say that what we are now witnessing is the rapid decolonisation of the education empire. A judgement has been made that schools and colleges, whether dependent colonies, mandated territories or protectorates, have reached a stage, along the evolutionary chain, where they both deserve and are capable of exercising considerable independence. Local authorities, therefore, have moved from the imperial grandeur of the India Office or the Colonial Office to the worthy and modest work of a Commonwealth Department.

If that is indeed the reality, then there is little to be gained by bemoaning the fact, but to look to authorities to exercise what residual powers they have with their undoubted skill and sense of commitment. They share the Secretary of State's concerns for quality in an education which 'promotes the spiritual, moral, cultural, mental and physical development of pupils at school and of society; and prepares such pupils for the opportunities, responsibilities and experiences of adult life'. With the implementation of the 1988 Act still in its infancy, the extent of those powers is uncertain, and likely to get better definition only from experience. This much, however, can be asserted – in management at institutional level, an LEA will have five principal tasks:

> to determine the overall level of investment in the service, and, through models of guidance and good practice, encourage governing bodies to exercise all their delegated powers wisely;

to monitor and evaluate the work of schools and colleges, and, through appraisal systems, the performance and achievements of teachers;

to provide training and guidance for teachers and governors; to prepare and deliver development plans for its area as a whole so that there is agreed direction and coherence;

to unify the work of the many agencies now involved in their several and practical ways in the work of institutions.

Albeit now of a different order, there is then a substantial amount to be done.

13 Communication and consultation

Communication

Methods of communication and consultation are changing year by year, especially as a result of recent legislation and new technology. They are becoming increasingly sophisticated and increasingly demanding, under constant public scrutiny and within a complex network of relationships. Formal communication in writing is still a major element in the education officer's work, but informed written and verbal skills are equally important whether for Committee and other public meetings, or at press conferences, on local radio or even in the television studio.

Formal communication

Some forms of communication are required by statute. For example, before a school is opened, closed or significantly changed in character, public notice has to be given of the LEA's intentions, in accordance with regulations issued by the Secretary of State. The Education Act 1980 required the LEA to publish information about its schools and its arrangements for admission to them. The Education (No. 2) Act 1986 and the Education Act 1988, however, reflect fundamental changes in the relationship between the LEA and individual institutions, so that the responsibility for formal communication with parents and the community rests much more with individual governing bodies. Increasingly, the statutory obligation of the LEA is to provide governors with the information and training necessary to enable them to execute a wide range of delegated responsibilities.

This does not in any way diminish the need for formality and accuracy, whether in respect of teachers' conditions of service and other employment legislation; formulae for the local financial management of schools and colleges; instruments and articles of government; curriculum policies, and many other formal obligations on LEAs, all of which have statutory force.

The Education Act 1988 increases hugely the powers and responsibilities of individual governing bodies while at the same time giving over 300 new powers to the Secretary of State. The LEA is left somewhat haplessly in the middle of this potential conflict, still with many responsibilities but relatively few powers.

Matters which are the subject of formal communication tend to be contentious and increasingly find their way into the courts. Cases relating to wrongful dismissal, breach of contract, non-attendance, personal injury and statements of special educational need are typical examples. Accuracy in the initial documentation is absolutely vital, therefore, and subsequently may save a great deal of time and public expense. The public is given to complaining about bureaucracy, but, properly conducted, formal communication avoids unnecessary subsequent work and, in fact, enhances public confidence.

Apart from formal communication on specific issues, an LEA will record its own actions in official minutes, most of which will be publicly accessible. Again, accuracy is essential, although the house style will vary from one local authority to another. A general rule might be that minutes should be as precise and concise as possible, without obliging the reader to refer to the original paper to understand what was discussed and resolved. In relation to papers presented to Committee, there is now a statutory obligation to declare all the sources of information which were drawn on in order to write them.

Formal communication, therefore, has to be exact and able to withstand public scrutiny. It may sometimes be necessary to add explanatory notes, but attempts to replace formal statements with explanations of them are generally misguided. For example, since public notices proposing to close a school are subject to the scrutiny of the courts, it has been established that an explanatory note at the foot of the notice does not constitute part of the notice and has no binding force.

At national level, statutory instruments have legal and binding force, whereas departmental circulars give advice and guidance but have no such force. At LEA level, it is useful to make a similar distinction – between obligatory regulations, of which there are likely to be fewer and fewer, and policy guidelines, which are an increasing means of communicating with and influencing individual institutions.

Committee reports

As with minutes, every LEA has its own house style, reflecting both tradition, relationships and the character of leading officers and elected members. Good report writing is not easy and should form an essential element in staff training. Ideally each report should enable the committee to come to a sensible conclusion based on the information therein. It should be based at all times on sound educational principles.

The general character of reports requiring a decision is, first, to state a problem, then draw attention to existing policies and practices. Next, they will offer a number of alternative ways forward, with costings and arguments for and against. Finally will come a clear recommendation.

It is not true to say that the more material reports contain, the better informed the committee will be. Long extracts from official documents and a proliferation of appendices are often a substitute for dealing concisely and analytically with the main issues. Most ineffective communication springs from a lack of clarity about what the writer wants to say. A good report to a public committee should be designed to enlarge understanding of an issue as well as to inform.

Major characteristics of local government are public accountability and openness. As far as possible, officers should work in partnership with their committees, or at the very least with their chairmen, and should be open and honest in the information they provide. Obviously, there is a facility for confidentiality, where reports are dealing with personal matters relating to named individuals or the interim stages of delicate negotiations.

It is also essential, in writing reports to committee, to anticipate how the information will be received and interpreted (or misinterpreted!): not only by the committee itself, but also by the press and the general public. It is vital that officers are seen to act on behalf of the public education service and not as spokespersons of a particular political party.

Letter writing

Most education officers deal with a massive amount of correspondence, much of which demands written replies. Similar principles apply as to the writing of committee reports.

Letters should be clear, concise and accurate and should take account of the person to whom they are written. That is not to suggest that they should ever be patronising or abusive but clearly one is likely to write in different terms to a particularly well-informed correspondent – say, to a head or a union official, than to a confused parent or a child. Jargon and acronyms should be avoided as far as possible in writing to the general public. Letters should not be seen as a means of scoring intellectual points or of outwitting an opposition.

One of the commonest complaints levelled at officers by correspondents relates to slowness, or even failure, to reply. There really is no excuse, in an age of word processors or standardised letters, for not sending at least a prompt acknowledgement. In principle, parents should be accorded the same service as members of parliament! Obviously officers have to draw up priorities in dealing with correspondence – most people accept that readily and are content to know that their enquiry has been received and is being dealt with.

Traditionally, all correspondence was with the Chief Education Officer and all replies bore his or her signature, generally either a rubber stamp or a forgery. Increasingly, letters are now signed by individual officers, at least down to section head level. This can be confusing to the public, especially when postholders change, but generally increases accountability and responsibility and avoids a feeling of anonymity. In most offices the CEO will still tend to sign personally letters to MPs, senior government officials, the Ombudsman and other persons deemed politically significant.

Sensitivity and fitness for purpose are also important. For example, sometimes standard letters are sent to employees leaving an LEA service. Unless these letters contain personalised elements, it is immediately apparent on comparison that what appeared a personal gesture of gratitude is no more than an empty piece of formality. The small saving in time by adopting a standard format of letter does not compensate for the bad public relations and loss of goodwill. This really is a potent message for people working in local government and a source of much ill will and low morale. It is vital in any organisation that people feel known and valued.

Other means of communication

Officers spend a great deal of time on the telephone and it is very tempting to use this as a substitute for written communication. Certainly it is a more rapid and effective way of exchanging views and exploring a particular issue, but it should be remembered that the risk of misunderstanding or misinterpretation is far greater. A good practice in a contentious call is to try to conclude by summing up what has been agreed and to keep at least a scribbled record of what was said.

Telephone manner should not be undervalued, especially where the caller has not met the officer to whom he is speaking. It is inevitable in the nature of telephone communication that junior staff may find themselves expected to handle complex situations on behalf of senior officers without the level of information or training necessary. Junior staff require considerable diplomatic skill in such circumstances.

A great deal of time is spent in formal and informal meetings as a further major medium of communication. Sharing information within the office sometimes appears to take up a disproportionate percentage of the working week but, if it is part of a structured network, can promote corporate endeavour and avoid duplication of effort.

Few officers receive adequate training in handling meetings, whether in one to one interviews, disciplinary cases, governing bodies, sub committees, union negotiations, task groups, management teams or receiving lobbies; yet a thorough understanding of group dynamics should form an essential element in their package of skills.

Consultation

The last ten years have seen a dramatic increase in LEAs' obligations to consult, either formally, principally as a result of statute, or informally, because of raised public expectations and political awareness.

It is important to distinguish between consultation and negotiation. Consultation is not a referendum but is undertaken with one party in a position to reach a decision, whether or not that confirms with the views of those consulted. Negotiation is essentially between parties each able directly to influence the decision ultimately reached. Consultation is a process by which those authorised to make a decision convey the nature of their proposals to those affected by them. It should be a two-way process and they should be ready to change their proposals, in the light of what is said to them, but they are not committed to do so. Most of the problems, and allegations that 'the consultation was a farce' arise from a misunderstanding of this.

Formal consultation

LEAs are involved in a wide range of formal consultation related to statutory obligations – not only in respect of Education Acts but also, for example, in respect of employment legislation or the Health and Safety at Work Act.

Education Acts contain many provisions requiring LEAs to consult other parties – sometimes parents, other authorities or agencies, but predominantly their own head teachers, principals and governing bodies. Examples are in respect of instruments and articles of government, admission arrangements, suspensions and exclusions, appointments and dismissals and changes in character.

The new legislation, however, reflects a dramatic shift in the power base, especially given the distinction between consultation and negotiation, whereas even in the Education (No. 2) Act 1986, the obligation to consult, and thereby the ultimate power, rests predominantly with the LEA – in the Education Act 1988, the position is dramatically changed. Only about half a dozen clauses require consultation by the LEA, the remainder give specific powers to the governing body or the Secretary of State. The role of the LEA is drastically diminished.

Informal consultation

Voluntary consultation takes place with a wide variety of people and organisations. Some is carefully structured and has a direct influence on the policies of the LEA, for example, in relation to recognised teachers' associations and other unions, employers, ethnic minority organisations and other community groups, diocesan authorities and parent groups.

Parent advocacy has a long way to go before it compares with, say, the United States but, nevertheless, the national federations are becoming increasingly well organised. The extent at local level to which they are broadly supportive of their LEA or alternatively adopt a generally critical stance depends to a great degree on officers of the authority. If they are seen to value the parents' views and promote a sense of partnership, then mutual understanding is likely to result. If, on the other hand, parents are kept at arm's length, either at LEA or school level, antipathies are bound to grow. Officers have had many occasions to be grateful to parents' organisations in the battle for resources for the education service, although officers can be put in a difficult position if they are seen to sympathise privately or publicly with the pleas of pressure groups contrary to the policy of their Council.

The whole process is extremely complex and it is vital that officers work in close collaboration with one another and call on expert assistance as appropriate, especially from lawyers and personnel officers. The days when an individual officer could write his own policies are over! Precedent becomes very important and a high level of professional skill and political sensitivity is called for.

It is in this particular context that systematic consultation between a local authority and its neighbours has become increasingly important. Sometimes this is done through meetings of CEOs or of elected members, sometimes through special interest groups such as further education officers, sometimes under the auspices of the Society of Education Officers. LEAs have been slow to recognise that many of the bodies with which they consult and negotiate are highly organised both nationally and regionally.

There is also an increasing need to consult government agencies – not simply the traditional encounters between officers and HMI but increasingly with bodies associated with external funding, especially of course the Manpower Services Commission. The emergence of the MSC is perhaps the most significant addition to education officers' network in recent years. Those working in post-14 education, whether in NAFE, TVEI, or adult education may well find themselves working more closely with MSC officials than with their own departmental colleagues.

Consultation is very time consuming and can generate difficulties in itself, for example, by raising public awareness and expectations, by offending groups who feel neglected if left late in the process, by drawing officers into party political in-fighting. Delicate decisions have to be taken, and sometimes played by ear, in respect of the amount of information to be shared. In public meetings, for example, detailed presentations and papers raise the quality of understanding but can give the impression that conclusions have already been reached and that the consultative process is a charade. On the other hand, inadequate information gives an impression of bad management and lack of concern. Also groups are becoming increasingly sophisticated in their ability to resist change and no assumptions can be made about the continuity of support from elected members or local MPs. In any public meetings, it is important to discuss in advance the respective roles of officers and elected members. Above all, officers must not be seen to take the platform on behalf of a particular political party.

Consultation is a demanding process for the education officer but is also potentially one of the most stimulating and rewarding aspects of the job.

Public relations

At one time, a Chief Education Officer's colleagues were covered by a cloak of anonymity and were seen by many as part of the army of 'faceless bureaucrats' who were supposed to control our every action. This has changed dramatically, however, in the last ten years with a great increase in demands to address public meetings, speak to clubs and societies, talk to the press, or appear on radio or TV. Whenever this occurs, the reputation of the LEA is in the hands of the officer, however junior, and his audience, whether 20 or 2 million will see him, for better or worse, as a personification of the service as a whole. There will be no allowances made for his lack of experience, for the fact that the area of work under consideration is not his normal responsibility or that he was called upon at the last minute. Nor can it be assumed that a meeting or an interview arranged to consider, say, cuts in the budget will not also be used as an opportunity to consider reading standards in primary schools. In other words education officers must have, or acquire, the ability to think on their feet as well as ensuring that they have a good general grasp of the activities of the whole department.

Nowadays all statements emanating from an Education Department, whether written or oral, marked confidential or told in confidence, are likely to be subject to public scrutiny either in the name of open government or, possibly, as a result of an investigation by the Ombudsman. This should not be used as an excuse for departments to 'clam up', but it does mean that communications with the public must be clear, explicit and consistent one with another.

Public relations work is shared, of course, with elected members, particularly with the Chairman of the Education Committee and its main sub-committees. Usually there is no clear cut division between responsibilities reserved to elected members and those undertaken by officers. In some authorities, officers have a much more subordinate role than in others. Generally, the principal and proper distinction is that officers confine themselves to factual issues and do not make any statements which could be interpreted as party politically biased.

Nowhere is the relation between Chairman and CEO more important than in public relations. If the Chairman is given to sweeping 'off the cuff' policy statements without consulting his officers as to the practicalities or the Chief Officer makes public pronouncements seriously at variance with the political attitudes of the majority party then good relations with the public are hardly likely to be sustained – nor for that matter are harmonious relations between members and officers.

Major policy pronouncements will normally be made by an elected member. Obviously policy is the responsibility of the

Education Committee or full Council, where press and public are in attendance. Usually the press will first learn of a particular policy issue via the papers submitted by the officers either to the committee or more usually to a sub-committee. At the committee meeting, the Chairman may even publicise his own or his party's view and the officer is likely to give a professional commentary.

It is important to remember, however, that, even with press officers, public relations officers and press releases, it is impossible to control what will appear in the media. Reporters are just as likely to emphasise interesting contributions from the floor as anything the Chairman or lead officer might say.

Few would question the fundamental duty of an LEA to inform the public in its area as effectively as possible. Despite the requirements of the Access to Information Act, the fact that virtually all formal meetings are held in public, and the readiness of MPs, the Ombudsman, the Secretary of State and elected members to challenge decisions and demand explanations, the public is still given to complain about lack of information. The role of publicist can be disheartening at times, but it is undeniably important.

The main principle should be that honesty is the best policy. Most of the time it is easy to be frank, even when one has to admit to a previous error; after all nothing endears us so much to others as the frank and unqualified admission of a mistake – as long as we do not have to do it too frequently. But occasionally an enquiry from press or parent may be difficult to answer fully without casting aspersions on colleagues, for example the head whose discipline is weak or who is insisting on unreasonably short, or longer, hair for boys or longer, or shorter, skirts for girls. Nevertheless in the long run, and perhaps the short run, it is better to be frank, and certainly if there are too many qualified responses the department's credibility with both press and public is likely to be jeopardised.

Effective public relations depend upon a sound grasp of the facts, a fundamental to efficient administration anyway, and an ability to present them clearly and briefly, not always a universal attribute of education administrators. That which cannot be said in 200 words will not be said at all in many newspapers. Equally regional TV or local radio programmes are unlikely to give a spokesman more than 120 seconds to get his message across.

Inevitably then the process involves simplification, both in the sense of separating the significant from the trivial and also in the use of vocabulary. Some education officers no doubt find the popularisation, and sometimes, trivialisation of information about educational developments distasteful, but it is inevitable and given that we are concerned to communicate with *The Sun* readers as well as *The Times* readers, usually justified.

One continual professional tension for education officers is the extent to which they should try to influence public and political opinion, rather than merely reflect it. It would be tragic if CEOs became silent political servants, but, at the same time, a CEO is a public servant and must be sensitive to political reality, whether in respect of the government or his local council. Advice should be forthright and fearless, but pragmatism should be as important as idealism.

There is one sense in which it seems reasonable for an Education Department to be selective, and that is in ensuring that bad news does not drive out the good. Obviously the issues which create a bad image must be faced squarely and a public response made speedily and efficiently. But it is pointless to spend hours pondering over a three-line counter to public criticism which may or may not be published. The time will be much better spent in presenting some achievement which will probably be of more value to the public than a long-running and much reported feud over a schoolgirl refusing to remove her ear-rings, or whatever. In other words to a degree an Education Department should co-operate with the press and media on the Department's terms, with the proviso that it does not 'cover up' or indulge in news blackouts when the going gets rough. Any Education Department may well issue two or three press releases each week explaining policy or describing healthy developments in the service as a whole or in individual institutions.

The media

Press releases, which explain issues in a succinct and interesting way are welcomed by the media and can often pre-empt unnecessary controversy. This is where the Public Relations Officer can be an invaluable ally. He will usually be an ex-journalist and consequently able to couch a press release in terms which will be acceptable to editors. A five-page memorandum on assessment and monitoring in primary schools prepared by an Assistant Education Officer may be appropriate as a basis for a committee's decisions but quite often will be difficult for journalists to digest, or if loaded with jargon even incomprehensible. It is the PRO's job to refine and summarise the essentials and to do so in such a way as not only to provide the local paper with a decent by-line but also give a reasonably accurate impression of the basic material. This requires skill of a high order and it also presupposes that the PRO has acquired a good working knowledge of the education service which he is representing.

The PRO is meant to be an intermediary between members, officers and journalists; if there is an insistence that all enquiries are funnelled through his office he can become an obstacle to communication rather than a channel. Some pressmen will ring the public relations office in the first instance but in many authorities they prefer to go direct to the Chairman, or more usually, to the Chief Officer, or officer immediately responsible for the matter under review.

Often the PRO will engineer news items; this does not imply improper manipulation. If the authority is proud of an outdoor pursuits centre for example it may combine a press conference with a visit to the centre. Similarly it may be important to reassure the teaching force – and parents – about the state of funding for the service in the coming year and a properly organised press conference will usually attract a good response from local papers, TV and radio, and often, the regional representatives of national papers.

Finally, but not least important, a specialist PRO should, through the example of his own activities, heighten the awareness of both members and officers to good public relations practice and, as well, improve the quality of communications between committee and senior officers and the many thousands working in the service.

Good public relations depend fundamentally upon cultivating a sound working relationship with the media. This does not mean that either members or officers should be so concerned with image building that 'the medium becomes the message' nor that journalists should be seduced into avoiding the awkward question or investigating weaknesses in the service; but that those speaking for the LEA are frank, not given to deliberate deception – and prepared to speak. The power of the media, particularly television, is now well understood; however assiduous members and officers are in speaking at meetings it is unlikely that on any issue they will reach a fraction of the people by this method that will be achieved by an appearance on regional TV. Obviously the impact in terms of how much information the viewer retains is another matter, but the majority who never attend meetings or 'great debates' are touched to some degree by television programmes.

Nor should the value of the local press be under-estimated. It is here that a more discursive approach is likely to be adopted to current issues. Indeed the cynic may wonder how some local papers will fill their news, editorial and letters columns if current comprehensive reorganisation issues are finally resolved. Many LEAs – particularly away from the large urban communities – can expect extensive coverage in the local press for virtually any item they sponsor, particularly if a press release is specifically prepared by the PRO.

In addition local newspapers are the vehicle for much of the authority's advertising, whether of vacancies, the publication of school closure notices (referred to in an earlier chapter) or of the adult education programme. It is often possible in association with the latter to persuade the local editor to undertake a special news feature on the local college or the provision of non-vocational educational opportunities throughout the area, particularly if the volume of directly commissioned advertising is substantial. Similarly a feature may be based upon a new community building with advertising drawn from the various contractors. Whilst some purists still deprecate this now widespread practice of associating special feature articles with advertising, it is certainly a most effective way of informing the public of the educational and recreational resources available to them. The school meals services are now much more entrepreneurial than formerly, and many LEAs undertake determined marketing campaigns.

Certain items have a natural appeal for journalists of all kinds, whether serving TV, radio or a newspaper – comprehensive reorganisation, allegedly falling standards in basic skill, indiscipline in schools, meat substitutes in school meals and so on. All can easily turn into 'knocking copy' but equally most can be turned to the advantage of the authority, not by falsifying the true situation but by emphasising the positive. However, if this is to happen it is important that an effective spokesman is available. TV, in particular, waits for no man; officers and members must be prepared to put themselves to considerable inconvenience. Perhaps the worst publicity of all is the statement after the news story 'nobody was available to comment on behalf of the Education Department'. In other words the case for the service should never be allowed to go by default, particularly when something has clearly gone wrong.

In certain circumstances the media can be of vital assistance. During a harsh winter most LEAs will find it necessary to close some schools, often at short notice. School transport may have to be cancelled, or heating fuel may run out, necessitating closure. Occasionally industrial action, particularly if sudden, will necessitate speedy communication with parents, either because of direct strike action within the service or perhaps because of food shortages compelling the abandonment of school meals provision but not necessarily school closures. In all these circumstances and no doubt others, the problem which faces Education Departments is how to communicate quickly with many thousands of parents often spread over a wide area.

Regional TV is now well used to passing information of this kind. Normally it will be generalised; it is too much to expect that they will carry during their brief news magazine programmes long lists of schools closed – or re-opening. But they will display emergency numbers to ring and describe the general situation.

Local radio, whilst not yet universal, provides a potent means of communication for many local education departments. Again availability is fundamental. Unless the elected member or education officer is prepared to turn up at the studio at 7.50 a.m. or to conduct an interview over the 'phone at home, inevitably in the middle of his favourite TV programme, then the opportunity will be lost. Schedules wait for no man.

Relationships with other bodies

The range of organisations and institutions with which an LEA needs to liaise in order to promote and develop its services is enormous and seems to grow in size and complexity year after year, especially as new initiatives and regulations repeatedly dismantle old relationships and demand new ones.

Whether or not an LEA has a university sited within its geographical area, it will depend to some extent upon one or more for in-service training of its teaching staff. The other common form of relationship is with the extra-mural department; most LEAs grant-aid them in order to facilitate the provision of university level part-time courses throughout their areas. In recent years the Open University has provided an increasingly valuable service both to the general public, often assisted by LEA funds, and also more specifically to trained teachers who are non-graduates. University and LEA controlling committees customarily have representatives from each other's sphere amongst their memberships.

Patronage of the arts having now passed from royalty and the nobility to central and local government, it is the education committees which provide major support from public funds in many areas. This takes the form of grants to regional arts associations, orchestras and local societies. Also LEAs are often partners in both capital and revenue financing of local theatres and other joint schemes, usually sport-orientated, undertaken in conjunction with district and parish councils and voluntary bodies. Such activities are obviously particularly vulnerable when LEAs have to cut into their budgets.

LEAs also have close relationships with examination boards, especially the GCE and GCSE boards, the Business and Technician Education Council and the CGLI. The relationship is not always an easy one: while the LEA is the principal source of finance for the examining bodies, there are other powerful vested interests, particularly the universities, the teachers' associations and employer groups.

Strictly speaking, relations with other departments of the Council are 'in-house'. Certainly the activities of the central legal, financial and architects departments in particular with that of Education Departments are completely inter-dependent as has been seen in earlier chapters.

A considerable impetus to the closer working together of Social Services and Education Departments – and District Health Authorities – came first from the report of the Seebohm Committee, concerned with the creation of an integrated social work service and from the Court Report reviewing the Child

Health Services. Currently the 1981 Education Act laying a responsibility upon LEAs to provide co-ordinated services for the handicapped as envisaged in the Warnock Report is a further spur towards partnership. Certainly it is now commonplace for local authorities to operate policies in relation to the under-fives and provisions for the handicapped and inner city areas for example across departmental boundaries. The past few years have also seen closer relationships developing between the Education Service, Social Services and the Police and Probation Services in relation to the prevention of juvenile crime and the treatment of young offenders.

Obviously interdepartmental jealousies still remain in some areas but in general there does appear to be a greater emphasis upon the needs of the 'client' rather than on preserving the scope for independent action on the part of one of the providers.

It is doubtful if the impetus for this coming together of the various professional providers for the community has resulted from the implementation of corporate management. In fact where that implementation has been most thoroughgoing, it sometimes seems to have stimulated inter-departmental jealousies rather than obviated them. The relative responsibilities of Education Committees *vis-à-vis* policy and resources committees and those of Chief Education Officers and Chief Executives has been a constant and diverting – in both senses – preoccupation in some local authorities. It is to be hoped that an equilibrium is being achieved between the centralisers and those educationists who would declare UDI if they could. Management theory and practice can, in the end, have only one justification, as has been demonstrated throughout the preceding chapters – that they enhance effectiveness at the chalk face, wherever that may be. It may well be that the threat recently presented to local government *in toto* by the determination of central government to control its affairs more tightly has led to a greater community of purpose amongst members and officers in most authorities.

The national scene

LEAs' responsibilities are by definition confined to their own geographical area, but education is 'a national service locally administered'. Therefore it is necessary for LEAs to have both well-established channels of communication with central government, and with each other, and also to make their views public on the educational issues of the day, particularly proposed new legislation. Before 1974 these functions and others such as proffering guidance on legal issues and other advice to Education Officers, were fulfilled by the Association of Education Committees whose title was descriptive of its membership in England and Wales but whose powerful executive contained both elected members of LEAs and Chief Education Officers.

Local government reorganisation in 1974 provided an opportunity for the local authority associations – the Association of County Councils and Association of Metropolitan Authorities – to assume the role previously played by the AEC and to create jointly the Council of Local Education Authorities (CLEA).

If local government is to remain local, it can never be so strongly organised as central government, but it does need an effective representative form and its people at the centre of affairs, whether members or officers, need to speak authoritatively on behalf of the service. When things are going smoothly, LEAs, understandably, want to be entirely free to act independently; when there are problems – industrial action or whatever – the associations may be under pressure to take a strong line on behalf of everyone.

Chief Education Officers act as advisers to the ACC and AMA education committees and the CLEA, and normally their views are influential in formulating policy nationally as they are at local level.

Education Officers also now have to relate to bodies charged with rationalising the provision of higher education in the non-university sector – a relationship which may not be easy during an inevitable period of contraction.

The County Education Officers have for many years operated as a group and meet before the ACC Education Committee to consider the advice which their representatives will proffer. There is thus a firm and continuing basis for the establishment of good relationships between Chief Education Officers, elected members and the officers of the ACC, particularly the Education Officer. The AMA Chief Education Officers have recently adopted a similar practice.

The Society of Education Officers has spoken increasingly not only for Education Officers as such but by extension for the local education service, both in relation to the DES and the public at large. Consequently the Society, which usually has in membership all Chief Education Officers and most other senior LEA officers, is able to analyse government green and white papers, express views on major reports of select committees and royal commissions and ensure that the views of those responsible for administering the service at local level do not go by default in relation to the education issues of the day.

The specialist educational press provides the forum for debate in which, of course, Education Officers take their full part, throughout the educational world. *Education* is a weekly published by the Councils and Education Press Limited, which speaks particularly to LEA members and officers. However its influence spreads far beyond them. The *Times Educational Supplement* is undoubtedly the broadest channel of communication throughout the education service, whilst the journals of particular organisations, the serious, and some less serious dailies and Sunday papers all maintain specialist education correspondents who usually have a ready familiarity with the workings of LEAs.

The international dimension

The traditional insularity of the DES has until recently been shared by most LEAs. However, under the impetus of our new European role and of almost instant communication across national boundaries this is slowly changing. Education Officers, and sometimes elected members, are prepared to consider what, say, Scandinavia has to teach us in relation to provision for the handicapped or West Germany in preparing youngsters for the world of work.

The European Community, through its specialist Education Officers based in Brussels, assisted by Social Fund monies has stimulated British administrators to seek out and learn from examples of good practice in the other member countries. Similarly OECD via its Centre for Education Research and Innovation has involved UK Education Officers with the help of the DES international relations branch, in working alongside educationists from the other 25 member countries on projects concerned with education in sparsely populated areas and provision for the handicapped, to mention but two of many recent examples. The Central Bureau for Educational Visits and Exchanges, the Council of Europe, the Commonwealth Secretariat and, of course, the British Council, all play a part in trying to see that our locally administered education service is not also parochial and closed to international influences.

The International Committee of the Society of Education Officers, in association with these other bodies, has developed a sophisticated programme of intensive study visits and administrator exchanges, which add a fascinating and valuable dimension to the professional experience of many Education Officers. It also facilitates the contribution of many officers to international seminars and consultancies and helps promote the image of the British education service abroad.

The ambassadorial role at home and abroad can be undervalued in the face of mounting domestic pressures but there is no doubt that where these wider responsibilities are discharged effectively, they make a major contribution to the health of the service as a whole.

14 Equal opportunities and race relations

Historically it is possible to represent the development of our society as progress, not always at a regular pace, towards fairness, justice and equal social opportunity for all citizens. Realisation of that ideal is still a long way short of achievement but from time to time public awareness gives rise to great forward surges. The Education Act 1944 with its requirement of free secondary education for all, education of the individual according to his or her age, ability and aptitude, access to higher education and the opportunity for life-long education, was surely such a surge. Much has been done to translate into practice the vision of 1944 but as has already been seen, educational administration has a hard task ahead to achieve what was envisaged in 1944.

Meanwhile our society has changed. Its composition in terms of ethnic groups and cultures is different, attitudes towards groups within the community have altered and education has revealed vastly increased potential in those formally deemed educationally or socially handicapped.

Statutory background

This heightened awareness has been embodied in legislation such as the Disabled Persons Employment Acts of 1944 and 1958, the Sex Discrimination Act of 1975, the Race Relations Act of 1976 and the Education Act 1981. A common feature of these Acts is the responsibility laid on local authorities to promote equality of opportunity within the particular area covered by the legislation.

The Disabled Persons Acts specify the proportions of disabled people who should be employed. The 1975 and 1976 Acts focus on discrimination which is defined in the 1975 and 1976 Acts as treating a person less favourably because of sex or race than another person would be treated in similar circumstances. Discrimination may be 'direct', if, for example it seeks to exclude women or black people as a group from a particular appointment; or it may be 'indirect', for example, by imposing certain conditions on an appointment which are more difficult for women or black people to meet, unless those conditions are justified by the nature of the job itself. Both types of discrimination are illegal.

Policy and administrative background

Awareness has been reflected in policy and administrative action. Many moves have been made by government in partnership with local authorities to afford equality of opportunity to those living in the 'educational opportunity areas' and in the inner cities. Special grants have been available to those coming to this country with disadvantages in language etc. National bodies, notably the Equal Opportunities Commission and the Commission for Racial Equality, exercise promotional and monitorial functions in those respective fields.

In statutory terms, the requirements on local education authorities related to discrimination are limited to issues of sex and race. In practice positive discrimination has been exercised in favour of other deprived sections of the community with the ultimate aim of giving them equal opportunities with the more fortunate. Sometimes policies have been implemented through the normal administrative structures. Some authorities have reinforced their commitment by setting up special committees for women and race and by appointing officers with specific functions related to these issues. Public advertisement and notices have been used to signal or broadcast the authority's employment policies, and some have extended their concern for minority groups to cover those, such as gays and lesbians, not coming within the terms of the various enactments. Those authorities which included homosexual groups within their equal opportunities policies will need to have regard to the provisions of Section 28 of the Local Government Act 1988, which requires that local authorities shall not intentionally promote homosexuality. Until there is case law, it will be difficult to say how this should be interpreted. In the meantime, teachers involved in personal/social education, for example, will need a clear indication of their LEA's position should the teacher be challenged under the Act.

A clear LEA policy statement is an essential starting point to demonstrate the authority's commitment. Essentially it is simply an integral part of good professional, administrative and management practice. Like other aspects of good professional practice, to be effective it must permeate all parts of the service from policy formulation to service delivery. It is important that it is developed in consultation with the groups with whom it is concerned and recent cases have underlined the importance of protecting all groups, not just particular minorities, against unfair discrimination. Consultation, open attitudes and close involvement are key factors. Authority guidelines to back up the policy and to give support to schools and colleges are very useful.

Areas for action

Wherever people are involved in the educational system, there is the potential for discrimination against particular groups, or conversely there is the opportunity for promoting sound and fair attitudes to such groups. LEAs and governors therefore need to direct attention to a wide span of activities, including particularly appointment and promotion procedures for both teaching and non-teaching staff; disciplinary arrangements; appointment of governors; curriculum development; books, resources and materials; teaching programme content; sensitivity to cultural and religious differences; training of teachers, governors and non-teaching staff; work of specialist staff; careers officers; psychologists; education welfare officers; youth and community workers; public relations; information and access; school, college and office procedures. The establishment of appropriate procedures in all of these areas is essential to support the delivery of statutory and policy objectives. Some of the key areas are examined further in this chapter in order to draw out administrative themes which are common to most.

Appointment and promotion of staff

It is the duty of governors who will appoint or recommend appointment of most members of staff in schools, and of the LEA to ensure that each school is run economically, efficiently and effectively. They clearly have therefore a responsibility to appoint the best and most suitably qualified person available to any vacant post. In doing so they will naturally have regard to guidance on racial, sex and other discrimination given by the LEA.

Even so, given the best-intentioned appointment of committees or panels, the appearance of unfair discrimination can arise and the governors or the LEA may have to appear before a tribunal to answer a charge of racial or sex discrimination. The tribunal is a necessary safeguard against bad practice and a fair means of arbitration, but the very fact of appearance before a tribunal argues a breakdown of relationships and potentially damages governors' or the LEA's integrity in this area. As employers therefore, governors and LEAs will seek to ensure that employment procedures embody precise job specifications and employee specifications.

Careful records will be kept of reasons for deciding to include or exclude candidates for shortlists and for making final appointments. Appointments will need to be recorded and monitored and practice reviewed from time to time to ensure that the cumulative effect of a series of appointments cannot be taken to indicate discrimination however careful and scrupulous the proceedings on each individual appointment have been. In this context it is important that the disadvantaged should not be discouraged but positively encouraged by building up confidence in the fairness and attention given to those who might possibly be the subject of discrimination.

Educational administrators need also to be aware that the elements of elimination of discrimination must permeate the whole educational system and that increasingly potential employees will need to have had any consciousness or suspicion of discrimination dispelled throughout their educational career.

Training

The cornerstone of an effective policy of non-discrimination is the training of teachers and others, particularly for all those involved in making appointments. This will need to cover work on general awareness about discrimination, followed by more specific training on appointment procedures and techniques. Given the greatly increased role of governors under the 1988 Education Act, the need for governor training becomes correspondingly more important. The administrative task is a considerable one and various techniques can be employed, including the use of video tapes – a cascade system of training through chairman and heads – as well as the issue of documentary guidance.

The wider issue of training for all teaching and support staff is a key to the development of understanding and attitudes which will foster an equal opportunities ethos throughout the service as part of normal good practice. Since the authority is involved in planning most training courses, it can ensure, without the need for major extra administrative effort, that all training courses, whoever they are aimed at and whatever their specific topic, should automatically embrace relevant equal opportunities issues as an integral element. It is a useful starting point if each course planner can consider at a formative stage just what equal opportunities issues can be tackled and reinforced in each particular course and its various components.

School and college action plans

Following the establishment of an authority policy and related guidelines, individual schools and colleges should be asked to draw up their own detailed action plans in the context of the authority's policy statement and in close consultation with their own staff and wider community. This should set a programme of specific objectives to be achieved within a given time-scale – to define their own policy statement – to review internal procedures – to examine curriculum and course content – to consider the 'hidden curriculum' – to examine books and other resources – and so on. Without specific objectives of this sort, action can lack direction and focus. As well as the practical outcomes, the process of discussion and formulation can fulfil an invaluable training function in itself.

Books and resources

Many resource materials in current use tend to reinforce rather than challenge some of the prejudices which an equal opportunities policy should aim to eliminate. Arrangements should be made, therefore, to ensure their careful and sensitive examination against LEA guidelines. This process may be lengthy and potentially expensive since some existing material which cannot be used positively will probably need to be discarded. Nevertheless, it is a necessary and revealing exercise to see how much material in common circulation may condition thinking in terms of white, male superiority – to overlook the contributions which black people and women have made to humanity – to assume that disabled people are unintelligent and entirely incapable – and so on.

It will be a matter within the annual budget cycle to examine priorities and to consider the need for targeted additional or re-directed resources to achieve some of these objectives, recognising that much can be done by change of attitude, direction or emphasis.

Some resource may be at hand in the form of grant under Section 11 of the Local Government Act of 1966. Although it is administered increasingly stringently by the Home Office, Section 11 may allow LEAs to obtain 75 per cent grant on the salaries of staff employed for the benefit of people of Commonwealth origin with particular needs greater or different in kind from the indigenous population. While there are arguments to be made that Section 11 is itself a divisive provision, nevertheless it exists for the time being and may be a useful source of extra funds.

Monitoring

Finally, as with any policy, continuous monitoring must be undertaken in order to track the success or failure of the various developments which have been undertaken. Systems operated in conjunction with the particular disadvantaged groups concerned will be welcomed particularly and will provide the opportunity for joint policy review and development.

15 The administration of education in Wales

The framework of the system in Wales is identical with that of England. The work of Welsh administrators is governed by the same Acts, orders, regulations and circulars as that of their English counterparts. Welsh teachers are paid on the same scales and are eligible for employment in England. Indeed, in the past teachers trained in Wales have found posts in England in large numbers. The eight Welsh LEAs are members of the ACC. Students at Welsh schools and colleges take the same range of examinations as those provided for institutions in England.

However, within this common framework there are differences. The most significant is the teaching and use of the Welsh language. For more than a century the use of Welsh as a medium was rejected by educators on the questionable grounds that it had no economic value and that its use would impede acquisition of control of the English language. In the last few decades the use of Welsh, over and above the teaching of Welsh as a subject, has acquired educational respectability. Its use as a medium has been enthusiastically supported by an increasing number of parents who have successfully pressed LEAs to establish designated bilingual schools in the more anglicised areas. Designated Welsh-medium primary schools have proliferated and these have been followed by bilingual secondary schools, most of which have grown quickly. Simultaneously schools in the Welsh heartlands have made increasing use of Welsh. More than one in four of the secondary schools of Wales now make some use of Welsh as a medium for teaching other subject areas. In turn some Welsh-medium teaching has developed at colleges of further education and in the University of Wales.

Provision of bilingual education presents the administrato in Wales with problems which do not exist in England. These of course, include the greater cost of bilingual education. The additional expenditure attributable to bilingual education is difficult to quantify, and local authorities have been reluctant to accept provision in the form of specific grant, but the 1980 Education Act made provision for specific government support for the Welsh language in education, over and above Rate Support Grant. Modest assistance has been provided through this means to support the expansion in provision made by local education authorities and the large number of other agencies involved in promoting and supporting Welsh language education. In 1986 the Welsh Joint Education Committee, at the invitiation of the Welsh Office, set up a Welsh Language Education Development Committee, whose remit is to provide a forum for discussion of policy by those responsible for Welsh language education, to coordinate the work of the various agencies concerned and to disseminate information, and to identify areas for research and priorities for developmental work.

Two administrative agencies which are concerned with the general range of the education service and which are peculiar to Wales are the Welsh Joint Education Committee (WJEC) and the Welsh Office Education Department (WOED). In addition the Wales Advisory Body for Local Authority Higher Education has a special role in a more limited field.

The Welsh Joint Education Committee

In 1946, the Minister of Education, Ellen Wilkinson, set up a working party to review the administration of education in Wales. It found a fragmented system. The Central Welsh Board was firmly entrenched as an examining board which had served generations of secondary school pupils. The Federation of Education Committees (Wales and Monmouthshire) was the Welsh equivalent of the Association of Education Committees. Two Advisory Councils for Technical Education existed in splendid isolation, one in the north, the other in the south. Both were represented on the Welsh Academic Board of Technology.

The Minister accepted the working party's recommendations for creation of a new central organisation to serve the collective interests of LEAs in Wales and on 9 July 1948 the Order establishing the Welsh Joint Education Committee was sealed.

Initially the Joint Committee was concerned with the functions outlined in the following clauses.

Clause 12 (I) The appointing councils shall refer to the Joint Committee the following questions:

   (a) The co-ordination of the provision of special educational treatment of pupils who suffer from any disability of mind or body.

   (b) The availability of existing boarding facilities and the provision of boarding schools.

   (c) The provision of colleges of further education including in particular colleges of art and adult education.

   (d) The co-ordination of the provision of further education.

   (e) The co-ordination of facilities for recreation and social and physical training for persons receiving primary, secondary or further education, including the provision of camps.

   (f) The provision of agricultural education.

   (g) The curriculum of schools maintained by the appointing councils, with special reference to the teaching of the Welsh language and culture.

   (h) The provision of refresher courses for teachers and youth leaders.

   (i) The need for research for the purpose of improving the educational facilities provided for Wales and Monmouthshire.

   (j) Such other questions of common interest to the appointing councils as the councils may from time to time refer to the Joint Committee.

   (II) The Joint Committee shall be entitled to make recommendations to the appointing councils on any matter, whether referred to them or not, affecting education in Wales and Monmouthshire.

Clause 14 (a) As from 1 April 1949 the Joint Committee shall conduct such examinations of pupils in secondary schools as were conducted before the said date by the Central Welsh Board.

   (b) The Joint Committee may conduct

examinations of pupils in institutions of further education.

Forty years have passed since those functions were identified. In that period constitutional developments have taken place, economic crises have curtailed action and educational thinking has changed direction more than once. The WJEC now engages in four broad areas of work: examinations, further and advanced further education, support of the Welsh language in education, and operating as an association of LEAs.

1. *Examinations*   The WJEC has been the only board in England and Wales charged with the responsibility of examining both for CSE, GCE 'O' and 'A' Levels and in the field of technical education. It was the constitutional inheritor of the Central Welsh Board system and could therefore be the only body to assume responsibility for GCE in 1951. It was essentially an LEA board and therefore was the natural body to undertake examining for CSE in 1965.

The General Certificate of Secondary Education has now replaced the GCE 'O' Level and the CSE. The WJEC is one of the examining groups for England and Wales. It is the smallest of them, but has the advantages not only of continuity of personnel and of relationships with schools and colleges but also of previous experience with both GCE and CSE and with pilot developmental work for the new examination.

Technical examinations had also been attributed to it by the 1947 working party. In 1962, the WJEC joined the other six technical examining bodies in England to form the Council of Technical Examining Bodies. In 1965, the seven bodies negotiated a Concordat which defined the field of examination in which each would function. At the same time each agreed to accept, as equivalent for all purposes, the certificates awarded by the others for their corresponding examinations.

The WJEC is a comparatively small agency in the field of vocational examinations as it is for GCSE and 'A' Level. It has therefore negotiated with larger examining bodies in order to be able more economically to sustain a wide range of activity. It will collaborate with the Northern Examining Association to extend its provision for GCSE, with the Joint Matriculation Board in regard to AS Level and with the City and Guilds of London

Institute and the Royal Society of Arts to mount a greater variety of techical examinations.

Over recent years a Certificate of Education, catering for the lower end of the ability range, has been developed to reflect a range of courses originally pioneered by one authority but now in widespread use in all authorities of Wales. The WJEC has also been engaged in developmental work in regard to records of achievement within its eight constituent authorities and to assessment of on-the-job and off-the-job training.

2. *Further and advanced further education* The WJEC is the Regional Advisory Council for Further Education for Wales and as such has the same advisory and co-ordinating functions as the nine advisory Councils in England. It is involved in the system of approvals for new courses, and, with the Manpower Services Commission, in promotion of development plans for non-advanced further education. The main thrust of its work is provision of a wide range of in-service courses for teachers of both advanced and non-advanced work, initiation and conduct of a number of projects to assist colleges to meet developments of industry and technological advances, and co-ordination of the work of agencies operating in the adult and youth fields and promotion of training for their personnel. It is concerned in development of new provision such as courses of retraining for a range of industries and for the adult unemployed. As part of its role in information-giving it is concerned to develop computerised data bases on non-advanced courses and computerised referral systems for adult enquirers. It has developed, and oversees arrangements for, forms of training for qualified teacher status for serving teachers of further and adult education.

Within the resources voted to it by the constituent LEAs the Joint Committee also engages in a range of activity on behalf of the schools as well as the colleges of the eight authorities It houses the Microelectronics Education Unit for Wales, i administers the National Youth Orchestra and the Nationa Youth Theatre of Wales, and its Regional Curriculum Base promotes a range of curriculum developments for schools and colleges and conducts related staff development.

3. *Teaching and use of Welsh* The contribution made by th

WJEC to use of the Welsh language in education has grown over the years. In 1968 it established the National Language Unit at Pontypridd. With the aid of working groups of teachers the Unit has produced courses and other teaching materials for primary, secondary and adult levels. Its officers make a substantial contribution to the in-service training programmes of the authorities. It arranges residential courses for sixth formers. It also carries out work in support of the teaching of modern languages and English in Wales. The large number of agencies which contribute to the teaching of Welsh to adults are brought together by the WJEC to consider ways of complementing one another's efforts and of meeting needs for materials and training.

Publishers in Wales are faced with the problem of a limited market. The WJEC has been involved in production of Welsh reading books for children and of course books for the different areas of the curriculum. It attends to editing and to other aspects of quality of production. Its schemes guarantee publishers a minimum sale in order to make publication of each of the books sponsored economically viable. Because of the lack of commercial incentive these schemes have been over the years a principal means of infusing new materials for Welsh language work in schools.

4. *Association of LEAs* The policy committees of the WJEC are forums at which major issues are discussed and the views of the eight authorities crystallised for submission to the Secretary of State. Unlike the two large local authority associations, the ACC and the AMA, the WJEC exercises functions only in the educational field and is an independent body without a constitutional link with the Welsh Counties Committee.

It is concerned to support and facilitate in regard to issues which authorities in Wales would find it advantageous to consider together. To this end not only has it arranged meetings and seminars for Chairmen, Chief Education Officers and deputies but it has increasingly brought together the authorities' officers concerned with policy for and management of various aspects of the service such as further education officers, advisers for Welsh, adult and youth officers, co-ordinators of in-service training, Chief Advisers, officers responsible for special education.

The Joint Committee exerts its influence, too, in other ways. In particular it has representation on many bodies. No major public body in Wales is without someone from the WJEC on its committees. Examples which illustrate the range are the National Library, National Museum, Welsh Books Council, University of Wales and its constituent colleges, Welsh Arts Council, School Curriculum Development Committee, Sports Council, BBC Schools Broadcasting Council, Christian Education Movement.

Representation is not confined to Wales. Members or officers participate in discussions at Elizabeth House, the National Employees' Organisation, Soulbury, City and Guilds, National Foundation for Educational Research, the Joint Standing Committee of Vice-Chancellors, Manpower Services Commission, Joint Councils of the Examining Boards, the LEA Associations, the Royal Society of Arts and many other bodies.

The Joint Committee consists of 116 members, 84 of these being county councillors and 32 being co-opted members representing educational and industrial interests in Wales. The Joint Committee meets three times a year to receive the reports of the following standing committees: Local Authorities, Finance, Establishment and General Purposes, Examinations, Further and Higher Education, Technical Examinations, Special Services, Welsh Language and Culture. The first three are composed of representative members only and deal with matters of policy and finance. The others comprise a mixture of councillors, added members and teachers. On the examination committees the teachers enjoy a majority. The panels which advise the committees consist almost entirely of practising teachers. A balance is maintained between democratic control and professional contribution.

Wales Advisory Body for Local Authority Higher Education

Higher education provision in the local authority sector, referred to as Advanced Further Education (AFE), is funded through an inter-county Pool – the AFE Pool – determined each year by the Secretary of State. Distribution of the resources from the AFE Pool is made by adjustments to the counties' rate support grant provision. The Secretary of State relates the AFE Pool allocation for each county to the number of students on AFE courses at the colleges in each county.

In the early 1980s the need was seen for AFE provision to

be planned on an all Wales basis. A new body, WAB, was established in 1983 to undertake this planning task. Since then it has advised the Secretary of State on the provision of AFE courses and student numbers in the colleges, on the approval of new AFE courses and on the distribution of the AFE Pool. WAB provides advice on matters affecting higher education in the local authority sector and has co-operated with the UGC and the University of Wales on matters of common interest to the two sectors.

The Welsh Office Education Department

Ministerial responsibility for education in Wales, other than for universities and a few other matters, rests with the Secretary of State for Wales whose duty it is to promote the education of the people of Wales and the progressive development of institutions devoted to that purpose, and to secure the effective execution by local authorities under his control and direction of the national policy for providing a varied and comprehensive educational service in every area (Education Act 1944). The Welsh Office, as the government department of the Principality, occupies a broadly similar position with regard to non-university education to that of the DES in England.

As a government department the Welsh Office dates from 1964 but the history of administrative devolution dates from 1907 when a Welsh department was located in the Board of Education.

Whereas WOED's responsibilities for the maintained sector in Wales are broadly the same as those of the Department of Education and Science in England, with which there is close collaboration, there are some distinctive features of education in Wales, notably bilingual provision for which the Welsh Office has sole responsibility. In both England and Wales direct control of schools and colleges rests, in the maintained sector, with the local education authorities who are responsible for funding, employment of staff and organisation of provision. The Secretary of State supports this provision through Rate Support Grant and specific grants by means of which the Secretary of State directs the allocation of funds for in-service training of teachers (INSET) and for a number of initiatives supported on a pump-priming basis. WOED is also directly responsible for funding educational provision outside the maintained sector.

WOED is primarily concerned with policy matters and has statutory responsibilities in respect of school curriculum and other organisation proposals, appellate functions in the areas of special education and needs and powers of direction in cases of unreasonable behaviour or a failure of duty. Another major area is the development of the Welsh language as a medium. An official in WOED acts as the Registrar of Independent Schools in Wales and has the responsibility of registering and maintaining standards at such establishments. The Department also has the duty of deciding whether certain independent schools are suitable for the admission of pupils with special educational needs.

WOED has been able to develop close relations with others working in the education field in Wales. Ministers consult regularly with the Welsh Joint Education Committee and the Wales Advisory Board. The small number of LEAs in Wales make it possible for meetings with officers of the LEAs, WJEC and WAB to take place frequently.

The primary duty of HM Inspectors in Wales is to advise the Secretary of State for Wales on educational provision in Wales and the performance of the system nationally. They do this on the basis of the formal inspections they carry out and their general knowledge of educational practice acquired through other inspection visits. They write reports on the institutions and aspects of practice which they formally inspect and also produce a range of other publications, all based on inspections, on matters of current educational interest and concerns. They have a particular duty to advise the Secretary of State on provision for the teaching of, and through the medium of, Welsh. HMIs' assessments influence the formation of policy and provide indications as to how effectively it is being implemented. HMI also maintain close contact with LEAs, with national bodies such as WJEC and WAB, and with a range of voluntary organisations active in education. They run a small number of short courses of INSET for teachers and of invitation conferences on major issues for practitioners and others involved in the educational system.

16 Administrative considerations arising from the Scottish educational system

O wad some Power the giftie gie us
To see oursels as others see us!   R. Burns

The role of the Education Officer is similar in all parts of the United Kingdom and there is, in consequence, considerable scope for career mobility in this sector of the education service. The similarity derives from the fact that, in all parts of the United Kingdom, the provision of public education rests on a partnership between central and local government. The role of the Education Officer is to advise the education authority on policies and to ensure that their policies are carried out. Education authorities operate within a legislative framework, and the differences in the role of the Education Officer in Scotland derive mainly from the different legislative framework in Scotland.

Like his counterpart in England and Wales, the Education Officer in Scotland has traditionally been a public figure of some standing in the community he serves. Discriminating critics have recognised the influence he can bring to the direction of the education service. In his book *Scottish and English Schools – A Comparative Survey of the past Fifty Years* G.S. Osborne quotes the Buchan poet, J.C. Milne, who earned his bread and butter first as a lecturer in logic at Aberdeen University, subsequently as the headmaster of a primary school and latterly as Principal Master of Method at Aberdeen College of Education. Milne gave this doubtful piece of vocational guidance to the lads and lasses o' pairts in the North East:

O dinna tak' to teaching, Ye clivver loons and quines.
Ye'll only haul the ploo-stilts, While Directors grip the rines.

It is a matter of debate and dispute as to the extent that the

Director of Education does hold the reins of the education service. A favourite theme of latter-day educational historians and commentators in the media has been the power struggle which has gone on for the control and direction of the public education service since it began in the 1870s. Administrators, head teachers, politicians, inspectors, teachers' organisations, the universities, the colleges of education, employers, parents and other interest groups have all had a hand in the struggle. The Manpower Services Commission is the latest organisation to have thrown its hat into the ring.

The Secretary of State for Scotland, who is a Cabinet Minister, is responsible to Parliament for the overall control and development of the education service in Scotland apart from the Scottish universities. Their funding, like that of the other United Kingdom universities, is the responsibility of the Secretary of State for Education and Science, working through the University Grants Committee. The Secretary of State for Scotland exercises his educational powers through the Scottish Education Department. The Scottish Office has personnel in both Edinburgh and London. The actual provision of public sector school and further education is the responsibility of the nine regional and three islands councils which are the education authorities.

The most significant event in the recent history of educational administration in Scotland was in 1975 when the 430 Scottish local authorities were reorganised into a two-tier system of nine regional and 53 district authorities with three all-purpose island authorities. The nine regional and three islands councils became the education authorities. They took over from the 35 previous education authorities in May 1975 after working for a year in double harness with them.

The estimated population of the education authorities in 1988 and their area is as follows:

Education authority	Estimated population	Land area (km²)
Strathclyde	2,332,537	13,537
Lothian	743,700	1,755
Grampian	502,863	8,704
Tayside	393,762	7,503
Fife	344,590	1,307
Central	272,077	2,632
Highland	200,608	25,389
Dumfries & Galloway	147,036	6,370
Borders	102,141	4,672
Western Isles	31,048	2,898
Shetland	22,429	1,429
Orkney	19,338	976
Scotland	5,112,129	77,171

Source: Registrar General - Scotland

Preparation and planning for local government reorganisation had been going on since the publication of a White Paper in February 1971. This White Paper was itself the outcome of consultation on the Report of the Royal Commission on Local Government in Scotland 1966–69, whose chairman was the Rt. Hon. Lord Wheatley. The Wheatley Report had criticised local government in Scotland for being fragmented and lacking coherent policies. 'There is unity in the parts,' said the Report, 'but disunity in the whole.' The aims of reorganised local government should be to create a powerful and effective system of democratic local government with popular involvement and provide strong, efficient public services. The hope was expressed that departmentalism would be replaced by corporate management and that local government in future would exhibit a total and coherent concern for the whole social and economic life of the community. The major departure that the Government made from the Wheatley recommendations in their White Paper was to give the housing function to the districts and not to the regional authorities. The primary role of the new regional authorities would be as strategic planning authorities. A working group appointed by the Scottish Local Authority Associations under the chairmanship of Mr. I.V. Paterson, County Clerk of

Lanarkshire, set out recommended patterns of organisations and management structures for the new Scottish local authorities, with a Policy and Resources Committee taking the major policy decisions of the new councils and a Chief Executive heading a Board of Chief Officers. The Paterson Report was the Scottish equivalent of the Bains Report. There have been recent indications that the Government may be prepared to consider another reorganisation of local government.

The main piece of legislation which deals with the education service in its local government context is the Local Government (Scotland) Act of 1973. This Act requires the appointment of an Education Committee which includes three church representatives and at least two teacher representatives. Education Committees lost their previously held statutorily delegated powers but educational matters stand referred to them. The Act empowers authorities to arrange for the discharge of their functions by committees, sub-committees, boards of management or officials. Each education authority devises its own internal framework of delegation and reference and sets it out in its standing orders.

It was part of the new strategy to give much greater weight to public participation in policy planning and the management of public services. Under Section 125 of the Local Government (Scotland) Act education authorities are required to appoint school and college councils to discharge such functions of management and supervision of establishments as the authority determines. Though there had been a tradition of College Councils in Scotland before local government reorganisation, there had not been the same tradition of managing and governing bodies for State schools in Scotland as there has been for the maintained schools in England and Wales. School councils include parent, teacher and church representatives and most include pupils. Further education college councils include representatives from local industry and commerce as well as staff and students. The normal pattern which has emerged in Scotland is that school councils are appointed for a group of schools comprising a secondary school and its feeder primary schools. Education authorities have tended not to delegate many functions to them. Some authorities involve school councils in non-teaching appointments but few involve them in teaching appointments. School councils tend to carry out functions such as the letting of schools and dealing with attendance problems;

they are proving perhaps most helpful in a consultative and advisory role. Regional councillors and officers use them as sounding boards of local opinion. There has been pressure from school councillors themselves to be given more say in determining the aims and goals of the school, and to be concerned with resource allocation and budgetary matters. So far, education authorities have tended to be more generous in their reference and delegation to further education college councils, who generally advise education committees on resource allocation, annual budgets and staff appointments. During 1987 the Government issued a consultative paper about the introduction of School Boards. This provoked considerable reaction and while the principle of greater parental involvement was unanimously agreed there was virtual unanimous rejection of some of the proposals. Even parents' representatives opposed the concept of parents being given wide ranging executive responsibility. The eventual legislation, the School Boards (Scotland) Act, 1988 creates a separate Board for most schools with a relatively small number of members but with a majority of parents. Initially the powers of Boards will be more extensive than those of School Councils but less than envisaged in the consultative paper. It is clear, however, that it is intended to increase the powers at a later date.

In the post-war period the Scottish Education Acts were consolidated in 1946, again in 1962 and yet again in 1980 and the Education (Scotland) Act 1980 contains the main body of legislation on Scottish education now current. Section 1 required that every education authority secure that there is made for their area adequate and efficient provision of school education and further education. The concept of school education includes provision for children aged three to five in nursery schools or nursery classes but the Act makes it clear that the provision of nursery schools and classes is a power and not a duty. Under Section 78 of the Act the education authority is required to employ a Director of Education who shall be 'the Chief Eduation Officer of the authority and shall hold office on such reasonable terms and conditions including conditions as to remuneration as the authority appointing him think fit'. The Secretary of State for Scotland has powers to make regulations prescribing the standards and general requirements to which every education authority shall conform in discharging their functions. In this connection the Scots have always been prepared to accept a much greater measure of central direction of their education service than their fellow Britons; and, to this extent, the Scottish system corresponds more closely to most continental systems. One significant difference between the Scottish and English Education Acts is that the Scottish Acts deem school and further education to include 'the teaching of Gaelic in Gaelic-speaking areas'.

Section 28 of the principal Act requires the Secretary of State and the education authorities to have regard in the exercise and performance of their powers and duties to the general principle that so far as is compatible with the provision of suitable instruction and training and the avoidance of unreasonable public expenditure, pupils are to be educated in accordance with the wishes of their parents. The rights of parents were substantially extended by the Education (Scotland) Act of 1981. This was the so-called 'Parents Charter' which amended the 1980 Act and gave parents much wider choice of schools for their children with an appeals procedure culminating if necessary in an appeal to the sheriff if the education authority refused to meet their placing request. The 1981 Act also made new arrangements for dealing with children with special educational needs. The former categories of children with special educational needs were abolished and records based on multi-disciplinary assessment were created for children with pronounced, specific or complex special educational needs. These recorded decisions have to be reviewed at fixed intervals. There is also an appeals mechanism in relation to recorded children and young people and to children who have been excluded from school. Authorities are required under the 1981 Act to undertake consultation with the public if they propose closing or changing the arrangements for a school, but the Secretary of State's control over most school closures was removed. The exceptions were Roman Catholic schools and schools where travel to the new school would be over five miles. A feature of the 1981 Act has been the extent to which the Secretary of State has felt it necessary to make detailed regulations describing the requirements to which every education authority shall confirm in discharging their functions under particular sections of the Act. The Education (Publication and Consultation etc.) (Scotland) Regulations 1981 prescribed the kinds of proposals which required consultation and the individuals and groups to be consulted. Amended Regulations were issued in 1987 after consultations with various interests.

In 1988 further amendments were issued hurriedly and without any consultation. The latter introduced the concept that when a school is more than 80 per cent full any proposal to change its status has to be referred to the Secretary of State. Whatever the reasons for this change the effect has been to reintroduce a large measure of control by the Secretary of State which he had relinquished in 1981.

Six education authorities - Strathclyde, Lothian, Grampian, Tayside, Highlands, and Dumfries and Galloway - established sub-regional functions in 1975. Some have already changed these arrangements while others are reviewing them. At regional level needs are assessed, policies formulated, provision planned and its implementation monitored. Where a sub-regional structure exists, administrative staff at this level are concerned mainly with executive functions, the details of staffing and supervision of educational establishments and resource allocation to them. Decisions are taken within a framework of policies agreed at regional level. For most Education Officers career satisfaction comes when they are involved in policy planning, advising the education committee and executing their policies. The larger authorities are still grappling with the problem of how career satisfaction can be ensured for officers who do not have a role in all these aspects of the education authority's work.

Policy planning is a function that is being given more conscious thought than before local government reorganisation. In 1975 the Secretary of State for Scotland issued a direction under Section 173 of the Local Government (Scotland) Act of 1973 requiring each of the Scottish Regional Authorities to prepare a Regional Report. The aim was to provide a framework of key information about the region. It would relate to population, their distribution in settlements, how they were employed, what natural resources were available and what public services were provided. The Regional Report would identify the main problems and issues facing the region. It would set out immediate and longer term policy matters and enable spending priorities to be settled in a coherent way. The district authorities were to be consulted in the preparation of the Regional Report; and, following its submission to him, the Secretary of State for Scotland would respond. The preparation of the Regional Report gave each local authority programming department, including education departments, an opportunity to describe the current situation, to review objectives, to articulate needs and to make recommendations for future development.

The Regional Report is essentially a policy planning document which reflects the corporate approach to local authority provision recommended in the Wheatley and Paterson Reports. As a corollary to it, new budgeting systems were introduced. The system of annual revenue budgets would appear to be much the same as used in England and Wales. The economic crisis of 1975 encouraged the Government to compel local authorities to abandon the old style political budgets, whereby annual estimates were prepared by service committees on the basis of perceived need and justified by advocacy. The new style budget is the economic budget in which upper expenditure limits are often fixed by Finance or Policy and Resources Committees on what is thought can be afforded. Central government at the time of fixing the Rate Support Grant gives indicative upper expenditure limits to each local authority. The Annual Public Expenditure White Paper published in January of each year since 1975 gives separate expenditure indicators for local authority services in Scotland at survey prices for the previous November. Revenue estimates at prices obtaining at November are prepared at the turn of the year for the financial year beginning the following April and a contingency allowance is made for inflation during the course of the financial year.

Policy proposals for capital expenditure are related to a new system of financial planning set out in Scottish Finance Department Circular 47/1976. Approval of building projects is no longer given by the Scottish Education Department on a 'starts' basis. Each authority is given a fixed allocation for building programmes with at present only a 5 per cent permitted carry-over of funds from year to year. Despite attempts by some authorities to increase the funds available by covenanting, the Secretary of State has introduced progressively greater controls over local authorities' total capital expenditure but has allowed greater freedom of allocation within the total available to each authority and has disengaged from the more detailed scrutiny of building activities. Chief Officers of service departments like education are now much more dependent on the skills of project planners. It has also been part of Government economic policy to reduce the public sector borrowing requirement, and considerably smaller amounts of capital expenditure are now available annually.

Certain fundamental values and concepts underpin the school and further education system in Scotland. Under Section 71 of the Education (Scotland) Act of 1981 an Advisory Council may be established to advise the Secretary of State for Scotland on educational matters. A generation ago towards the end of the Second World War the Advisory Council took stock of education in Scotland and reviewed its way and purpose in three separate reports on primary, secondary and further education. These reports have been very influential and though some of what they had to say is now out of date, much of what they said is still relevant. During the years 1946–52 the Advisory Council sought to see education in Scotland within its social, cultural and economic framework, not as an isolated professional activity or as a body of techniques but 'primarily as the energising of a society consciously striving to preserve and enrich its inheritance amid changed and changing conditions'. The Advisory Council was conscious throughout of the unity and continuity of the educational process from nursery school to adult education. It articulated the aim of education as 'to foster the full and harmonious development of the individual' but went on to claim that an individual can only develop to his full stature through the society of which is he a member.

Deriving from this the most important part of the Caledonian educational system is seen as the point of contact between client and field worker, be they pupil and teacher, student and lecturer or club member and youth leader. It is here that relationships are established and the curriculum transmitted. Scots tend now to use the word 'curriculum' to mean all the activities planned and organised by the institution; and each institution will have its formal, informal and hidden curriculum. The formal school curriculum consists of courses, normally, in Scotland, subject-related, organised within the timetable of the school. It links with the informal curriculum which may infiltrate the timetable but may be carried on outwith the school timetable and in part at least outwith the school day. Both the formal and informal curriculum take place within the context of the 'hidden' curriculum which relates to the ethos, code of discipline, standards of behaviour, attitudes and values which obtain within the school or college; what is caught, rather than what is taught.

Closely associated with the curriculum are pedagogy, assessment and certification. Most Scots place considerable value on them but the radical school reform movement in Scotland led by notable educationalists like A. S. Neill and R. F. Mackenzie have claimed that excessive emphasis over the years on formal curricula, examinations and classroom teaching have not been conducive to the full and harmonious development of individual pupils in a free society. They were particularly critical of the continuing, even if much diminished, use of the tawse in Scottish classrooms. The Secretary of State for Scotland asked education authorities to discontinue the use of corporal punishment in schools by the end of session 1983/84. In common with authorities in England and Wales the Technical and Vocational Initiative has been piloted and is now fully developed in a number of areas.

The Secretary of State for Scotland has not in recent years used his power under Section 71 of the Education (Scotland) Act to establish an Advisory Council. Instead, he has, from time to time, appointed committees with remits to advise him on various aspects of education. The most important of these is the Consultative Committee on the Curriculum which was set up in 1965 to advise the Secretary of State on all matters concerning the school curriculum. The Scottish Education Department recently undertook a major review of the CCC. As a result the structure of the organisation has been considerably changed and its detailed remits altered. The CCC has established a range of working parties and published many papers over the years. For example, in 1971 there was a report on nursery school provision entitled 'Before Five'. It appraised the best practices in nursery schools and classes and commented on the principles on which pre-school education should be based. Advice was given not only on the curriculum of the nursery school or class but also on staffing and buildings.

The publication which has had most influence on the development of primary education in Scotland in recent years, however, was a memorandum published in 1965 called 'Primary Education in Scotland'. It was prepared by a committee representative of the teaching profession, the Colleges of Education and Her Majesty's Inspectors of Schools. Its purpose too was to provide an up-to-date appraisal of the best practices in primary schools in Scotland and of the principles on which in the view of those most closely associated with its development primary education should be based. 'Primary Education in Scotland' struck a balance between traditionalism and radical change. It gave prominence to the notion that the primary school child learns best to think by doing things:

I hear and I forget,
I see and I remember,
I do and it becomes part of me.

Teachers were enjoined to reject what they could no longer justify, particularly much of the formal and repetitive work in English and Arithmetic. They were encouraged to look more broadly at the curriculum. A suggested time allocation was introduced: roughly one-third to language and arts, one-third to environmental studies including mathematics, and one-third to artistic, aesthetic, moral, social and health education. The serried rows of desks disappeared gradually from Scottish classrooms; there was more activity and discovery, more pupil learning and less teacher teaching; resource and library areas made their appearance; the use of TV sets, tape recorders and other teaching aids became more widespread; there was more staff consultation and more team teaching; non-teaching staff were appointed to undertake non-teaching tasks; parents were more in evidence in schools. HMIs make progress reports on the development of primary education since the publication of the 1965 memorandum. There have been two influential progress reports, one on 'Children with Learning Difficulties' and the other on 'Pupils in Primary IV and Primary VII'.

Pupils in Scotland normally transfer to secondary school a year later than in England. Organisationally, separate infant schools are much less common in Scotland than in England; and secondary schools, unless in sparsely populated areas, are normally six-year comprehensive schools. There has never been the opposition to comprehensive secondary education in Scotland that there has been in England, since the traditional Scottish secondary school was the multilateral or omnibus school. There is not the same variety of secondary schools in Scotland as in England. The middle school and the sixth year college have not caught on here. Secondary schools are organised in three phases. In the first two years S1 and S2 classes are normally taught in mixed ability groups and are 'set' by ability for different subjects at the end of S2. S3 and S4 take pupils up to the statutory leaving age and to the first batch of public examinations at Scottish Certificate of Education, Ordinary grade and, increasingly, its replacement, Standard Grade. The SCE 'O' grade examination was changed from a pass/fail examination to a banded examination like GCE 'O' level in 1973. Awards are made on a subject basis and are banded A to E with A to C equivalent to the former pass. The Government has in hand the implementation of a development programme for the reform of curriculum and assessment in S3 and S4, deriving from the Munn and Dunning Reports. The SCE 'O' grade is being replaced by the SCE Standard grade with courses at Foundation, General and Credit level assessed on a seven point scale by grade related criteria. At the end of S5 pupils take the SCE at Higher grade which is the normal standard for entrance to university and higher education in Scotland. At the end of S6 there is an opportunity to take the Certificate of Sixth Year Studies. The Scottish Sixth Year is looked upon as a preparatory year for Higher Education and the CSYS includes in addition to a formal syllabus an opportunity for independent work recorded in an enquiry, dissertation or project. The Government has also in hand the implementation of an Action Plan published in January 1983 for the 16 to 18 year-olds. The Plan is being implemented both in schools and Further Education Colleges. Its main feature is the development of new courses based on a collection of learning units of 'modules', usually of 40 hours study. The first modules were ready for teaching in colleges and schools in 1984/85. The 16–18 Action Plan also proposes a new 16–18 certificate listing modules successfully completed whether in school or college. These modules are revisions of courses developed by the Scottish Business Education Council (SCOTBEC) and the Scottish Technical Education Council (SCOTEC). These two bodies were merged in January 1984 into a single Council, the Scottish Vocational Education Council (SCOTVEC). The SCE Higher Grade syllabus is being revised and changes will be introduced progressively. It will be for consideration whether the process of bringing awards into a single certificate should be extended to include all forms of academic and vocational awards for the 16–18 group and whether there also needs to be some fundamental change in the relationship between Higher Grade and CSYS. Teacher training arrangements are different in the two countries.

Colleges of education in Scotland are not run by local authorities; like that other part of the non-university higher education sector, the Central Institutions, the colleges of education have their own Boards of Governors and are funded directly by the Scottish Education Department. The Association of Directors of Education in Scotland appoints members of the Directorate to serve on College of Education Governing Bodies.

A unique feature of the Scottish system is the General Teaching Council which was constituted in February 1966 in terms of the Teaching Council (Scotland) Act 1965. Its functions are to keep under review the standards of entry to training, to make recommendations on supply, to keep itself informed of the nature of instruction given in colleges of education, to keep a register of qualified teachers and to determine whether registration is to be withdrawn or refused. Teachers elected by their colleagues are in a majority on the council. Three Directors of Education are among the appointed members. All teachers holding permanent posts in school education must be registered with the General Teaching Council. This condition does not yet apply to further education teachers.

Teachers' salaries and conditions of service in Scotland are negotiated in two committees set up by Section 14 of the Education (Scotland) Act of 1981. One committee deals with teachers employed in school education and the other with lecturers in further and non-university higher education, although the Government has given notice it intends to abolish the latter committee. Teachers, local authorities and the Secretary of State are represented on the first committee; the second includes, in addition, representatives of lecturers and of the governing bodies of the Central Institutions and the Colleges of Education. There is provision for arbitration in the event of the committees failing to agree settlements and awards.

The Scottish Teachers Service Conditions Committee which existed prior to the 1981 Act went some way to providing national conditions of service for Scottish teachers and lecturers. In schools, for example, there is a normal working week of 35 hours. In primary schools there is a maximum of 25 hours class contact time and in secondary schools a maximum of $23\frac{1}{2}$ hours. The normal maximum class size in primary schools is 33. For practical classes in secondary schools the normal maximum size is 20.

This committee has drawn up models for settling grievances, and established model disciplinary procedures.

The promoted post structure in Scotland schools is more uniform than in England. In primary schools there are only three grades of promoted post, the head teacher, deputy head teacher and the assistant head teacher. The secondary school promoted post structure is more elaborate and has seven grades. It differs from the English arrangements in that any teacher who receives a responsibility payment always has duties in addition to classroom teaching. A large secondary school will have a head teacher, a deputy head teacher, one or more assistant head teachers, principal teachers if the departments are sufficiently large, and principal and assistant principal teachers of guidance. Thus, promoted staff in Scottish secondary schools have, in addition to their teaching duties, responsibilities in the areas of policy, administration, curriculum development, social education, vocational guidance, personal guidance and leisure activities. New patterns of school organisation were published as a discussion paper in February 1971 in a memorandum entitled 'The Structure of Promoted Posts in Secondary Schools in Scotland'. It accompanied SED Circular No. 780.

The problem of what constitutes an adequate complement of teaching staff for a school has exercised the Scots over the past decade. Guidance on staffing standards in primary and secondary schools was given in SED Circular No. 1072 dated 25 August 1981. In the agreement reached on teachers' pay and conditions in January 1987, following the Report of the Main Committee, the Secretary of State agreed that current staffing needs and their resource implications should be reviewed. This review was completed early in 1988. Its conclusions produced considerable changes in the method of calculating staffing requirements. Planned financial provision for primary teachers in 1988/89 was sufficient to support the basic complements in Circular 1029 plus an addition of 8.2 per cent. In reality most authorities were staffed to a much higher level, the cost being met by rateborne expenditure. The new formula is supposed to take account of the number of classes needed, the time required by promoted staff to carry out management and other non-teaching responsibilities, the time needed for visiting specialists or learning support staff and short term absence cover. It is expressed as follows:

Pupil roll	Teachers (FTE)
Up to 19	1.2
20 – 150	1.5 + 0.39 × pupil roll
Above 150	1.67 + 0.0377 × pupil roll

The number of teachers (FTE) derived from the application of this formula is augmented by a 'flexibility' addition of 6 per cent to allow for the staff resources needed to provide, for example, for secondments of serving teachers to curriculum development at national and authority level, and the release of teachers for programmes of staff development.

A great deal of work was done in Scotland in the early 1970s on teaching staff standards in secondary schools and the timetabling of secondary schools. A comprehensive investigation was carried out by the Scottish Education Department into the organisation and staffing of secondary schools in Scotland with the primary aim of establishing more objective criteria than had hitherto existed for assessing staffing requirements. The investigation had two parts. First of all there was a factual enquiry into the organisation and staffing of all education authority and grant-aided secondary schools in Scotland at January 1970. Secondly, theoretical studies of staffing requirements were carried out using modelling techniques. These studies are set out in a three-volume staffing survey published in 1972 and they were followed by a report which set out the proposals for new staffing standards as guidance. This report, pillar box red in colour and entitled 'Secondary School Staffing', was published in 1973. The Red Book, as it is known to every Scottish secondary teacher, gave tables for ascertaining the staffing complement of different sizes of schools. For 1988/89 the financial provision made for the cost of secondary teachers was sufficient to allow for Red Book complements plus an addition of 6.8 per cent. Many authorities were staffed to a higher level. The new formula is supposed to provide for what SED calls, but does not describe in detail, recognised curricular assumptions such as the breadth of subject choice appropriate for pupils in S3/S4 and for FTE pupils/students (including adults) in S5 and S6. It is also supposed to take account of staffing needed for smaller practical classes; support for pupils with learning difficulties, etc. The basic formula is:

Teachers (FTE) = 10.24 + 0.059 × pupil roll and incorporates an allowance for non-class contact time for promoted posts calculated as follows:

Promoted post time = 2.05 + 0.0046 × pupil roll.

Less central guidance is available on establishments of non-teaching and ancillary staffs in schools. Two working parties were set up at the end of 1972 to consider the need for ancillary staff and other non-teaching staff in secondary schools. The working party chaired by Principal Ruthven of Moray House College of Education considered what level of administrative and clerical staff, technicians and auxiliaries required to be provided in secondary schools and concluded that a reasonable level of provision of these three categories of ancillary staff in relation to school roll was a ratio of 1:80. The non-teaching staff in secondary schools which came under the scrutiny of a working party chaired by Principal Stimpson of Dundee College of Education were youth and community workers, librarians and instructors. The working party took the view that the person best equipped to give tuition in any subject whether part of the formal curriculum or informal curriculum is the qualified teacher, but, until there is an adequate supply of qualified teachers of instrumental music, they conceded that a period would have to elapse during which instrumental instructors without teaching qualifications would be employed. They also gave qualified approval for a limited period of temporary posts of swimming instructors and dance instructors. They recognised that qualified youth and community workers and qualified librarians could have an important role in a secondary school, provided their activities were clearly defined and acceptable to them, to the head teacher and to members of the school staff whose interests might be affected by their activities. It was the working party's view that a qualified librarian should be appointed to the professional staff of each secondary school with more than 600 pupils. He should operate from a library/resources centre. The reports on non-teaching and ancillary staff in schools were published in 1976 at a time when there was substantial reduction of educational expenditure. It is clear that their full implementation will have to wait until the economic climate is more favourable.

As in England and Wales, each education authority has a cadre of support staff to schools, though the scale and scope of support services vary widely depending on the size of the authority. Only the largest authorities have a comprehensive support system; and some small authorities have very few advisers. Unlike England and Wales, Scotland has no education authority inspectors – only education authority advisers. Curriculum development and in-service training are seen in Scotland as the major roles of education authority advisers, who have close links in this work with the colleges of education and with HM Inspectors. They also advise on the design of educational premises, the choice of supplies and resources, the selection, deployment and utilisation of staff and the solution of management and timetabling problems.

The Child Guidance Service became mandatory by the 1969 Education (Scotland) Act and its provision was embodied in Section 4 of the Education (Scotland) Act of 1980. This Act also sets out the functions of the service – the study of handicapped, backward and difficult children, giving advice on educational methods and assessment to teachers, and counselling parents and Social Work Department staff. There are some differences, mainly historical, in the practice of educational psychology in Scotland and in England. Whereas in England there was for a long time a dual system with a medically dominated Child Guidance Service in which educational psychologists played a part and a separate School Psychological Service, in Scotland there has only been one service which grew up as an integral part of the education service. Educational psychologists in Scotland already undertake most of the duties ascribed in the Warnock Report to the advisory and support service, with the exception of curriculum development. Following the Disabled Persons (Services Consultation and Representation) Act 1986, the name was changed to the Regional Psychological Service.

There are considerable variations within education authorities in Scotland in the provision of school welfare and attendance services. Most authorities employ attendance officers. A few use school-based educational social workers employed either directly by education departments or in association with social work departments.

The Careers Service and the School Health Service are broadly similar in Scotland to those in England and Wales. Both these services derive their powers from United Kingdom legislation. In the case of Careers Officers, this is the Employment and Training Act of 1973 and legislation is now embodied in Sections

126 and 128 of the Education (Scotland) Act of 1980. Careers Officers are an integral part of education departments and participate with secondary school guidance teachers in careers programmes for all pupils. This starts in S1 and S2 with an introductory talk on careers guidance and the importance of the educational choices to be made at the end of S2. There follows throughout the pupil's secondary course an attempt to broaden his awareness of himself and the world of work, and more specific study of careers and jobs and further and higher education courses. Special assistance is given to handicapped young people. Careers officers liaise with a number of agencies including the Training Services Agency and Manpower Services Commission, and they visit employers regularly to keep up to date their knowledge of job and employment trends. They visit education and training establishments and they organise and participate in careers conventions. With the considerable rise in youth unemployment, careers officers have to be knowledgeable about the various special measures programmes for training and retraining and, with a rapidly changing employment pattern, the Careers Service is a branch of the education service which is growing in importance.

The School Health Service has since April 1974 been a function performed as an integral part of the National Health Service by Area Health Authorities in close co-operation with education authorities. The aim of the School Health Service is to foster the health of all children at school, so that they can obtain maximum benefit from their education. It also seeks to provide an advisory service for teachers and a counselling service for parents.

HM Inspectors have the right under Section 66 of the Education (Scotland) Act 1980 to enter schools and other educational establishments for the purpose of inspection. One of their principal functions is to report to the Secretary of State on education in schools and other educational establishments, and a feature of their work in recent years has been their readiness to share this information with education authority officers and advisers. With effect from the beginning of school session 1983/84, their reports were made public. The Inspectorate in Scotland numbers about 112 and is headed by a Senior Chief Inspector and two Deputy Senior Chief Inspectors. There are 10 Chief Inspectors, seven are centrally based and three are outstationed and have general oversight over the three territorial divisions into which Scotland is divided for the purposes of inspection and liaison.

HM Inspectors assess the quality of the educational process and advise on aspects which call for improvement. As the Secretary of State's principal professional advisers their role is to seek to ensure the most effective use of available resources for the education service and to initiate and stimulate desirable developments within the resources available. The independence of their professional judgement is preserved by their organisation as an entity under the Senior Chief Inspector and by giving him the right of direct access to the Secretary of State. The decision to publish reports of the Inspectorate rests with the Secretary of State but any report which he decides to publish is published as written by the Inspectorate. In a policy statement on the Inspectorate by the Secretary of State for Scotland in March 1983, the role of the Inspectorate as a 'catalyst for change' was stressed. Various changes have taken place in the organisational structure since 1982. These sought a closer integration of inspectors within the sectors of school education and between school education and post-school education and took account of new initiatives and changing priorities.

At HMCI level seven of the posts are deployed as follows:

  (i) 5–14
 (ii) 14–18
(iii) Further education and informal further education including
      pre-school education.
 (iv) Vocational education and training.
  (v) Higher education.
 (vi) Research and intelligence/management of educational
      resources unit.
(vii) Teacher education and supply.

A number of inspectors have national responsibility for particular subjects or aspects of education. The remainder are based in the territorial divisions combining specialist and general duties. HMIs act as liaison officers between the SED and the education authorities, the Consultative Committee on the Curriculum, the Examiner Board and other agencies. They regularly produce reports on particular aspects of education and frequently follow them up by planning seminars in conjunction with Directors of Education. The small numbers of regions make this form of follow up possible.

While between 80 and 90 per cent of most education authority budgets are spent directly or indirectly on school education, the indicators are that an increasing proportion will be spent in future on further education. The great growth in the local authority sector of further education occurred in Scotland, as in England, in the 1960s, and has gone along similar lines. The marked differences found in the school education sector are not so obvious in the FE sector. Since the Houghton Committee recommendations of 1974 brought further education college lecturers' salaries in the two countries into line, there has been considerable pressure from further education lecturers in Scotland to have their conditions of service brought into line as well. The courses, examinations and certificates of the City and Guilds of London Institute have always been a common factor in further education colleges north and south of the border, but the other major body offering courses mainly at technician and equivalent levels is already devolved. Its role is to devise and develop courses in the business and technical education sector of employment; to investigate and develop suitable methods of assessing standards of attainment, to arrange for the conduct of examinations and the awards of certificates and diplomas. It is possible that there may be a further merger of SCOTVEC and the Scottish Examination Board (SEB) at some future date. The Tertiary Education Advisory Council was appointed by the Secretary of State for Scotland to have an overview of all non-university tertiary education in Scotland and advise him on its future development. This body was abolished in 1983 and its successor, the Scottish Tertiary Education Advisory Council, has also been abolished.

That part of further education which is not specifically vocational was examined in the early 1970s by a Committee of Inquiry appointed by the Secretary of State for Scotland under the chairmanship of Sir Kenneth Alexander. The Alexander Report, entitled *The Challenge of Change* was published in 1975 and recommended that adult education should be subsumed in the term 'community education'. The Alexander Report made the plea for the concept of education to be a lifelong process. It spelt out the contemporary tasks for adult education and how it could help modern man preserve his status as an individual in a changing pluralist society. Distinctive features of the Scottish community education scene are an interest in the community school concept, healthy university extra mural departments of adult education, a buoyant interest in distance learning systems, a concern for adult illiterates, the disadvantaged and the unemployed. The community education service has taken a leading role in promoting life and social skills courses as part of MSC special measures funding. There is a Scottish Community Council which exists, among other things, to advise the Secretary of State, who appoints the members, about the development of adult and community education in Scotland.

The focal point of educational research in Scotland is the Scottish Council for Research in Education which celebrated its sixtieth anniversary in 1988. It was founded in 1928 on the initiative of the main teachers' organisation, the Educational Institute of Scotland, and the Association of Directors of Education in Scotland. Over the years it has contributed significantly to research in education and has produced an impressive array of publications. In 1972 the council extended considerably its cadre of professional full-time staff. Prior to this period most of the emphasis had been on the school education sector, but, increasingly, the council has contributed to new areas of enquiry, in particular further education and the 16–19 age group. There has also been a new emphasis on 'policy-oriented' research which is increasingly required by educational administrators and planners. The major part of the council's programme is contract research or research sponsored by grant-giving bodies such as the Social Science Research Council. Successive directors of SCRE have been internationally minded, and one of them wrote the final and summarising volume of the influential 'Six Subject Survey; an empirical study of education in twenty-one countries' sponsored by the international Association for the Evaluation of Educational Achievement.

An achievement of some political significance was the agreement in 1975 of the regional, district and island authorities to have only one local authority association in Scotland. This is the Convention of Scottish Local Authorities (COSLA). COSLA has an Education Committee with representatives on it of all 12 authorities; it is a convenient forum where the Conveners and Directors of each authority can consider together their approaches to policy planning and can confer and consult on specific issues. COSLA is proving both a partner and a counterpoise to central government in policy planning and development at a time when there is considerable controversy about the weight to be given to Scotland opinion in UK developments.

Further reading

Scottish and English Schools - A comparative Survey of the Past Fifty Years, G. S. Osborne, Longmans, Green & Co, 1966.

The History of Scottish Education (Vol. 2) 1870 to the Present Day, James Scotland, University of London Press Ltd, 1969.

The Educational System of Scotland, issued by the Scottish Information Office for the Scottish Education Department, Her Majesty's Stationery Office, Edinburgh, 1977.

Royal Commission on Local Government in Scotland 1966-1969 (The Wheatley Report), HMSO, Edinburgh, 1969 (Cmnd 4150).

The New Scottish Local Authorities - Organisation and Management Structure (The Paterson Report), HMSO Edinburgh, 1973.

Local Government (Scotland) Act 1973, HMSO London.

Education (Scotland) Act 1980, HMSO London.

Education (Scotland) Act 1981, HMSO London.

The Schools (Scotland) Code 1956, HMSO London.

The Schools (Scotland) Code (Amendment No. 1) Regulations 1972, HMSO London.

The Schools General (Scotland) Regulations 1975, HMSO London.

The Government's Expenditure Plans 1979-80 to 1982-83 (Cmnd 7439), HMSO London, 1979.

Primary Education, A Report of the Advisory Council on Education in Scotland, HMSO Edinburgh, 1946 (Cmnd 6973).

Secondary Education, A Report of the Advisory Council on Education in Scotland, HMSO Edinburgh 1947 (Cmnd 7005).

Further Education, A Report of the Advisory Council on Education in Scotland, HMSO Edinburgh 1952 (Cmnd 8454).

The Structure of the Curriculum in the Third and Fourth Years of the Scottish Secondary School, Scottish Education Department. Consultative Committee on the Curriculum (The Munn Report), HMSO Edinburgh, 1977.

Before Five, Scottish Education Department, HMSO Edinburgh, 1971.

Primary Education in Scotland, Scottish Education Department, HMSO Edinburgh, 1965.

Primary Education - Organisation for Development, Scottish Education Department, HMSO Edinburgh, 1971.

The Education (Scotland) Act 1918 with annotations, Edited by John Strong, Oliver and Boyd, 1919.

Teaching Council (Scotland) Act 1965, HMSO London.

Remuneration of Teachers (Scotland) Act 1967, HMSO London.

The Structure of Promoted Posts in Secondary Schools in Scotland, memorandum by the Scottish Education Department, HMSO Edinburgh, 1971.

Secondary School Staffing, Scottish Education Department, HMSO Edinburgh, 1973. A Report on Secondary School organisation and staffing in Scotland with proposals for new staffing standards ('The Red Book').

Ancillary Staffing in Secondary Schools, Scottish Education Department, HMSO Edinburgh, 1976. Administrative and Clerical Staff, Technicians, Auxiliaries (The Ruthven Report).

Non-teaching Staff in Secondary Schools, Scottish Education Department, HMSO Edinburgh, 1976. Youth and Community Workers, Librarians, Instructors (The Stimpson Report).

Adult Education: The Challenge of Change, Scottish Education Department, HMSO Edinburgh, 1975 (The Alexander Report).

The IEA Six Subject Survey: An Empirical Study of Education in Twenty-One Countries, David A. Walker, Almquist and Wiksel, 1976.

Scottish Office Finance Division Circular 64/1975 (Current Expenditure).

Scottish Office Finance Division Circular 47/1976 (Current Expenditure).

Scottish Education Department Circular No. 780 February 1971 – The Structure of Promoted Posts in Secondary Schools.

Scottish Education Department Circulars No. 1029 December 1978, No. 1053 June 1980 and No. 1072 August 1981 – Primary and Secondary School Staffing.

Assessment for All, Scottish Education Department, HMSO Edinburgh, 1977. Report of the Committee to review assessment in the third and fourth years of Secondary Education in Scotland (The Dunning Report)-

Truancy and Indiscipline in Schools in Scotland. Scottish Education Department, HMSO Edinburgh, 1977 (The Pack Report).

The Education of Pupils with Learning Difficulties in Primary and Secondary Schools in Scotland, A Progress Report by HM Inspectors of Schools SED, HMSO Edinburgh, 1978.

Learning and Teaching in Primary IV and Primary VII, A Report by HM Inspectors of Schools SED, HMSO Edinburgh, 1980.

Report into the Pay and Conditions of Service of School Teachers in Scotland, HMSO, Edinburgh, 1986 (The Main Report).

The Education (Publication and Consultation etc.) (Scotland) Amendment Regulations 1987.

The Education (Publication and Consultation etc.) (Scotland) Amendment Regulations 1988.

Review of Staffing Standards in Schools, Scottish Education Department 1988.

The School Boards (Scotland) Act 1988.

17 Manpower Services (Training) Commission: education and training

Introduction

Until recently it was a truism that whilst technological change is fast and getting faster, institutional change is slow, and attitude change slower still. Yet the 80s will in fact have seen more institutional change in this and other parts of the education sector than anybody could have contemplated six years ago. It is deliberate institutional change, not as an end in itself but as a means of promoting attitude change to attain a clearly perceived goal: a more competitive and effective economy.

By the time this chapter is read the Employment Act 1988 will have been implemented and the 1988 Education Act will be on the statute book. In different ways the two acts represent the culmination of the same trend: the destruction of local authority and trade union 'monopolies' and their replacement by a different, much more centralised regime, operating within a local framework relying on competition in provision. The Education Act leaves the LEA much reduced in real power and control within the further education system. The Employment Act sees the end of the MSC, replaced by the Training Commission (TC), with the concomitant end of the partnership concept which gave MSC such power throughout the 80s: henceforth the Training Commission and all its local and regional committees will have an employers' majority, if not quite a monopoly. The previous edition of this chapter identified both LEA and MSC as major partners in the provision of education and training, with the latter rapidly encroaching on the duties, powers and resources of the former. Within five years the LEA has been effectively supplanted by a centralising process in which local government is being replaced by local administration, with MSC (now TC) as the arm of central government in the area of post-16 education and training. The DES role throughout has been shadowy and it is hard to see now whether this will change in any substantial way, in this sector of education.

MSC always had the inclination to act as the arm of government at local level, but under successive chairmen (not excepting David Young, as he then was) it was also prepared to modify its policies at point of delivery and offer unpalatable advice to Government. The further education colleges are being substantially removed from the real control of LEAs who will retain essentially 'strategic' responsibilities, but even these could in turn be greatly affected by the cross-area responsibilities of the new local arms of the Training Commission. Both the colleges and TC will have one thing in common: statutory provision of significant employer representation within the bodies that direct them: not less than 50 per cent in the former and a majority in the latter.

Other reasons for this massive change are not hard to find. They relate in part to a deep mistrust and dislike of local government on the part of central government and a belief that the only way to ensure that the country's long term industrial and economic performance can be permanently changed is by ensuring that employers 'own' the new arrangements for training in a way in which they have never done before, unlike their colleagues in other competitor countries. There is a firm belief that the minimising of the LEA role, the freeing of colleges from local political control, the further encouragement of entrepreneurial skills within them, the operation of supply and demand in the provision of training across them and employer providers, all within a strategic framework determined by Government through TC will solve the issues of an 'under-trained, under-educated and immobile workforce' identified at the time of the New Training Initiative at the start of the decade. In this way, the prize of a more competitive and effective economy will be attained and ensure that this country enters the next century as a winner. The school 'reforms' are seen as the other side of the same coin. In the interests of this goal constitutional change of a substantial order is being undertaken. To understand the strength and importance of this approach it is necessary to look briefly at the history of education and training in this country, and in more detail at the developments in this area over the last five years. At the start of the decade LEAs saw MSC as the Leviathan, now they realise that Leviathan has always been central government.

From one perspective the history of public education since 1870 can be seen as an unsuccessful search for a system which would provide the kind of educational and training climate which would restore this country's position as an international economic leader: the concept of an industrial nation with an anti-industrial culture is still with us to this day. The 1870 Act was quickly seen to be an effective way to produce clerks, domestics and shop assistants, but failed to produce the craftsmen, technicians and technologists needed by British industry. Similarly the public and grammar schools were adept at producing imperial administrators and civil servants but much less effective at providing the entrepreneurs and inventors needed for world industrial and technological leadership. It is significant that from Samuelson in 1884 to HMI in 1986 the model sought was that of Germany, where even earlier Fichte in his 'Addresses to the German Nation' had expatiated upon an education system subordinated to the industrial and social needs of the state. The Lewis Report in 1917, the 1918 Education Act, Spens in 1930, the 1944 Act with its plans for county colleges, right up to the Industrial Training Act 1964, reveal a history of good ideas and promising starts, but ultimate disillusion. The absence of an effective training system had effects at all levels, from shop-floor to management.

Employers remained stubbornly uncommitted to training and the education system saw training in a systematic, comprehensive way as second order business. Whilst comparatively full employment obtained, it did not seem to matter too much. Public debate over grammar and comprehensive schools or over the future of the independent sector were couched more in terms of privilege and social justice rather than in providing analysis of the products of the various systems and relating these to individual and national needs. Throughout this period the further education system continued to respond to demand, providing traditional high quality and expensive training on request from employers and Industrial Training Boards; it also continued to expand, often on a second chance basis, its provision of GCE courses. But the dominant theme of the entire system was its wastefulness, especially of human resources. A system in which over 50 per cent of young people could spend 15,000 hours of compulsory schooling and still leave without credible qualifications to enter jobs without access to systematic training and further education was in little position to take credit for the greatly improving examination performance of the minority. The absence of an integrated system of education and training opportunities reinforced the belief that the country was on an irreversible downward economic path.

In 1974 the British economy entered a period of very severe cost inflation which rapidly affected public spending in general and local government in particular. In the same year both the new local authorities and MSC came into existence and started work. The latter was a product of the Heath Government's Employment and Training Act 1973, but with its concept of employer/union partnership to tackle the employment and training problems of the country it was a body through which the new Labour government would have little difficulty working. The last major report of the old Central Youth Employment Council – 'Unqualified, Untrained and Unemployed' – clearly identified at least one constituency at which the new body's work would be directed. The massive increase in unemployment, including youth unemployment, which was to take place over the next ten years substantially dictated MSC's agenda throughout the period: succeeding governments and MSC had to put much effort into attempts to provide jobs or alternatives to jobs. Yet MSC's main purpose on establishment was to provide a training system and training opportunities which would reverse the historical experience identified earlier, eliminate skill deficiencies and lead the way to improved economic performance.

The two issues of unemployment and improved training systems brought MSC from its earliest days into direct contact (and sometimes conflict) with LEAs. Its strengths in this relationship were the perceived failure of the existing system, MSC's comparative freedom from resource constraints, support from both unions and employers, support from government, the weakness of LEAs following the 1974 reorganisation and a clear perception (following the OECD study) of DES impotence to get LEAs to do much more than remove air-raid shelters from playgrounds.

318   *Manpower Services (Training) Commission*

The work of MSC

It is helpful to look at MSC's work in two main phases: the first, tentative stage up to 1981, and the second more incisive stage from then to the present. Before doing so it is important to identify the main characteristics of the organisation and its way of working. The first point is that in comparison with the multi-purpose LEA, the MSC's remit and targets have always been sharply defined and this together with its effective organisation have enabled it to carry out work at a much greater speed than traditional government departments and the LEAs. The Commission itself was of a manageable size (ten, initially) and it has been served by very effective chairmen and an effective and highly-talented bureaucracy. Its techniques have always involved two levels of operation: nationally, *ad hoc* task groups (representing the interests involved, but especially CBI and TUC) to analyze the constituents of a particular issue and to make recommendations for development, working within tight time and resource constraints but assisted by an able and energetic secretariat. The result has usually been a compromise package of proposals. Locally, provided the centre held (i.e. the Commission agreed), the proposals were translated into reality by a well-organised local force working to numerical targets and timetables; national decisions were sometimes softened at the edges locally, but they stuck. Except in the earliest years, MSC has used local committees and office organisations having boundaries coterminous with LEAs, but they have always avoided local organisations with one-to-one relationships with LEAs. This was true of local manpower committees, special programme boards and area manpower boards, and the proposed new Local Advisory Boards appear likely to follow the same pattern. Whatever the reason it has added to LEA uncertainty and difficulties and emphasised the element of competitiveness and instability.

Phase 1

After tackling the early problems of developing the central secretariat and incorporating the potentially separatist Training Services and Employment Services Agencies, MSC rapidly became involved in the development of the Job Creation and Work Experience Programmes, followed by an expansion of the Training Opportunities Scheme and work with the Industrial Training Boards. In 1977 the Holland Report proposed a new Youth Opportunities Programme; implemented from April 1977, it provided a throughput of 230,000 young people a year receiving training, work experience and further education. At the same time there was a further increase in centrally funded careers officer posts. Oversight was in the hands of national Special Programme Boards and in the localities some 30 area boards were established to oversee the development of YOP and the new successor to JCP – the Special Temporary Employment Programme. Co-operation between LEAs and MSC was probably at its best, under the old terms, in this period and is perhaps exemplified by the AMA/MSC joint publication: 'Making YOP Work'.

But by the end of the decade unemployment was continuing to increase and concerns about levels of youth unemployment were reinforced by the inexorable rise in the size of age groups attaining normal school leaving age; in addition there were increasing criticisms about the quality of YOP both from LEAs and from the young people experiencing it. The new government established the Macfarlane Committee to examine the educational needs of the 16–19 age group. By its composition and its terms of reference it was another missed opportunity: there were MSC assessors, but its remit was to avoid MSC spheres of influence. The result was a flawed document which examined the issues only partially and failed to tackle the overall needs of the age group and the system which was supposed to cater for them.

The New Training Initiative (NTI) consultation launched in May 1981 by MSC in effect bridges the gap between phases 1 and 2. By early 1981 MSC were not only deeply concerned about the general unemployment position but also shared the gloom about the longer term training outlook. After two years of Conservative government, levels of unemployment were worsening. Reactions to the work of ITBs amongst employers were very strong and overall training levels (especially of apprentices) were declining steeply alongside the loss in manufacturing. In the previous decade apprenticeships had declined by more than a third and other traineeships by 55 per cent. In May 1981 MSC issued the consultative document on

NTI. It represented a change of potentially great significance in the history of training and education in this country.

It identified the need 'to invent, to innovate, to invest in and to exploit new technologies' for prosperity and growth. It also identified a number of weaknesses in British industrial and economic performance, and suggested several contributory factors which included training inadequacies, attitudes of employers and employees, and the working of the education system. It proposed three objectives for training for the rest of the decade:

1. The development of skill training (including apprenticeship) to enable young people entering at different ages and with different educational levels to obtain agreed standards of skill appropriate to the jobs available and provide them with a basis for further progression.
2. The establishment of a position by which all young people under the age of 18 had the opportunity either of continuing in full-time education or entering a period of planned work experience with training and education.
3. The creation of widespread opportunities for all adults to obtain, increase or update skills and knowledge throughout their working lives.

It argued that employers, employees and the education service all had much to gain from involvement in achieving the three objectives. It therefore required them all to contribute something: for all three it would mean the abandonment of traditional attitudes and practices, together with considerable commitment including the application of resources. The actual costs of development should be shared by employers, employees and the public purse.

Phase 2

In December 1981, following responses to the consultative document, two documents were simultaneously issued: the Secretary of State's White Paper (Cmnd 8455): 'A New Training Initiative: A Programme for Action', and MSC's 'A New Training Initiative: An Agenda for Action'. The former contained a proposal for a youth training scheme essentially for the unemployed: about 300,000 places costed at £1.1 billion. It met with considerable hostility, especially for its presumed attack on young people. MSC's 'Agenda for Action' was, on the other hand, broadly welcomed. In particular the proposal to establish a youth task group (YTG) to look urgently at the problems raised by NTI was welcomed.

1. Youth Training Scheme (YTS)

YTG produced a compromise package of proposals, unanimously endorsed by MSC and the governing bodies of TUC and CBI. It was subsequently accepted by the Government and formed the basis of the Youth Training Scheme. YTS offered a guarantee of a one-year traineeship to all unemployed 16-year-old leavers and sufficient places for 16-year-olds in work as well as those leaving full-time education at 17 who became unemployed in the first year after leaving. The traineeship was to last about a year and to include a minimum of three months off-the-job training and/or relevant further education and was assumed to cover 460,000 youngsters in total. There were two types of sponsor: public or private employers (including local authorities and LEAs) providing a complete programme for the trainee; and MSC acting as a sponsor for opportunities such as training workshops and community projects. The first group were to provide 300,000 of the places and MSC the remainder. A Youth Training Board (YTB) supervised the scheme nationally and 54 local boards with boundaries coinciding with LEA boundaries vetted all proposals for inclusion in the schemes, assessed the quality and content of all opportunities in their area, supported and supervised a network of managing agencies, mobilised local support, monitored and evaluated the progress of the scheme.

The YTG report placed considerable emphasis on quality assurance within the new scheme and recommended MSC to establish nationally a group of professionals with expertise in initial training, vocational preparation, standards and scheme design (for young people who had left full-time education) to advise the national supervisory board. MSC were also asked to establish a small but effective field force from practitioners from industry, the education service etc. to act as 'inspectors' and a system of in-service training including a network of accredited centres. MSC had learnt the lessons of the 'never mind the quality, feel the width' criticisms of YOP and intended from the start to emphasise the issue of quality assurance: anything LEAs could do, MSC intended to do better. YTS was important for a further reason: announced in June 1982 and fully operational by September 1983, it marked a clear departure to an essentially employer-based concept, with public bodies providing merely a safety net. It is not without significance that this same period witnessed the abolition of two-thirds of the ITBs in response to employer pressure. The ITB bureaucracies with their instrumental training targets and built-in tripartite co-operation of employers', employees' and educational interests were seen as burdensome by many employers and did not suit the new climate.

2. *TVEI (Training and Vocational Education Initiative)*

From YTS onwards the local authority associations and local authorities have been fighting what appears in 1988 to have been an ultimately unsuccessful rearguard action, against MSC and government infiltration. It may be fanciful to think that successive Secretaries of State and leaders of MSC studied 'blitzkrieg' techniques, but their method of operation showed all the signs of first identifying the LEAs' soft spot, establishing their strong points there, and then rolling up behind the lines. Certainly the words 'schwerpunkt und aufrollen' were never used but perhaps government regard for the German model went further than just its economic success.

Paragraphs 7.9 to 7.11 of the YTG Report had drawn attention to the importance of the last two years of compulsory schooling and the need in those years to prepare young people to face the world of work. They indicated the need for higher levels of competence in numeracy, literacy, oral expression, social relationships and understanding of the world young people faced outside education in order to make them more likely to benefit from the new traineeship. This pointed to the heart of the main secondary school curriculum and it was followed by the Prime Minister's announcement of 12 November 1982 of a new Technical and Vocational Education Initiative. An unusual device was used to bypass

LEAs – the Secretary of State for Employment, on behalf of the Prime Minister, wrote to MSC inviting it to develop a TVEI Pilot Scheme for 14–18 year olds, 'where possible, in association with LEAs'. If YOP and YTS were encroachments on LEA territory, this was full-scale invasion. There was never any chance that MSC would reject the invitation nor any doubt that they had the powers and resources to carry it out, if necessary without LEA involvement. Much of 1983 was spent by the authority associations in trying to retrieve the position by the establishment of a joint MSC/LAA steering group to consider bids from LEAs and recommend successful ones for inclusion in the scheme. The fourteen initial pilots were later followed by extensions to the scheme and over the next three years it was extended to more and more LEAs until in 1986 Cmnd 9823 ('Working Together – Education and Training') announced a ten-year £900 million expansion across the country. Over the years the LEAs have been able to exert increasing influence over the scheme, but they have developed the educational underpinning of the proposals as they have gone along, trying to ensure that TVEI did not subvert the comprehensive principles on which most secondary schools are provided. That outcome could not be known at the time and certainly David Young's view expressed to CLEA in 1983 that he had no 'further territorial ambitions' in the education service rang hollowly to many delegates at Canterbury. For the time being the LEAs were able to work in with the proposals, but the clear threat to work outside the LEA system had been a real one and would arise again in different contexts later.

3. 'Training for Jobs' (Cmnd 1935)

If 1983 was the year of YTS and TVEI, 1984 was the year of 'Training for Jobs'. The White Paper reiterated the aims of the New Training Initiative and explored its main themes: 'Britain lives by the skill of its people. A well-trained workforce is an essential condition of our economic survival. Training must be . . . firmly work-oriented and lead to jobs'. It rehearsed the importance of developments such as YTS and TVEI and drew attention to the significance both of MSC's Open Tech programme (introduced a year earlier) and the DES Professional, Industrial and Commercial Updating Programme (PICKUP). It drew particular attention to MSC's proposals for an adult training strategy which included the following elements: a national awareness campaign on the need for adult training, national action to improve the coherence and responsiveness in the machinery for providing adult training and education, encouraging local collaboration between employers and providers and restructuring MSC's own adult training programmes to contribute more cost-effectively to meeting the needs of industry and commerce. The White Paper went on: 'We endorse this strategy as entirely in line with the market-oriented approach to training that is now required'. It also affirmed the need for clarity of roles if vocational education and training were to be improved . . . 'The Government is now asking the Commission to extend its range of operation so as to be able to discharge the function of a national training authority'. To facilitate this, it was proposed that within two years about a quarter (£200 million) of LEA expenditure on work-related non-advanced further education (WRNAFE) would be removed from rate support grant and recycled to MSC to increase its purchasing power: 'It is envisaged that the great bulk of the resources, though not necessarily all, will continue to be spent within local authority colleges'.

If TVEI was regarded as invasion, the WRNAFE proposals were seen as annexation. There were many in the local authorities who believed that there should be no co-operation at all with the proposals; they said, rightly, that a system which would require a quarter of WRNAFE to be planned in conjunction with MSC, put the rest of WRNAFE and even the whole of NAFE potentially *en pris* and that this was just another, if more blatant, example of the Government trying to replace LEAs. Other arguments eventually prevailed: LEAs needed to get their money back, colleges needed to be maintained, and perhaps there would be a greater chance of ameliorating the worst aspects of the proposals if LEAs were part of the arrangements from the start. Even so it took nearly eighteen months of negotiations between MSC and the authority associations before outright LEA opposition was translated into a form of co-operation and an agreement acceptable to the LEAs was produced: in the case of AMA at least, it was accepted for only a year in the first instance. In the event local authorities found themselves able to work effectively with local MSC officers and the early introduction of two national bodies (the NAFE Implementation Group and the NAFE Evaluation Group) with joint MSC/LEA membership has kept a helpful dialogue at national level. The main issues of contention have been the levels of money held back by MSC from distribution in the interests of promoting development schemes and the fact that MSC's much-vaunted local labour market information has been totally inadequate in facilitating planning. Overall the effects of the WRNAFE initiative have been to tighten up LEA planning in the FE sector and to give MSC a real bridgehead into the LEA system: it has given MSC the opportunity to see the weaknesses of the FE system at close quarters and some of the resources to start developing alternatives to it. Above all it has provided Government with a staging post on the way to total emasculation of LEA powers in the post-16 sector; time spent on producing WRNAFE development plans in LEAs suffering from constrained resources must have diverted attention from other tasks related to improving the quality of the provision made. Whether there has been the promised improvement in the quality and responsiveness of the training provided remains doubtful.

4. 'Education and Training for Young People' (Cmnd 9482)

In March 1985 the Chancellor's budget statement announced a proposal to expand YTS to a two-year scheme; it was prefaced by the following words: 'One of the most long-standing problems in this country is our failure to prepare our school-leavers adequately for work. Since it was first launched in 1983, the youth training scheme has proved to be a very successful bridge between school and work. It has also helped to make young people's pay expectations more realistic. But too many trainees are still reluctant to accept rates of pay which reflect their inexperience, and too many employers still fail to recognise that training is an investment in their own interest . . . In the long run, we would expect employers to

meet the full cost as those in other countries do, but I recognise
that such a major change in attitude may take time.'

The following month the Government issued Cmnd 9482.
As well as reflecting the themes identified above, it formally
announced the expansion of YTS and TVEI. It also reflected
a concern expressed in 'Training for Jobs': the need for a system
of nationally recognised qualifications. It proposed a review
of vocational qualifications to reform the structure and content
of such qualifications and the introduction of methods of
certifying vocational competence in YTS. Cmnd 9482
effectively restated most of the issues surrounding our
inadequate vocational preparation system for decades and
attempts to provide the answers. The inadequacies of the school
curriculum were to be addressed by the continued reform of
school curricula (new examinations, economic literacy and the
like) and by the planned expansion of TVEI. The issue of
student/trainee support was simply ignored – there was to be
no increase in the trainee allowance and there was the threat
of compulsion by withholding benefit from 'refuseniks'. The
traditional reluctance of most employers to commit themselves
to training was tackled by stick and carrot: in two-year YTS,
the trend towards private employer schemes was intensified
by abolishing the old modes A and B and introducing a single
form of administration to make it more acceptable, but the
Chancellor's longer term threat was still there. The local
authority and other safety net schemes were retained but much
reduced in numbers and the next two years were to see a real
squeeze on training costs in LEAs and voluntary provided
schemes. Within a year YTS(2) was to be introduced and full
entry onto the labour market was effectively postponed to the
age of 18. The full effects of this change on the relevance of
16+ examinations and on the labour market in the light of
demographic change have still to be worked out.

One of the earliest criticisms of YOP had been the quality
of the experience provided for young people and, the other
side of the coin, the LEA insistence that effective training was
expensive. MSC response had been effectively that training was
bound to be costly if it were provided in expensive LEA colleges
with their restrictive union practices. YTS(1) with its system
of managing agents and contractors had opened up this system
to stern competition, but there remained nagging doubts within

MSC about quality and quality-control, those most elusive beasts. A start had been made in YTS(1) to tackle these issues through MSC's own quality control mechanisms, but there was an even greater prize to be attained: a total clearance of the jungle of vocational qualifications.

The Review of Vocational Qualifications (RVQ) was instigated by Cmnd 9482 and reached fruition a year later in the RVQ Report which recommended a clear, coherent and comprehensive system of vocational qualifications based on the assessment of competence directly relevant to the needs of employment and the individual. This was to be overseen by a National Council for Vocational Qualifications with responsibility for accrediting the awards of the examining, validating, professional and industry based bodies. This new system was to develop a new framework, links with GCSE and A levels, and was to have universal recognition, credit accumulation and transfer, as well as acceptability as entry qualifications leading to higher education and professional institutes. NCVQ was also to develop a register of professional bodies and seek to eliminate incompatibilities between them, as well as providing a national database of vocational qualification. These recommendations were accepted and following the White Paper of 1986 (Cmnd 9823 'Working Together – Education and Training') which formally established the National Council for Vocational Qualifications, are being implemented, although it is fair to say that the work is still in its early stages.

5. *MSC's remit*

In February 1986 the newly appointed Commission was given an indication by Government of the way in which it would like to see it develop in the ensuing three years. It was essentially to develop a total training and vocational education system which 'will provide rapidly and flexibly the skills employers and individuals will need, and to promote enterprise and employment so that we accelerate the growth of new jobs and also provide specific measures to help long-term unemployed people get back into the labour market'. This new remit required it to take 'a leading role in developing and modernising our vocational education and training arrangements and gaining the commitment of all parties – employers, individuals and providers – to vocational education and training'. Other areas included the following: MSC to work to increase the labour market relevance of NAFE; to develop closer links with NAB and UGC on planning the contribution of HE to the supply of highly qualified manpower; to promote further the adult training strategy by seeking changes in training arrangements and improvements in the operation of the market; to follow up RVQ with the education departments and develop quality audit and approval of training organisations for training and vocational education; to develop a progressively 'more effective contribution towards curriculum change and the spread of existing good practice through input into programmes and by seeking closer association with the work of the Further Education Unit'; to develop closer association with the FE Staff College; to take a 'positive role' in pulling together and improving arrangements for FE staff development and the training of trainers; to promote enterprise and employment and help long-term unemployed people back into the labour market; to inform Government of the ways in which it intends to improve formal and informal links with the education service.

Much of MSC's activity since 1986 can be explained in terms of this revised remit, which is quite clearly based on the premise that MSC, not a department of state, was to be the engine which would drive the wheels of change. Nowhere is this clearer than in MSC's attempts to tackle the third and most difficult area of its NTI strategy: adult training.

6. *Adult Training Strategy*

The 'Training for Jobs' White Paper, as indicated earlier in this chapter, had rehearsed the initial developments in this area, including the promotion of Open Tech and the recommendations following upon the initial Adult Training Strategy consultation. From the start the issue was not simply one of training the workforce, but also involved an attempt to tackle the problems of the increasing numbers of unemployed adults, including the long-term unemployed. 'Training for

Jobs' endorsed MSC's proposals to develop an industry-focussed programme to give job-related training directed to known employment needs in industry and commerce and to help the creation and growth of businesses; these were directed at both employed and unemployed. It also endorsed the proposal to give basic training to the unemployed through work preparation courses and through community and voluntary programmes. Although there was considerable activity in these areas the increase in the numbers of long-term employed continued and the various initiatives seemed to the cynical as a means of massaging the unemployment statistics rather than a positive approach to a national system of training. Increasing concern about the numbers of long-term unemployed led MSC and DHSS to introduce the Restart Programme in 1986. Long-term unemployed people were invited to a Restart interview at which failure to attend 'without good reason' would result in suspension of benefit. At the interview the individual was counselled about future action which included options such as attending a restart course, obtaining a job, entering the Community Programme, entering an enterprise allowance scheme, undertaking training, attending a Job Club, joining a voluntary projects programme or obtaining a Jobstart allowance. This too was criticised for adopting a recruiting-sergeant approach instead of making a genuine attempt to provide training.

In the autumn of 1986 MSC introduced the Job Training Scheme (JTS) as a pilot in nine areas to test the feasibility of offering those under 25 and had been out of work for six months or more either a job, membership of a Job Club, a place on the Enterprise Allowance Scheme or a place on the JTS. After a ten-week pilot MSC announced that 'it appears feasible to deliver what is an ambitious combination of integrated training and practical experience . . .' Government asked MSC to extend the pilot and the latter proposed a 50,000 place scheme, but in response the Government determined that it should be 110,000 by September 1987 and 250,000 in a full year. The killing feature for many was that recruitment would be mainly through the Restart Programme. Even more important was the fact that in order to pay for JTS, it was proposed to remove £26 million from the budgetary provision of existing ATS/TOPS courses in LEAs and that would rapidly have a direct effect on the provision made by LEA colleges; in addition JTS was considered to be a recipe for inadequately funded training. Many LEAs refused to participate in JTS and there were strong indications that MSC's heart was simply not in the massive expansion proposed by Government. In some LEA areas the scheme went ahead but from the start it was an obvious failure; even in those where it did not, there were clear and significant losses of income to colleges who found other adult training courses discontinued at short notice.

Following the failure of new JTS, the Government announced early in 1988 in 'Training for Employment' its decision to bring together all the existing programmes for unemployed people over the age of 18 into a single unified training for employment programme to start from September 1988 and to provide up to a year's training and 600,000 places; the two main components are the Community Programme and JTS and the scheme takes up virtually all of MSC's adult training work. It is run by the Training Commission following acceptance by Government of the MSC's proposals unamended. Included amongst them are five cardinal principles: that the scheme should be voluntary, that it must offer and assure high quality training, that the individual must count, that there must be incentives to take part in it and that it must be locally planned and locally delivered. As with YTS, MSC is being currently advised by a national task group and proposes the establishment of an Adult Training Board on lines similar to YTB. Despite the emollient words and principles, there remain considerable doubts about the funding of the new scheme; equally it is clear that neither the White Paper nor the MSC submission to Government makes more than a passing reference to LEAs and their colleges. There will be no national agreement on fees for providing the new programme to which the common point of entry will be Approved Training Agencies, independent of training providers. MSC intends to strengthen its Training Standards Advisory Service to oversee the new programme, which will have to follow a local training plan to be produced by MSC area managers with advice from the new Local Advisory Boards.

For some weeks the authority associations and TUC held back from expressing support for the scheme but they have now endorsed it and the objections of AMA have been substantially withdrawn. Neither of these actions prevented the resignation of one TUC Commissioner and an indication from two of the major local government unions that they would encourage their members not to participate; NATFHE on the other hand said they would take part. There is a sense of *deja vu* about it all: the words from MSC are substantially the same as in 1982 about YTS; many of the attitudes are the same. But the difference for LEAs is that there are now well-established consortia such as local employer networks and voluntary agencies ready and willing to bid into the new scheme; LEAs have suffered or are suffering major income losses from the ending of 'traditional' adult training work such as TOPS courses and the effect of the Education Act on their ability to deliver involvement at college level must be problematic.

The Education Act 1988

There is provision in the Act for further education colleges to attain corporate status although there have been some ministerial assurances that unlike the major establishments and polytechnics (which will be required to attain it under the legislation), it will have to be with maintaining LEA approval. For those that continue to be LEA maintained, there will be new governing bodies having a minimum of 50 per cent membership of 'employer' representatives and LEAs will be required to submit schemes of delegation for all but the smallest colleges (less than 200 FTE students). Although DES guidance does not provide a model scheme, it makes clear in detail what the Secretary of State will 'have in mind' when he considers scheme submissions from LEAs. On the one hand LEAs are to retain strategic responsibility for planning the system of further education in their areas, but on the other, colleges may operationally decide to ignore ('with good reason') the resource allocations which flow from the strategy. There will be some twelve major areas in which LEAs will have to satisfy the Secretary of State about the form and content of their arrangements for the strategic planning of their further education. The Secretary of State considers that the strategic planning of FHE provision and the preparation of college budgets should be part of a single process.

The LEA will be able to establish both a development and a contingency fund and there will be certain areas exempted from delegation, but there are detailed requirements including a formula approach based on weighted student numbers for allocating the bulk of funds to colleges. Once these indicative allocations are made college governors will have maximum discretion to vire and the potential to carry forward overspends and underspends into the next financial year. The process in fact exhibits all those aspects of discontinuity for which ministers criticised RSG: one set of factors determines the size of the cake; another set determines how it should be divided; and finally the recipient can decide the way in which his/her share is to be consumed, in accordance with yet further factors. There is an equally clear discontinuity between the LEA's plan and its delivery by the college: the college can vire most parts of its indicative allocation, and the only action open to the LEA is retrospective.

If, as seems likely, colleges do become even more competitive and 'responsive', there could well be an increase in the duplication of provision, especially in the light of the demography over the next few years. One hope seems to be that the employers (not less than 50 per cent) on the college governing bodies will get together with the employers who will be in the majority on the Training Commission's Local Advisory Boards and the employers on the Local Employer Networks to ensure that the LEA's strategic plan (broadly in line with its WRNAFE plan agreed with TC) is implemented. Perhaps it is not fanciful to imagine that the employers in question will be the same people wearing different hats. If they are not, how will business be able to sustain these demands on them?

The FE sections of the Act seem to provide a *reductio ad absurdum* of the Government's view of LEAs held with an evangelical intensity. Somehow, within all the planning and monitoring activity, LEAs will have to try to stitch together networks of principals, employers, administrators, local politicians and TC to develop co-operative working in the interests of the entire system. Otherwise these sections of the Act could put at risk the potential of the developments introduced in the last eight years. If this attempt is not made, or if it fails, local competition between colleges, and between colleges and other providers will not only increase duplication in the short-term, but in the long-term will mean the effective end of LEA provision of post-16 education and training for its area.

Appendices

1 Budgeting for expenditure on education

The national process

The national process of budgeting for education expenditure is highlighted twice a year so far as local government is concerned. Early each year a Public Expenditure White Paper on the Government's plans for all services for the three years from the following April is published and in July outline proposals for local government expenditure and central government grant for the following financial year are announced. This is followed by more detailed decisions normally in November.

As with local government, a major part of the national educational budgeting process is the assessment of existing levels of spending, followed by an expenditure forecast on the assumption of a continuation of current policies and the maintenance of standards. Central and local government officers work closely together on this exercise. The formal link is the Expenditure Steering Group for Education, commonly known as ESGE. This group is chaired by a Deputy Secretary of the DES, and has members from the DES, including the other Deputy Secretaries, Senior Chief Inspector and the Finance Branch, together with officers and advisers of the ACC and AMA and an observer from the Treasury. Representatives of the Department of Employment join for careers service discussions.

The membership of the ESGE forecasting sub-group, charged with assembling the facts and preparing forecasts for the Steering Group, comprises representatives of the Finance Branch of the DES and local authority treasurers and education officers, together with the Under Secretaries (Education) of the ACC and AMA. Additional *ad hoc* sub-groups are established to deal with problems remitted to them by ESGE. Valuable reports have been produced giving analyses of changing expenditure patterns leading to improved forecasting of expenditure and better estimates of the costs of possible policy variations.

In the spring and early summer forecasts of expenditure for the following financial year and an outline for a few subsequent years are prepared by the forecasting sub-group. These are based on the most up-to-date statistics available and take account of the expenditure implications of any new policy decisions taken by the Government since the last forecasts were prepared. They are measured against the limits set by the forecasts underlying the most recent Public Expenditure White Paper or any other guidelines issued by the Government and possible economy measures are identified.

At this stage of the cycle, the expenditure base for forecasting has to be the last actual out-turn of expenditure, i.e. for the last financial year but one. For the year just ended, and for the current year, estimates by local authorities of their expenditure levels are available, but experience suggests that these are likely to be somewhat above actual out-turn. The Steering Group's forecasts of actual out-turn are often nearer the truth than the figures implied by the aggregate of estimates from individual local authorities.

In the summer, therefore, ESGE can report to the Consultative Council on Local Government Finance its estimates of the cost of continuing existing policies in the following financial year and the probable costs of any proposed policy changes compared with the figures underlying the last White Paper. If the forecast is higher than the government's plans allow, the report is likely to give a range of options for expenditure reductions which might have to be considered unless additional finance is provided. ESGE reports over the years have been marked by a very high degree of agreement between the central and local representatives. However, from the mid-1980s it became increasingly common for Department of Education and Science representatives to record marginal, but significant areas where they felt that expenditure reductions should be made; such areas included the number of teachers to be employed, school meals expenditure, administration, taking school places out of use. After discussion with the Local Authority Associations, the Secretary of State for the Environment, normally at the end of July, gives general guidance to local authorities on expenditure targets.

During the autumn the details of local authorities' actual expenditure in the previous financial year are known. More up-to-date knowledge is available about the numbers of pupils and students in the system. Apparent discrepancies can be investigated so that trends can be forecast as accurately as possible.

In parallel with these discussions small groups of officers representing central and local government will discuss any suggested changes in the methods of calculating the Grant Related Expenditure Assessments for the education service. Any recommended changes can then be considered by the Secretary of State for the Environment for incorporation in the overall GREs of local authorities.

Subsequently, usually at the end of November, at the statutory meeting of the Consultative Council, the Secretary of State for the Environment gives details of the Government's decisions on estimates of relevant expenditure for the following year, any amendments that he and other Government Ministers have made to service estimates, together with the policy implications and the details of the percentage and distribution of Revenue Support Grant for that year. Details will include grant penalties for authorities spending in excess of Government expectations, and the nomination of any authorities whose community charge is to be 'capped'. Finally, Statutory Orders are laid before Parliament to implement the Government's decisions.

The Government's annual public expenditure survey, which begins each spring, looks at the last forecasts in the light of later information and the current economic situation and usually adds another year, so that plans for the next four-year period can be made by the Government and published early in the following year when the annual national budget cycle then starts again. For local authority expenditure on education the most recent estimates adopted for Revenue Support Grant form the starting point for the forecasts. This means that, although the local authority associations and their advisers are not directly involved in the public expenditure survey, they make, indirectly, a substantial contribution to it.

The local authority process

The financial year in all authorities is from 1 April to 31 March, the following year. Although this overlaps the academic, September to August, year and therefore one financial year's estimates contain provision for parts of two academic years, the overlap is, in practice, helpful. The time between April and September is often the minimum necessary to allow for staff recruitment or other resource provision, although, partly because of employment legislation, it is often too short for sensible staff redeployment. In spite of the advantages of planning ahead most authorities do not make final decisions about expenditure until February or even March before the financial year starts, although this may be because it is often not until late November or early December that the Government grant for the ensuing year to an individual authority is known and the effect of the different levels of expenditure on the community charge can be calculated. Some authorities do, however, produce draft estimates for more than one year ahead.

It is not easy to generalise on budget-making in a local authority because practices vary considerably. The introduction of schemes of delegation may add to the variety of approaches by individual authorities in the way in which information is presented.

Estimates of income and expenditure for any one financial year are presented to the Council, usually towards the end of the previous financial year. They are likely to be broken down under a number of main headings, such as:

Nursery education
Primary education
Secondary education
Special education
Education provided otherwise than at school
Further and higher education
Adult education
Youth and community service
Provision of school milk and meals
Administration and inspection
Careers service
Government grants

Approved estimates, and probably revised estimates, often referred to as probable out-turn for the current year are likely to be given for comparison and sometimes, also, the previous year's actual expenditure. Under each heading the estimate may be analyzed to show the changes because of (*a*) inflation, (*b*) demographic change, (*c*) agreed policy changes, (*d*) suggested changes in policy or practice, (*e*) full year effect of items included for only part of the previous year, (*f*) the effect of capital projects coming on stream, (*g*) estimate 'adjustments', which may be a rectification of the earlier year's 'poor' estimates. The 'poor' estimate may be due to circumstances entirely outside the control of the estimator; for example, an unexpected increase in the number of students entitled to mandatory awards or pupils requiring special education.

Before the introduction of statutory delegation to school and college governing bodies estimates of expenditure and income were normally sub-divided into a number of sub-headings for each main category. For example expenditure on primary schools would be given as follows:

Salaries and wages of employees
National Insurance
Superannuation
Other employees' expenses

Repair and maintenance of buildings and grounds
Alterations and improvements
Fuel, light, cleaning materials and water
Rent and rates

Cleaning, domestic and administrative equipment
Capitation (or Furniture, Equipment, Books, Stationery and Materials separately).

The introduction of statutory financial delegation to most school governing bodies and all colleges from 1990 onwards means that governors will be free to decide their spending priorities, once the budget has been allocated, and they will not be bound by any sub-division determined by the authority. Authorities may therefore in future include a single line figure of 'governors' expenditure' in the estimates for each category of institution. Items excepted from the delegation scheme may be shown on a sub-divided basis, for example, structural repairs, transport of pupils from home to school, maintenance allowances, in-service training of teachers, special school and small primary school budgets. As an aid to governors' decisions about individual institution budgets an indicative breakdown may be given over expenditure sub-headings showing the assumptions made by the authority in arriving at the total budget for schools or colleges.

The estimates documents of some authorities include statistics which help an understanding of the finances – numbers of pupils, teachers, meals, student hours, unit costs and year on year comparisons, for example.

Estimates of cost are built up largely on an historic basis and adjusted for projected changes in pupil or student numbers, and other known changes such as school reorganisations, policy changes, new statutory requirements. The pattern of spending on premises costs will not vary greatly from one year to the next. The assumptions included in the authority's funding formula about staff/student ratios or costs per pupil on books will affect the total spending requirement as student numbers change, but the assumptions themselves may need to be reviewed from time to time to reflect the cumulative effect of individual spending decisions by governing bodies.

The costs for the education service of central departments, such as finance, architecture and legal services, together with office costs, are likely to be apportioned centrally. Contingency allowances are included to cover such needs as pay awards not determined at the time the estimates are made, possible inflation, changes in interest rates, revised scales of assistance for grants to students and pupils. These may be included in the education estimates – especially for school and college budgets – or a general allowance provided to cover all of an authority's services.

It is a fortunate coincidence if the sum of all the requests for education expenditure is the same as the amount the local authority is prepared to agree. There seem to be a few cases each year where the Education Officer is asked to increase the estimates. It is more common, however, for some requested improvements not to be approved. In recent years many authorities have decided that, often because of government cash limits or penalties, they cannot continue to maintain the level of services. Usually this results in difficult discussions and amendments to expenditure proposals not long before the estimates are finally approved. In a few isolated cases discussions between members about expenditure reductions to balance the budget have continued well into the financial year sometimes leading to late decisions and more substantial effects on the service than if decisions had been made at the proper time before the year began. Other authorities have decided at an early date that lower levels of service will be necessary, or inevitable, and estimates have been prepared on that basis.

2 Sources of statistics

The note under each title is intended to give only a general indication of content.

1. *Department of Education:* 'Statistics of Education'
   (i) Statistics of Education was published annually by HMSO up to 1979. All England and Wales unless otherwise stated and except for 1978 and 1979 Vol. 1 and 2, by which time Wales had assumed responsibility for school statistics.
   (*a*) *Vol. 1 – Schools*
   > Schools; pupils; teachers; class sizes; courses of study.
   (*b*) *Vol. 2 – Schools Leavers CSE and GCE*
   > Destination (employment or further education), external examination achievements of leavers, and of further education students.
   (*c*) *Vol 3 – Further Education*
   > Students by age, mode of attendance, type of institution, qualification aims, subjects of study, release from employment, degree, diploma and certain other attainments.
   (*d*) *Vol 4 – Teachers*
   > Initial training; in-service training courses; teacher numbers of age, subject qualification, level of post held, type of school, movement from/to maintained schools.
   (*e*) *Vol 5 – Finance and Awards*
   > Current and capital expenditure including that on educational building; meals and milk statistics; adult education; teachers' salaries; awards to post-graduate, undergraduate and other students.

   (f) Vol 6 – Universities (UK)
  (ii) The post 1979 publications retain the title 'Statistics of Education' but contain just the two volumes *(a)* and *(b)* above and relate to England only.
  (iii) *Education Statistics for the United Kingdom*
    The main statistics for the whole UK, prepared annually by DES in collaboration with the Scottish Education Department, the Welsh Office, the Department of Education for Northern Ireland, and the University Grants Committee.

2. *Scottish Education Department*
 Scottish Abstract of Statistics. Annual.
3. *Welsh Office*
 Digest of Welsh Statistics. Annual
 Welsh Social Trends. Annual
 Statistics of Education in Wales. Annual
4. *Department of Education for Northern Ireland*
 Northern Ireland Annual Abstract of Statistics
5. *Statistical Bulletins*
 Published regularly on selected aspects by the Department of Education and Science, Scottish Education Department and Department of Education for Northern Ireland.
6. *Education Statistics Estimates*
 Published annually by the Chartered Institute of Public Finance and Accountancy.
 Financial and non-financial statistics for individual LEAs based on approved estimates and covering the whole range of an LEA's responsibilities.
7. *Central Statistical Office: Annual Abstract of Statistics*
 Published annually by HMSO.
 The 'Education' section, contains a selection of the statistics contained in the DES *Education Statistics for the United Kingdom* with more detailed information on staff and students at Universities, post-graduate students and expenditure on scientific research. Schools health service expenditure is now included in Government expenditure on the National Health Service.
8. *Central Statistical Office: Monthly Digest of Statistics*
 Some relevant tables, e.g. employment and unemployment; manpower; population and vital statistics.

9. *Central Statistical Office: Social Trends. Published annually by HMSO*

Each chapter, which generally reflects an administrative function of Government, presents social data in either chart or tabular form backed up by extensive commentary. The education chapter contains sections dealing with the stages of education, school leavers and resources. Wherever possible data are on a United Kingdom basis.

10. *Central Statistical Office: Regional Trends. Published Annually by HMSO*

The Education section gives regional and county data on a number of educational topics. There are also many other regional figures of general interest on related subjects, e.g. population, social characteristics, housing, etc.

11. *Office of Population, Censuses and Surveys*

Population projections by OPCS.

Historic and forecast population figures by age groupings for regions, counties and metropolitan districts. Historic and projected live births, fertility rates.

12. *Numerous other sources of statistical data, largely DES publications*

(a) DES, *Reports on Education*, published intermittently, often contain statistical data

(b) Reports of the Assessment of Performance Unit (APU).

(c) Reports of Committees of Inquiry established by the Secretary of State may contain statistical material or appendices,

(d) DES Consultative Documents.

(e) University Grants Committee

University Statistics (supersedes *Statistics of Education Vol 6, section 1(i) above*)

Volume 1: Students and Staff

Volume 2: First destinations of university graduates

Volume 3: Finance

Published annually from 1980 by Universities Statistical Record for the University Grants Committee.

(f) Education Year Book

Education Authorities Directory and Annual.

13. *Reference Works and Indices*

   Government Statistics – a brief guide to sources (CSO)

   United Kingdom in Figures (CSO)

   Central Statistical Office: *Guide to Official Statistics* (HMSO gives the published sources of official statistics (covering occasional reports and articles as well as regular services) including education and related subjects.

   Central Statistical Office: *Statistical News,* a quarterly journal (HMSO) lists recently available statistical publications

   Register of Educational Research in the United Kingdom(National Foundation for Educational Research)

3 The role of Local Authority Associations in the education system

The structure of the associations

Individuals with common interests, and organisations of all kinds, find it desirable to create associations or other bodies to represent them to other individuals or organisations, to the media, and perhaps above all to Government. Individual local authorities, and local government as an institution, are no exception.

Local government in Scotland is served by a single organisation – the Convention of Scottish Local Authorities. In England and Wales local education authorities may look to one of two Associations to represent their interests and views (although in Wales there is additionally a unique statutory body – the Welsh Joint Education Committee, which has defined functions and a particular role in consultation with Government – see also Chapter 15). The education interest for the non-metropolitan county councils, which cover approximately three-fifths of the population of England and Wales, is served by the Association of County Councils, while the education interests of the metropolitan areas are represented by the Association of Metropolitan Authorities. Both Associations have a voluntary membership and the object of serving the interests of 'their' authorities.

The general structures of the Associations are similar and reflect those of their member authorities. Each has a senior council or executive which receives reports from committees representing service interests (for example planning, fire and police and – of course – education). One difference in emphasis between the Associations and individual local authorities is, however, worth noting: having no direct operational responsibilities for running services, the service committees' business is largely comprised of policy items relating to the particular service interest. It has not been the practice to develop a structure of supporting sub-committees, although working parties and smaller representative groups of members meet from time to time on specific issues. Broad issues of general policy which affect all or several services are normally referred to a Policy Committee, after consideration by the committee for the service concerned (or its officer advisers) where that is appropriate.

The elected membership of the Associations is composed typically of senior and experienced members of local authorities. In education, most of their members hold or have held the chair of the Education Committee and the double burden of representation at national level and of local responsibility can be very considerable indeed. Both Associations go to some lengths to ensure that the views of all member authorities can be taken into account.

The Associations' secretariats are small and, in the case of education and recreation services, are headed by an Education Officer assisted by no more than three or four professional and administrative staff. This inevitably means that a great deal of the Associations' work and advice is heavily dependent on the contributions that are made by Chief Officers and their colleagues in LEAs. There are strengths, as well as obvious difficulties, in this diversity. On some topics the secretariat staff may be immersed in detail, and have the advantage of the wide view which contact with other national bodies and practices in a number of LEAs can give. They would not claim, however, to have detailed knowledge on all business and they must rely considerably on the expert and up-to-date knowledge of colleagues in the field. The problem of representing a collective view from a diversity of circumstances is compensated for by the breadth of knowledge and experience of LEA officers currently engaged in providing the service.

The purpose and work of the associations

The purpose of the Associations is to promote the interests and defend the independence of their member authorities. This task has clearly become more difficult in recent years as successive governments have taken more controls over local government and, more recently, removed some of its powers. Financial and other pressures from outside have increased the problems for local authorities and much of the Associations' work is therefore defensive and reactive, but much of it is also concerned, perhaps less dramatically, with the 'nuts and bolts' of a service that affects more members of the community than any other.

This concern for the running and administration of the service is best illustrated by reference to the time which elected members, officer advisers, and the Associations' secretariats spend on negotiations and discussions of matters of pragmatic detail – for example fees, awards, conditions of service, draft legislation and draft Government regulations and circulars. This is the every day 'bread and butter' work involving links with teacher unions, with Government agencies (increasingly with MSC), with several Government departments in addition to DES and with a whole range of national bodies. Much of this work involves the details of the framework within which the education service operates. It does not have a party-political content, although some of it will stem from previous political decisions. It is routine and it is vital to the running of the service. A survey in one Association indicated that it constituted over 75 per cent of the work-load.

The remainder of that work-load is largely taken up with representation of LEA interests in discussion of policies – again with a multiplicity of groups but most often, of course, with Ministers and senior officials of the Department of Education and Science. The pattern and rhythm of consultation have varied over the years and in the recent past the Associations have been concerned about decisions which have been taken without consultation. The ensuing discussions on implementation are no less important as they may have to fill in the practical gaps which open up as a result of the previous absence of real consultation. As the drive towards greater centralisation continues, the Associations' task in representing LEAs' interests and ensuring that policies are workable – and to the benefit of the people served by LEAs – become no less difficult or unimportant.

Relationships with the other partner in the education service – the professional interests represented principally by the teachers' unions – are similarly subject to changing winds of opinion but consistently close. They involve negotiations on salaries and conditions of service although, in the case of school teachers, the employers' power to negotiate was removed by the Government through legislation in 1987 and the more permanent arrangements which might take the place of the 'quango' which Government set up to advise itself on pay and conditions have yet to be settled. In addition they range – as needs indicate – over other matters of concern to the service and may take place in informal and *ad hoc* meetings as well as in the more obvious formal bodies such as the National Joint Council for FE.

A single voice?

Discussion about the case for a single Association to represent the whole of local government in England and Wales dates back over many years and revives from time to time. Whatever the merits of the theoretical case, the Associations have gained a good deal of experience of both the advantages and the difficulties of a common approach in the years since 1974.

During the discussions leading to the reorganisation of local government, there was a clear recognition of the particular needs of the education service. As a result the Council of Local Education Authorities was established in 1974 to provide a single body on which senior members of the Education Committees of the two Associations concerned could meet to discuss matters of common interest. (The Welsh Joint Education Committee is also represented on CLEA.) The composition of CLEA (12 senior members of the Education Committees of ACC and of AMA plus professional advisers) has not been varied since. The body is served by the education staff of the Associations' secretariats and a jointly appointed administrative officer. It acts for both Associations in a wide range of matters and is responsible for some of the liaison between the Associations and outside bodies.

CLEA's activities are often, and rightly, indistinguishable from those of the Associations. Meetings with Ministers may take place with representatives of CLEA or of the Associations. The members involved are usually the same people and their concerns are the same. The constitutional differences are preserved by an Association veto. The fact that it has seldom been used demonstrates the essential unity of view and interest.

Members and Officers have become accustomed to working

through CLEA when that is operationally the more effective forum and, particularly, when it presents an opportunity to demonstrate a unity of views amongst local education authorities. The most recent example of this developed from a resolution passed at CLEA's 1987 Conference to establish a Standing Conference on Education. CLEA was in a position to bring together a large number of organisations and associations connected with education and ranging from providers, through Trade Unions, to include consumer groups such as parent interests and industry. The Conference met on a number of occasions to consider in particular detail the Government's proposed legislation for the education service. The outcome demonstrated the value of CLEA's role in providing a national forum for those interested in the maintained education service.

Further reading

Baron, G. and Taylor, W. (1969). *Educational Administration and the Social Sciences*, Athlone Press.

Baxter, C., O'Leary, P. J. and Westoby, A. (1978). *Readings in Economics and Education Policy*, Longman.

Birley, D. (1970). *The Education Officer and his World*, Routledge & Kegan Paul.

Blaug, M. (1972). *An introduction to the Economics of Education*, Penguin Press.

Bush, T. and Kogan, M. (1982). *Directors of Education*, Allen and Unwin.

Dent, H. (1961). *The Educational System of England and Wales*, University of London Press.

Dobson, L., Gear, T. and Westoby, A. (1975). *Management in Education: Some techniques and systems*, Ward Lock O.U.

Drucker, P. F. (1969). *The Age of Discontinuity*, Heinemann.

Drucker, P. F. (1955). *The Practice of Management*, Heinemann.

Fielden, J. and Pearson, (1978). *Costing Educational Practice*, Council for Educational Technology.

Fowler, G., Morris, V., and Ozger, J. (1973). *Decision Making in British Education* Heinemann, O.U.

Fowler, G. (1974). *Local Government of Education*, O.U.

Greenaway, H. and Harding, A. G. *The Growth of Policies for Staff Development* (Surrey University Monographs). Society for Research into Higher Education.

Hepworth, N. P. (1970). *The Finance of Local Government*, Allen & Unwin.

Kogan, M. (1971). *The Politics of Education*, Penguin.

Kogan, M. and van der Eyken, W. (1973). *County Hall. The role of the Chief Education Officer*, Penguin.

Mann, J. (1979). *Education*, Pitman.

Maclure, J. Stuart (1973). *Educational Documents England and Wales 1816 to Present Day*, Methuen.

Peacock, A. T. Glennister, H. and Lavers, R. (1968). *Educational Finance, its Sources and Uses in the U.K.*, Oliver and Boyd.

Taylor, G. and Saunders, J. B. (1976). *The Law of Education* Butterworth.

Taylor, G. and **Saunders, J. B.** (1980). *The Law of Education,* First
Supplement to Eighth Edition, Butterworth.
Vaizey, J. E. and **Sheehan, J.** (1968). *Resources for Education,* George
Allen & Unwin.
Vaizey, J. E. and **Chesswas, J. D.** (1967). *The Costing of Educational
Plans* UNESCO.
Woodhall, M. (1970). *Cost Benefit Analysis in Educational Planning,*
UNESCO.
HMSO:
  Royal Commission on Local Government in England 1966–69 (Cmnd
    4040).
  The New Local Authorities Management and Structure (Bains Report,
    1973).
  Local Government Finance (Layfield Report, 1976 (Cmnd 6453).
  Annual Report of Department of Education & Science.
  A study in School Building (DES 1977).
  Statistics in Education. Annual Publication of DES.
  A New Partnership for our Schools (Taylor Report, 1978).
  Primary Education in England, HMI Survey (DES 1978).
  Special Educational Needs, Warnock Report (Cmnd 7212, 1978).
  Local Authority Arrangements for the School Curriculum, Report
    on the Circular 14/77 Review (DES 1979).
  Aspects of Secondary Education in England, HMI Survey (DES 1979).
  The School Curriculum (DES 1981).
  Mathematics Counts, Cockcroft Report (DES 1982).
  Teaching Quality, White Paper 1983 (Cmnd 8836).
  Better Schools, White Paper 1985 (Cmnd 9469).
  Conduct of Local Authority Business, 1986 Widdicombe Report (Cmnd
    9797)
  Rate Support Grant, annual reports on Rate Support Grant
    negotiations.
  The Government's Expenditure Plans, Annual White Paper.
  Commission on Industrial Relations (Cmnd 4803).
Local Government Training Board. *Staff Engaged on Personnel Work*
(Training recommendation No. 8).
LACSAB *Employee Relations Handbook – Local Authorities Conditions
of Service Advisory Board* (1977).
Manpower Services Commission. *Young People and Work* (Holland
Report). *A New Training Initiative A Programme for Action,* White
Paper 1981 (CMnd 8455).
Youth Task Group: *Outline of Youth Training Schemes* (1982)
OECD:
  *Budgeting, Programme Analysis and Cost Effectiveness in Educational
    Planning – 1968*
  Public Expenditure on Education – 1976.
Open University. *The Finance of Education. Block IV of Economics
and Education* (1971).
Society of Education Officers:

Winter, G. *The Position of the Education Service Following Local Government Reorganisation* (1977).

The Role of the Education Officer (1977).

Nice. D. *Education and the Law*, 1986.

Brooksbank, K. and **Anderson, K.** (1987). *School Governors*, Second edition, Councils' and Education Press.

Brooksbank, K., Revell, J., Ackstine, E. and **Bailey, K.** (1982). *County and Voluntary Schools*, Sixth Edition. Councils' and Education Press.

Councils' and Education Press, *Education Year Book*.

Note: For publications on statistical sources, see p. 343 ff; on Scottish system, see p. 312 ff.

Index of statutes

General Index

Directors of Education, 303
Directors of Education in Scotland, 311
of County Councils (ACC), 40, 105, 178, 272
of Metropolitan Authorities (AMA), 40, 105, 178, 272
attainment surveys, 131
targets, 239
Audit Commission, 104, 253
Auld, Robin, 154, 155
awards, 139

Bains Committee, 140
Report, 199
Baker, Kenneth, 163
balance of power, 37
Baron, George, 154
Barraclough, Frank, 137
BBC Schools Broadcasting Council, 288
Before Five 1971, 300
behaviour, 163
Better Schools 1985, 153, 157
bids for primary schools, 78
secondary schools, 78
bilingual provisions, 289
schools, 282
birth rate, 211
Black Paper 1969, 155
Block Grant System, 115
Board of Education, 27, 153
books, 242, 277, 280
borrowing money, 105
branch structures, 198
British Council, 30, 274
economy, 318
industrial and economic performance, 321
budget forecasts, 53-54 (see also finance)
formulae, 108
shares, 108
systems, 280, 298
building bulletin on fire prevention, 82
cost analysis, 180
maintenance, 241
of new schools, 82
planning, 53
processes, 79
programmes, 73
projects, 82

repairs, 241
Burgundy Book, 142
Burnham Committee, 144, 221
salaries agreement, 194
Business and Technician Education Council, 270
Butler, R. A., 249

Callaghan, James, 155
capital allocations, 79
expenditure, 77, 89, 105, 108, 239, 242
grants to voluntary organisations, 108
spending plans, 76
capping of community charges, 104
career guidance, 3, 127
mobility, 291
Careers, 139
Advisory Officers, 32, 194
advisory service, 204
education report of 1987, 158
guidance, 131
officers, 115, 277, 307
Service, 307
Service Sub-Committees, 24
caretaking, 151, 241
catering, 131, 140, 212
Central administration, 4, 5-6
administration inspectors and advisers, 242
Bureau for Educational Visits and Exchanges, 274
government initiatives, 47
government's dislike of local government, 316
provision of equipment, 96
purchasing, 95
Welsh Board, 283
Youth Employment Council, 318
Centre for Educational Research and Innovation, OECD, 273
Certificate of Education, 286
Sixth Year Studies, 302
Secondary Education (CSE), 161
CGLI, 270
Challenge of Change 1975, The, 310
change, 52
channels of communication with local government, 272
charges, 118-120
Chief Education Officers, 5, 8, 21, 27-

Inner London Education Authority, 18

innovations and improvements in the curriculum, 160

INSET, 124

Advisory Committee, 64

programmes, 247

inspectorates, see Her Majesty's Inspectorate

institutions' management, see Management

Instrument and Articles of Government, 221

Instrument of Government, 219

Instruments and Articles of Government for Polytechnics, 232

for Special Schools, 232

insurance, 13

inter-departmental relationships, 186

inter-disciplinary working, 50

International Committee of the Society of Education Officers, 274

interventionist governments, 46

investment costs, 133

James Report, 149, 213

Jewish community, 25

Job Clubs, 330

Creation Programme, 320

related training, 330

specifications, 278

Training Scheme (JTS), 330, 331

Jobstart allowances, 330

Joint Councils of the Examining Boards, 288

Matriculation Board, 285

schemes with district councils, 94

Standing Committee of Vice-Chancellors, 288

ventures, 58

Joseph, Sir Keith, 160, 163

juvenile crime, 271

keeping of records, 124

Kingman Report on English 1988, 167

language centres, 253

law, see Index of Statutes

Layfield Report 1976, 102, 120

legislative programme, 4

levels of competence in numeracy, literacy, oral expression and social relationships, 323

Lewis Report 1917, 317

library areas, 301

work, 131

licensed teachers, 149

life-long education, 275

links with colleges and schools, 247

overseas countries, 180

Local Administration, 4

Advisory Boards, 319, 331, 333

Authorities, 6, 82, 156

allocation, 78

chairmen, 55

inspectorates and advisory services, 188

joint committees for specific purposes, 40

management functions, 248

local competition between colleges, 333

connections, 247

education and administration, 7-9

Local Education Authorities (LEAs), 4, 17, 19, 22, 47, 76, 78, 165, 227, 270, 315, 332 (see also building; Chief Education Officers; communication; management; office; personnel; planning; rules; Scotland; Wales

Education Authorities' administration structure, 57

advisers, 32

annual submission, 76

capital programmes for building, 127

communication with the DES, 38

control of education expenditure, 101

financial planning, 105-106

inspectors, 32

officers, 178, 273

planning role, 46

plans for longer-term developments, 248

policy statements, 277

powers, duties and responsibilities duties, 15, 66, 239

provision of post-16 education and training, 333